New World Economies

New World Economies

━∽∾∽━

*The Growth of
the Thirteen Colonies
and Early Canada*

MARC EGNAL

New York   Oxford
Oxford University Press
1998

Oxford University Press

Oxford   New York
Athens   Auckland   Bangkok   Bogotá   Buenos Aires   Calcutta
Cape Town   Chennai   Dar es Salaam   Delhi   Florence   Hong Kong   Istanbul
Karachi   Kuala Lumpur   Madrid   Melbourne   Mexico City   Mumbai
Nairobi   Paris   São Paulo   Singapore   Taipei   Tokyo   Toronto   Warsaw

and associated companies in
Berlin   Ibadan

Published by Oxford University Press, Inc.
198 Madison Avenue, New York, New York 10016

Oxford is a registered trademark of Oxford University Press

Library of Congress Cataloging-in-Publication Data
Egnal, Marc.
New world economies : the growth of the thirteen colonies and
early Canada / Marc Egnal.
p.   cm.
Includes bibliographical references.
ISBN 0-19-511482-5
1. United States—Economic conditions—To 1865.   2. United States—
History—Colonial period, ca. 1600–1775.   3. Canada—Economic
conditions—To 1763.   I. Title.
HC104.E37   1998
330.973'02—dc21   97-50483

9 8 7 6 5 4 3 2 1

Printed in the United States of America
on acid-free paper

For my parents, Abraham and Leah Egnal

Preface

In the 1750s most white settlers in Canada and the Thirteen Colonies lived better than their parents did. These gains were not as spectacular as those recorded in the nineteenth century or the first half of the twentieth. Nor were the fruits of progress evenly distributed. But the advances were unmistakable, and colonists remarked on the changes in their world. This book is about that process of growth.

What shaped the course of development? Several influences affected the New World economies. Shifts in prices and the influx of funds were important, while additions to the capital stock, gains in productivity, and patterns of culture had an impact. But at the heart of the process of growth were the ties with the metropolitan power. The central argument of this book is that the pace of economic development in the colonies reflected the rate of growth in the mother country.

This argument rests on a theoretical foundation as well as a broad empirical base. The first chapter explores the theory that shapes the book. The paradigm presented builds on the "staple thesis" but goes well beyond this traditional formulation. It includes sectoral analysis and an emphasis on economic long swings. The balance of the work examines the economies of the Thirteen Colonies and early Canada. These chapters elaborate the framework presented in chapter 1 and draw on statistical series, literary evidence, and the findings of many secondary works. Over a hundred graphs, some based on newly compiled series, accompany the text. Appendices A to E present these original data.

Given the abundance of graphs, how should this book be read? Early in the writing of this work, a friend advised me to eliminate, or at least reduce, the number of graphs — or risk scaring the chartophobic reader. Some individuals might wish I had taken that advice and might regard the figures as distractions, or at best as adornments to the text. They are neither. The charts are every bit as important to this book as reproductions of paintings would be to a study of an artist. They make the arguments convincing and permit the reader to test the conclusions. These figures show, for example, the shape and amplitude of long swings. They allow comparisons between larger trends and the prosperity of a single firm.

Other individuals might approach this book from a very different vantage point. They may assume that the complete story is contained in the graphs, and that the text is simply a gloss on these figures. This too is a perilous tack. Much of the evidence in *New World Economies* is drawn from nonstatistical sources. Readers should be especially wary of drawing firm conclusions from individual graphs. Skyrocketing land values in an older county may suggest prosperity. But when these data are set against soaring rates of foreclosure, rising poorhouse admissions, and complaints about the growth of tenancy, a different, more balanced picture emerges.

Ideally readers will take the text as a starting point but will use the charts to assess the arguments of the book. The graphs do more than illustrate — they encourage participation. I've tried to make them "user friendly." Each one has a caption discussing its significance. Few of the charts are far removed from the tabulations they represent. The theory in this book does not slide into hypothetical constructs or abstruse equations.

The conclusions in *New World Economies* also should be set in a broader context. The differences between regions as diverse as the northern and southern Thirteen Colonies and French Canada cannot be understood simply by focusing on economic variables. I have written a companion work, *Divergent Paths: How Culture and Institutions Have Shaped North American Growth* (New York: Oxford University Press, 1996), which examines the impact of long-standing patterns of thought and behavior on economic development. The two books deal with the same regions, but *Divergent Paths* looks at a broader time span. It begins with the Old World origins of settlement and concludes with the late twentieth century. To be sure, *New World Economies* can stand on its own. Close ties with the mother country guided the course of growth in the seventeenth and eighteenth centuries. But if we want to understand the longer term and the transition from the "household economy" of the eighteenth century to commercial and industrial capitalism in the nineteenth, we must examine far-reaching differences in culture and institutions. Chapter 1 briefly discusses the findings of *Divergent Paths*. The two works should be considered together for a full understanding of the process of development.

Many individuals strengthened this book. I've been blessed with readers who had no hesitation in pointing out my mistakes and who have provided incisive, often lengthy critiques. These scholars have graciously shared their own data and insights and promptly replied to my requests for clarification of disputed points. These individuals include John Bosher, Ken Carpenter, Lois Carr, Jay Cassell, Joseph Ernst, Yves Frenette, Allan Greer, Matthew Laird, Gloria Main, Jack Main, John McCusker, Dale Miquelon, Jeanette Neeson, Fernand Ouellet, John Robinson, Nicholas Rogers, Jacques Rouillard, Lorena Walsh, Thomas Weiss, and Thomas Wien. My research assistants—Elaine Naylor, Richard Gilmour, Michelle Geller, and especially Sarah Elvins—helped track down errant sources, iron out knotty problems, and construct the graphs. Pat Bilbao checked proof for this text, as she has for my previous two books. I'm also grateful to two editors at Oxford University Press. Andrew Albanese and Thomas LeBien had faith in this somewhat unusual work, with all its graphs, tables, and appendices. The Social Sciences and Humanities Research Council and York University provided funding that allowed me to broaden this study.

My family helped in ways that every historian's family should: it slowed down the writing of this work. (Several housing moves helped too.) Benjamin, our ten-year-old, dragged me to the basketball court, patiently explaining what "bricks" and "alley-oops" are. Barton, our teenager, guided me through the intricate world of Warhammer battles; lining up my elven archers against his orcs was usually the break I needed. My wife, Judith Humphrey, involved me in her ever-expanding business. She also remains my best reader and has buoyed my spirits during the seemingly endless revisions that characterize every book I've written.

Finally, this work is dedicated to my parents, Abraham and Leah Egnal. I gained my love of history from them. My father was a high school social studies teacher, my mother a weaver. Both of them were politically active during long careers stretching from the 1930s to the 1990s. They fought in various ways for their vision of a better world and spoke out against injustice during years when many others kept their heads down. The dedication is one way of expressing my appreciation for all they have done.

Toronto, Ontario   Marc Egnal
February 1998

Contents

Figures and Tables

Figures

Tables

Abbreviations

BL   British Library, London

DCB   *Dictionary of Canadian Biography*, 13 vols. (Toronto, 1966–94)

HSP   Historical Society of Pennsylvania, Philadelphia

JEH   *Journal of Economic History*

PRO   Public Records Office, London

RHAF   *Revue historique de l'Amérique française*

WMQ   *William and Mary Quarterly*

New World Economies

—✺—

ONE

Introduction

A Brief March through the
Thickets of Economic Theory

adwallader Colden, the lieutenant governor of New York, was
right. Economic growth was unmistakable in colonial North
America. "The manner of living among all ranks of people," Colden remarked
in 1764, "is now at a much higher rate than formerly."[1] By the mid-eighteenth
century settlers in the Thirteen Colonies and Canada had more possessions
and more disposable income than was the case even a few decades earlier.
Homes—such as those in Anne Arundel County, Maryland (fig. 1.1)—were
now more likely to have knives, forks, and plates on the table; sugar or molasses in the cupboard; and imported cloth on their shelves. To be sure, the rate
of growth was uneven, the distribution of wealth hardly uniform, and the pace
of development far slower than in the nineteenth century. But for most white
colonists there were tangible gains.

This book explores the process of growth in the Thirteen Colonies between
1713 and 1775 and in Canada from 1665 to 1760, and examines the reasons
the standard of living improved. Key to any understanding of progress in the
New World is the close connection between the metropolitan powers and their
dominions. Hence the central argument of this work may be simply stated: the
pace of economic development in the colonies reflected the rate of growth in
the mother country.[2]

The ensuing chapters elaborate this proposition and examine in detail the
patterns of growth in the North American colonies and the metropolitan powers.
The text draws upon many statistical series as well as qualitative information.
But an explanation requires a sound theoretical framework as well as extensive

3

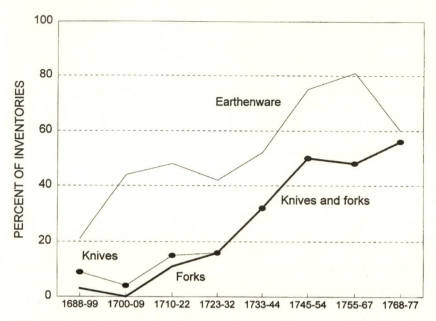

Figure 1.1. *Forks, knives, and earthenware in Anne Arundel County, Maryland, 1688–1777.* This series measures the presence of these amenities in households of "middling wealth" (estates valued between £50 and £94) in rural Anne Arundel County. Material conditions improved for these farm families. [*Source:* Lois Green Carr and Lorena S. Walsh, "The Standard of Living in the Colonial Chesapeake," WMQ, 3d ser., 65 (1988): 144. This figure, and others that measure the ownership of goods or total personal wealth, are based on probate records—the valuation of estates after death.]

data. This Introduction helps make that framework explicit. The Introduction begins with an analysis of the staple thesis, a widely accepted but flawed approach to early North American growth. The next section sets forth a model that better explains development. It is one that emphasizes sectors and long swings as well as the importance of price movements and capital flows. The final two sections elaborate this model by examining the principal and the secondary forces that boosted the colonial standard of living.

The Staple Thesis

The staple thesis is a convenient starting point for a discussion of early North American growth. No single paradigm is so well known within the scholarly community. The merits of this approach—with its emphasis on the role of staple exports—are clear. But this hypothesis also has serious shortcomings that highlight the need to introduce other bodies of theory.

The staple thesis asserts that the export of primary products was the engine of growth for the colonial economy. It also affirms that the nature of these exports shaped the pattern of regional development. Thus a study of early Canada must emphasize the commerce in furs, while an analysis of the Lower South should concentrate on rice and indigo. Moreover, each major staple created a social structure and course of development. For example, tobacco culture in the Upper South fostered a society marked by extremes in wealth, large plantations, and few towns. By contrast, the cultivation of grain in Pennsylvania and New York created a world of middle-class farmers and burgeoning urban places.[3]

This framework also focuses attention on the "spread effects" of the export sector. Each of the major staples promoted growth in several ways. These exports encouraged *backward linkages*—investments that aided the production and shipment of the staple. Such spin-offs include the roads built to move the barrels of grain or tobacco, the tools made locally that allowed farmers to better cultivate their crops, and the shipping and shipbuilding industry, which helped carry the staples to their markets. The major staples also produced *forward linkages*—activities that added value to exports. Flour mills and bakeries, for example, increased the worth of wheat. The rise of the export economy also fostered *final demand linkages*—local enterprises that provided consumer goods for individuals producing the staples. The increasing number of weavers in the countryside is an example of such a connection.

Taken all together, the spread effects suggested by the staple thesis point to the diversification of productive activities, and the gradual transformation of the economy. Eventually—in the nineteenth century—industry rather than agriculture and North American demand rather than foreign markets became the engine of growth. In the mid-eighteenth century, however, such developments seemed far off. Colonial exports, much as the staple thesis suggests, dominated the pattern of growth.[4]

Despite its strengths, the staple or "export-led" explanation has weaknesses that point to the need for other paradigms. These problems can be briefly reviewed.

1. *The staple thesis rests on broad generalizations rather than measurable norms.* From its inception in the work of Harold Innis, the staple thesis has been marked by a qualitative approach to questions that demand quantitative precision. Innis's work on the Canadian economy emphasized the importance of a series of staples on growth, but included few numbers to support the descriptive material. Economist Mel Watkins observes that for Innis, "the staple approach became a unifying theme of diffuse application rather than an analytical tool fashioned for specific uses." But the efforts of Watkins and others to make this theory more precise have been to little avail.[5]

Consider two problems that cry out for quantification. One is the question of just when is the staple thesis applicable? Clearly, the major exports are central to any explanation of North American growth in the eighteenth century. But what of the nineteenth century? In *The Economic Growth of the United States, 1790–1860*, Douglass North applies the export-led paradigm to nineteenth-century America. He argues that the export of cotton was "the most important proximate cause" of development in the United States between 1815 and 1843. But North's conclusions have been roundly and justly criticized. Several writers note that even during the 1830s and 1840s cotton exports amounted to no more than 4 percent of the Gross National Product (GNP). There is a need for a yardstick—perhaps the value of staple exports as a proportion of GNP—to help us judge when this thesis is applicable. But the writing on export-led growth provides little guidance.[6]

A second issue that demands greater precision is that of linkages. "Forward" and "backward" linkages are not concepts that readily lend themselves to quantification. The upcoming discussion of the role of capital goods suggests a direction such analysis might take.

2. *The staple thesis focuses on one aspect of the economy, and ignores other important reasons for growth.* While the sale of staples was important, it was not the only cause of growth in early North America. Impetus for development also came from the funds provided by the mother country, investments in capital goods, gains in productivity, and the nonstaple sector. The staple thesis is silent on all these concerns, or deals with them only indirectly.

3. *The staple thesis ignores the impact of culture and long-lived institutions on growth.* Crops did not dictate the social system. Consider these contrasts. Along the St. Lawrence grain growers lived in a hierarchical, feudal society with seigneurs and an established clergy. In Pennsylvania grain farmers could point to a more open egalitarian environment. In Virginia grain was often raised by slaves toiling on large plantations. Clearly, the demands of particular crops were not the only determinants of social structure. Over the long run, French Canada and the northern colonies (later states) followed very different paths of development—despite many similarities in the staples produced. The impact of deep-rooted patterns of behavior on development is slighted by this export-led hypothesis.

4. *The staple thesis has an odd, static quality, and does not shed light on the rate of growth.* With its descriptive emphasis, the staple thesis ignores questions about the pace of development. Was improvement more rapid in the colonial era or later? Were changes in the standard of living smooth or discontinuous? Economic historians vigorously debate these issues—but the discussions occur outside the literature on this export-led paradigm.

In his 1960 work, *The Stages of Economic Growth: A Non-Communist Manifesto,* W. W. Rostow provided one set of answers to such questions. Rostow argued that economies experience a sharp break—a "takeoff"—from a long era of no growth to one of rapid development. For modern industrialized countries Rostow typically located this discontinuity in the nineteenth century and treated the earlier period as one of stagnation. Most economic historians now feel the evidence does not support such a conclusion. The discussion below of long swings provides an alternative and more cogent explanation of changes in the pace of economic development. However, the dialogue involving Rostow and long-cycle theory stands apart from writing on the staple thesis.[7]

Of course, the staple thesis can be stretched to accommodate such challenges. From one vantage point its very vagueness is part of its strength. But an enlarged and redefined staple thesis would bear little resemblance to the literature on this hypothesis. It seems wiser to accept the contribution of this paradigm—an emphasis on the chief exports—and look at other reasons for growth and other frameworks for analysis.

Beyond the Staple Thesis: A New Framework

If the staple thesis is unsatisfactory, what can replace it? Any model that works must be sensitive to the range of factors that propelled growth. And it must emphasize change over time. The paradigm that underlies *New World Economies* responds to these concerns, and can be briefly stated: the regional economies of colonial North America grew in a series of long swings that were shaped primarily by changes in the terms of trade and capital flows. We might add that these long cycles also reflected additions to the capital stock, gains in productivity, and patterns of culture.[8]

The balance of this chapter explores this model. This section discusses three concepts that help frame the hypothesis. They are the regional nature of the colonial economy, sectoral analysis, and long swings. The next section examines the leading factors—movement in the terms of trade and capital flows—forming these cycles. And the final section looks at the other concerns shaping these swings.

REGIONAL ECONOMIES

Any analysis of the European settlements in North America must begin with regional divisions. While Canada[9] can be treated as a unit, the Thirteen Colonies must be divided into sectional components: the northern colonies, the Upper South, and the Lower South. Chapter 3 examines the areas that comprised the Thirteen Colonies, and discusses the reasons for this threefold division. These regions are fundamental to the organization of the book and to the analysis of data.

SECTORAL ANALYSIS

Within the regions, sectoral analysis makes possible a systematic investigation of the reasons for economic development. This approach views the economy in each geographical area as the sum of distinct activities. The deepest fault line was the one separating staple production from commerce and manufacturing. We can understand the sectoral approach better by examining staple production, commerce and industry, and finally the overall balance.

Staple Production. Staple production was unquestionably the most important source of wealth in each regional economy. The value added by the individuals who harvested the grain, fish, furs, tobacco, rice, indigo, and other exports was far greater than the wealth produced by merchants and artisans. Within the realm of staple production, the leading exports define the areas of analysis. Canadians, for example, shipped furs and wheat. Both activities must be scrutinized. Similar segmentation was evident in each of the regions. A series of pie charts, which display the value of regional exports, suggests the relative importance of the several staples (figs. 4.18, 5.10, 6.1, and 9.8).

Two problems may be noted here. One is classifying the activities of the fur traders. A case could be made that the voyageurs and others who ventured west were engaged in commercial activities. After all, unlike farmers, fur traders were not primary producers. They bartered European goods for the pelts that the native peoples harvested and prepared. Still, in their narrow focus on a single staple and in their dependency on the urban merchants, the fur traders seem more akin to farmers than to shopkeepers or importers. In this study they are grouped with the other staple producers.

A second problem lies in assessing the role played by the subsistence sector. Only between 20 and 25 percent of the produce raised on a typical small (120-acre) farm in Canada and the Thirteen Colonies was shipped overseas or purchased by town dwellers. The rest was consumed on the farm itself or in the local community. On the large tobacco, rice, and indigo plantations of the South the proportion exported was greater; close to half (by value) of the crops harvested on those estates were sold abroad. Taking the colonies as a whole local, nonmarket production was far greater than the output directed to distant entrepôt.[10] In discussing the 1690s David Galenson and Russell Menard estimate that tobacco accounted for 20 percent of total income in the Chesapeake region if subsistence production is included, but two-thirds of regional income when output for local use is excluded.[11]

Giving full weight to goods produced for local consumption would misrepresent the process of economic growth. World markets, not local ones, set prices and helped determine how rapidly output expanded. In small communities goods were typically valued at market prices, even in dealings where no money changed hands.

However, wholly ignoring the subsistence sector also creates a distorted analysis. This production raised the local standard of living and contributed to the development of secondary industries such as milling and weaving. The chapters that follow strike a balance in dealing with the subsistence economy. The emphasis is on the export of staples, because it provided the impetus for growth. But notice is also taken of local consumption.

Commerce, Industry, and Towns. Commerce and manufacturing made a significant contribution to the economy, but they were clearly less important than staple production.[12] Several sets of figures help delineate the size of the commercial sector. Nineteenth-century data indicate that individuals engaged in commercial and artisanal activities generated, on average, twice as much wealth as those involved in farming. A similar ratio seems to hold in the colonial era. City dwellers were decidedly wealthier than farmers. At mid-century, for example, Boston claimed 8 percent of Massachusetts residents, but paid 17 percent of the provincial tax. Similarly, Charlestonians cut a broad swath in the South Carolina economy. In 1768, the Charles Town elite owned nearly one-third of the taxed rural land in South Carolina.[13]

Since most commercial activities were focused in the cities, the size of the towns casts light on the magnitude of nonfarm enterprises. In both Canada and the Thirteen Colonies the portion of the population living in urban centers declined during much of this period. Fully 28 percent of Canadians lived in Quebec, Montreal, and Trois Rivières in 1667. The proportion gradually fell to 26 percent in 1712, 21 percent in 1739, and 20 percent in 1760 (fig. 8.2). In the northern Thirteen Colonies about 10 percent of inhabitants resided in towns in 1700; by mid-century, the figure was only about 6 percent. The percentage of town dwellers in the North recovered to about 8 percent by Independence (fig. 4.11). (In the southern Thirteen Colonies fewer data are available. But towns were home to about 1 percent of southern inhabitants in 1760, and about 2.5 percent in 1776.) Doubling these percentages probably provides a rough approximation of the urban contribution to the economy.[14]

The decline in the percentage of town dwellers, it should be noted, was *not* the result of a slump in urban growth. The numbers in the chief Canadian centers expanded at almost 30 percent a decade between 1660 and 1760. Growth in the cities of the northern colonies averaged more than 20 percent between 1710 and 1750. Instead, the diminishing proportion in the towns reflected the redefinition of the economy. In both Canada and the Thirteen Colonies, the fur trade — with its small work force and significant demand for urban support — gradually declined in importance. At the same time agriculture boomed, shifting the balance between city and countryside.[15]

Some commercial and industrial activities lay outside of the towns, even if links of investment and trade connected these enterprises to the urban centers. Iron plantations were located in rural areas, as were mills for grinding grain. Weavers assisted farm families in the production of cloth. Storekeepers in the small towns and crossroads settlements were part of the dense web of commercial relations evident throughout the colonies.[16]

Bringing It All Together. If the data were available, this sectoral approach could be set upon a firm mathematical foundation. One might say for the northern colonies in 1770 that commercial and artisanal activities accounted for 20 percent of the domestic product, grain production for 30 percent, fishing for 15 percent, and the wealth added by a broad assortment of other products (livestock, whale oil, flaxseed, lumber, iron, rum, and the like) the remaining 35 percent. But the data do not exist for any exact analysis. Such figures would simply be a "guesstimate" and give the reader a false sense of precision. This broad concept, however, underlies the information presented in the chapters that follow.

LONG WAVES OF GROWTH

Just as regional and sectoral analysis helps organize the forces for development, so long waves bring together the data on change over time. Analysis of these broad fluctuations also demonstrates the strong relationship between changes in the mother country and colonies. But what are long waves, and why are they so useful for an analysis of colonial North America? We begin with definitions, then explore the forbidding terrain of long-wave theory.

Every economist who has studied business conditions recognizes that the many activities making up an economy do not fluctuate independently. There are patterns that emerge above the "white noise" that characterizes chance events. Short-term fluctuations are often called business cycles, and are generally less than ten years from trough to trough. Variables such as employment, output (in a range of industries), prices, interest rates, and trade figures rise and fall in ways that suggest these measures have a strong relationship to one another and to changes in the economy as a whole.[17]

Most economic historians also recognize oscillations that are longer than business cycles. These swings comprise extended periods of rapid economic development followed by many years of slower growth. For scholars the identification of these long waves emerges from a close study of the data. In the decades before the American Civil War, economic historians point to the patterns established by exports and imports, prices, land sales, immigration, tonnage on the Erie Canal, and urbanization. Reflecting on such data, Stanley Engerman and Robert Gallman observe that "the economic history of the years 1793–1860 divides into three major expansions and perhaps two and a quarter contractions." In the U.S. context, such long swings range between fifteen and twenty-five years, and are often called "Kuznets cycles." The name honors economic historian Simon Kuznets, whose work helped define these fluctuations.[18] Some economic historians suggest that even longer cycles organize economic activity. In the 1920s a Russian economist, Nikolai Kondratieff, argued that there were recurrent cycles about fifty years in length. Unlike the presence of business cycles (universally acknowledged) or Kuznets cycles (widely accepted), the existence of Kondratieff waves is hotly debated.[19]

If we grant that there were fluctuations longer than business cycles, we must ask *why* did long swings characterize economic activity? Economists have set forth a bewildering array of explanations for these oscillations.[20] Joseph Schumpeter, an influential Austrian economist, asserts that these long swings reflect the tendency of innovations to come in clusters.[21] Others emphasize the role of wars in shaping long cycles.[22] Many of these explanations focus on modern, industrialized economies. Researchers looking at cycles before 1800 have found underlying factors in food production, population growth, and weather.[23]

Where does this enormous body of cycle literature leave us? Perplexed perhaps, and aware that even the experts vigorously disagree with one another. Indeed, many researchers contend that there is no uniform or simple explanation for these swings. In a survey of nineteenth century U.S. growth, Diane Lindstrom remarks: "Economic historians have identified Kuznets cycles or long swings but their sources and their impact in the growth process are obscure."[24]

This book affirms the importance of long cycles in the economies of England, France, and North America. This position does not emerge from adherence to one school or another of long-wave theory, but rather because these oscillations help us understand the evidence. Many of the relevant data are presented in the graphs that accompany the chapters. Are the long swings in *New World Economies* (a) Kondratieff waves; (b) Kuznets cycles; or (c) neither? The best answer is (c). The evidence suggests that they are cycles whose lengths consistently fit neither one paradigm or another. For Great Britain and the Thirteen Colonies/States, this text dates the long swings (from trough to trough) as 1713 to 1745 and 1745 to 1783. For France and Canada, the two long swings had very different dimensions. The first stretched from 1660 to 1713, and the second—at least for the mother country—from 1713 to about 1789. The similar fluctuations in the mother country and colony were not a matter of coincidence. Strong ties of trade and credit transmitted these changes from the metropolitan power to the New World.

New World Economies provides an eclectic explanation for the long swings in Britain and France. Changes in population and weather, the impact of war, and the relative prosperity of the agricultural and industrial sectors all helped shape these cycles. It is worth emphasizing that these cycles are descriptive, not predictive. No single set of forces generated long waves with uniform or regular spans.

The discussion of long swings points back to our central argument: the pace of growth in the colonies reflected the pattern of development in the mother country. Still, this emphasis on long swings, regions, and sectors simply provides a framework. We next must look at the influences that affected the particular sectors and helped shape the cycles of growth in the New World.

Shifts in the Terms of Trade and Capital Flows Shape the Long Swings

Two primary concerns—changes in the terms of trade and capital flows—shaped the timing and amplitude of the long cycles in North America. These factors may be explored in turn.

SHIFTS IN THE TERMS OF TRADE

Movements in the terms of trade were usually the most important influence on colonial incomes. The terms of trade are the ratio between export prices and import prices. Settlers in Canada and the Thirteen Colonies were fortunate that the price of the staples they exported rose more rapidly than the value of their chief imports, textiles from the mother country.

The value of imported cloth remained level or rose only slightly between the 1720s and 1770s (figs. 2.3–2.5, 4.21–4.24, and 9.11). To be sure, no technological breakthroughs reshaped the manufacture of cloth (typically woolens) during these years. But there were improvements in the organization of production, and cloth makers in the Old World were able to expand output without raising prices.[25]

During this same period, 1720 to 1775, the prices commanded by the leading colonial exports climbed. The increases were not steady, or uniform from one staple to the next, but the direction was clear. Rising prices were evident in the sales of beaver pelts, fish, wheat, bread, flour, corn, beef, pork, tobacco, rice (after 1745), indigo, and barrel staves. Relatively fixed quotations for imports and inflating prices for exports meant a favorable movement in the terms of trade — and mounting prosperity for the colonists. A barrel of flour or a hundred pounds of beaver skins commanded almost 50 percent more cloth in the 1750s than in the 1720s (figs. 4.25 and 9.12).

More broadly, there was a strong correlation between fluctuations in the prices of the chief staples and the well-being of the colonists. During those brief periods when export prices declined, colonial incomes slumped as well. Indicators such as probated wealth or per capita imports fell along with quotations for the chief exports. The disastrous drop in beaver prices, between 1695 and 1710, signaled depression in Canada, just as low rice prices in the early 1740s hurt the Lower South. Similarly, surging quotations — for example, the ascent of flour prices between 1745 and 1760 — underwrote eras of rapid growth. Fortunately for the colonists, the overall trend of staple prices was upward.

Movements in the terms of trade must be understood in the broad context of the supply and demand for colonial staples. Generally, supplies of most agricultural products expanded steadily over the long term. The key variable in establishing the trend of prices was shifts in demand from England and the European continent.[26]

The limitations of growth based on favorable price movements also must be underscored. Higher export prices provided a fragile base for prosperity. Without the creation of capital goods, such growth was temporary, much like the prosperity that Spain and its dominions enjoyed during the sixteenth century when gold and silver poured into the kingdom. There were ties (or *link-ages*, as the staple thesis would say) between higher export prices and spending in other areas of the economy. But buoyant staple prices did not provide a secure foundation for sustained growth.

THE INFLUX OF FUNDS FROM THE MOTHER COUNTRY

Probably the next most important influence on colonial development was the influx of funds from the mother country. These credits boosted consumption as well as spending on capital goods. They affected the pace of growth in both the staple and commercial sectors.

Funds arrived in a variety of ways. Some came with the settlers themselves, although most individuals were unable to pay for their passage and relied on an employer to cover these costs. Governments forwarded money to their New World dominions, particularly during war years. For Canada these subventions outweighed all other sources of financial support. Mercantile houses provided lengthy credits that facilitated the sale of imported wares. In the Thirteen Colonies such credits accounted for most of the funds the settlers received.

The amounts that private houses extended to the colonists were sizable. Barlow Trecothick, a prominent London merchant, reported in 1766 to the House of Commons on the monies the Thirteen Colonies owed to British firms:

The Committee of the Merchants of London trading to
North America . . . do unanimously authorize me to give it as
their opinion that at the lowest compilation there is due the
merchants of London only   £2,900,000

The agent for the merchants in Bristol authorizes in the
same manner to say that there is due that town   800,000

Ditto from Glasgow (Virginia and Maryland only)   500,000

Ditto from Liverpool   150,000

Ditto from Manchester   100,000
                                                          _____
                                                           £4,450,000

Besides sums due to Lancaster, Whitehaven, Birmingham,
Sheffield, Leeds, Norwich, Wakefield, Halifax, and other
manufacturing towns, which must considerably augment the
balance due from North America.[27]

The indebtedness of the Thirteen Colonies continued to climb after 1766. Similarly, Canadians owed substantial and growing amounts to French houses.

As with other factors, the increase in the flow of funds to the New World was neither steady nor uniform from region to region. During downturns in the mother country, loans from trading houses and government funds were harder to obtain. These periods of contraction slowed the rise in the colonial standard of living.

In sum, fluctuations in the terms of trade and capital flows were the most important concerns shaping the pattern of growth in the colonies. These two factors helped link the economies of the New World and the metropolitan power.

Other Factors That Influenced the Long Swings

Along with shifts in prices and the flow of investment funds, other influences shaped the long swings in North America. These secondary factors included additions to the capital stock, gains in productivity, and patterns of culture.

THE ROLE OF CAPITAL

He was an absent-minded professor, known to wander far from his home in Edinburgh dressed only in a nightgown. He was also a brilliant scholar, famous for his writings in the fields of moral philosophy and political economy. Above all, Adam Smith was the author of a masterpiece, *The Wealth of Nations*, published in 1776. In his wide-ranging book Smith explored a variety of topics, including the division of labor, the way markets functioned, and the harm wreaked by the mercantile system. Most of these separate strands led back to Smith's concern with long-term growth. And close to the heart of that issue was the crucial role played by the stock of capital, the goods that produced other goods. Hence Smith's views provide a good starting point for an analysis of the role of capital in the development of early North America.

For Smith, a growing society needed *capital*, which was an investment in the future, as well as *revenue*, outlays that satisfied present needs. "Wherever capital predominates, industry prevails," Smith observed, "wherever revenue, idleness." He continues: "Every increase or diminution of capital, therefore, naturally tends to increase or diminish the real quality of industry, the number of productive hands, and consequently the exchangeable value of the annual produce of the land and labour of the country, the real wealth and revenue of all its inhabitants."

Savings, typically undertaken by wealthy individuals, make such investments possible. "Whatever a person saves from his revenue," Smith remarks, "he adds to his capital, and either employs it himself in maintaining an additional number of productive hands, or enables some other person to do so, by lending it to him for an interest, that is, for a share of the profits."[28]

Smith's ideas have been refined and modified by many generations of scholars. The role he assigned capital, however, remains one of the most durable aspects of his work. Most modern economists feel that, without such investments, growth cannot take place. The converse, however, is not necessarily true: high levels of investment do not guarantee development. In his study of underdeveloped countries, Ragnar Nurske summarizes a widely accepted viewpoint: "Capital is a necessary but not a sufficient condition of progress."[29] This generalization applies fully to early North America. Capital was a requirement for long-term growth, although it never was the only reason for economic expansion.

Two questions must be answered before we can fully understand the role of capital in colonial North America. To begin with, what constituted capital in the Thirteen Colonies and Canada? Estimates for England, presented in table 1.1, provide a point of comparison. These figures make clear that for England (and Great Britain) land was overwhelmingly the most important capital good. Land, livestock, and farm implements comprised 72 percent of English national capital in 1688. This agricultural category kept its preeminence well into the nineteenth century. In 1798, when Britain was in the early

Table 1.1. *Capital Goods in England, 1688, and Great Britain, 1798*

Capital Goods	Gregory King's Estimates for England, 1688	H. Beeke's Estimates for Great Britain, 1798
Land	64.0%	55.0%
Housing	17.5	13.8
Livestock and other farm goods	8.0	8.7
Industrial, commercial, financial, and other capital	10.5	22.5
All capital goods	100.0	100.0

Source: Phyllis Deane and W. A. Cole, *British Economic Growth, 1688–1959: Trends and Structure*, 2d ed. (Cambridge, Eng., 1967), 270–71.

stages of the Industrial Revolution, land and farm implements still accounted for almost 64 percent of the total.[30]

The distribution of these investment goods in the northern Thirteen Colonies and Canada broadly resembles that of England in 1688. Table 1.2 presents Alice Hanson Jones's figures for the productive resources held by free property holders in the Thirteen Colonies in 1774. In the colonies, as in England, land, livestock, and farm equipment were overwhelmingly the most important grouping. This category made up 94 percent of the capital goods in New England and 85 percent in the middle colonies. These figures also make clear that the colonies lagged far behind the metropolitan powers in the proportion of funds invested in commerce and industry. Colonial North America had no London or Paris. While the "industrial and commercial" category amounted to 10.5 percent in England in 1688 and 22.5 percent in Britain in 1798, the comparable grouping ("Nonfarm equipment and business inventories") in the Thirteen Colonies was only 2.1 percent of all capital goods. In New England such business capital amounted to 4.0 percent of capital goods and in the middle colonies 4.7 percent.

Because of slavery the distribution of producers' goods was different in the southern Thirteen Colonies. Economists regard slaves both as consumers and as capital goods, depending on the framework selected. Viewed as producers' goods, slaves made up 36 percent of the capital stock in the colonial South. Land, livestock, and farm equipment accounted for 61 percent, and business capital an insignificant 0.4 percent. Perishable goods, such as crops, made up the balance of producers' capital.

Next we must ask whether there was any increase in the capital stock in the New World, relative to the population. Periods of growth typically are linked

Table 1.2. *Capital Goods of Free Property Holders in the Thirteen Colonies, 1774*

Capital Goods	Thirteen Colonies	New England	Middle Colonies	South
Slaves and servants	21.3%	0.5%	4.3%	35.6%
Land/real estate	59.7	81.1	68.5	48.6
Other producers' capital				
Livestock	10.0	8.7	12.6	9.4
Farm equipment	3.2	3.9	3.6	2.7
Perishables	3.7	1.8	6.3	3.2
Nonfarm equipment & business inventories	2.1	4.0	4.7	0.4
All capital goods	100.0	100.0	100.0	100.0

Source: Alice Hanson Jones, *Wealth of a Nation to Be: The American Colonies on the Eve of the Revolution* (New York, 1980), 98. Perishables include crops for sale and household materials. In pounds sterling the totals are: Thirteen Colonies, £232.1; New England, £141.9; Middle Colonies, £168.7; Southern Colonies, £372.3. Columns above may not add to 100.0 because of rounding off.

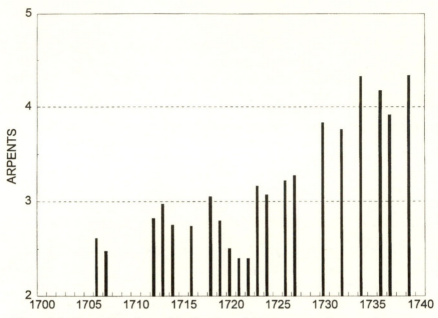

Figure 1.2. *Per capita cultivated land in Canada, 1706–1739.* After 1713 the amount of land under cultivation rose more rapidly than did the population. Since land was the most important form of capital in Canada, this series argues strongly for an increase in capital for each person. [*Source:* A. J. E. Lunn, "Economic Development in New France, 1713–1760" (Ph.D. diss., McGill Univ., 1942), 443–44. Note: 1 *arpent* = 0.85 acre.]

to high rates of capital formation. New producers' goods allow individuals to create more output. The evidence, while far from conclusive, suggests that North America grew more capital intensive during the eighteenth century. Censuses taken between 1706 and 1739 in the St. Lawrence colony show that the amount of cultivated land per person increased strongly (fig. 1.2). The Canadian censuses also reveal an upward trend in the amount of meadowland (fig. 9.9) and number of sheep per person. Findings for the Thirteen Colonies are less clear cut. We lack figures for the whole population, comparable to those for Canada. So we must extrapolate from local studies. Gary Walton and Duane Ball's study of farms in Chester County, Pennsylvania, finds only a slight rise in cultivated land per farm between 1714 and 1770, although the value of farm implements climbed steeply (fig. 1.3). Data for Maryland counties suggest that during the eighteenth century the average household was increasingly likely to own a spinning wheel or other clothmaking equipment (fig. 1.4) and a plow (fig. 1.5).

The rising proportion of slaves in the population of the southern colonies also indicates that New World society became more capital intensive. The percentage of African-Americans climbed in Maryland, Virginia, North Carolina, and Georgia. Only South Carolina, where by 1720 blacks made up more

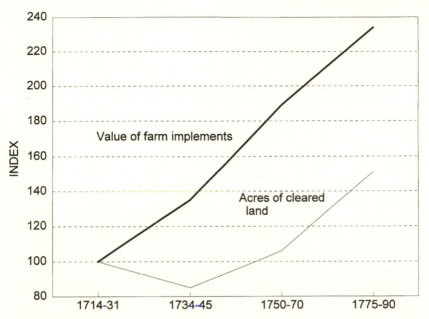

Figure 1.3. *Cleared land and farm implements on an average farm in Chester County, Pennsylvania, 1714–1790.* Although the amount of farmland per person increased only slightly during the colonial era, the value of farm implements soared. The index is based on 100 = average, 1714–31. [*Source:* Duane E. Ball and Gary M. Walton, "Agricultural Productivity and Change in Eighteenth-Century Pennsylvania," *JEH* 36 (1976): 106.]

than 70 percent of the population, did not record increases in its percentage of African-Americans during the last fifty years of the colonial era (fig. 1.6).[31]

There is, to be sure, no one-to-one connection between the creation of this capital stock and the well-being of the colonists. But over the long term such investments were crucial. They helped boost incomes during the eighteenth century, and laid the foundation for more rapid growth in later eras.

GAINS IN PRODUCTIVITY

Advances in productivity also raised the standard of living, although in most instances these improvements had only a modest impact. Productivity gains foster development because the same resources now create a larger output.

Economists discuss productivity in several ways, but probably the most useful concept for understanding growth in colonial North America is *labor productivity*. This is a measure of the change in the output of workers. If slaves engaged in rice production harvested, on average, 2,000 pounds of rice each in 1740 and 3,300 pounds in 1770, they recorded a 65 percent increase in labor productivity. For a single crop, labor productivity can be measured in quantities, such as bushels or barrels per person. When an entire economy is

Figure 1.4. *Wool processing equipment in St. Mary's County, Maryland, 1713–1774.* This series shows the proportion of estates with spinning wheels and wool cards. It illustrates one way in which colonial farms became more capital intensive. [*Source:* Lois Green Carr and Lorena S. Walsh, "Inventories and the Analysis of Wealth and Consumption Patterns in St. Mary's County, Maryland, 1658–1777," *Historical Methods* 13 (1980): 95.]

studied, value — livres tournois and pounds sterling per person — becomes the yardstick.

Several factors heightened labor productivity in early North America. One was additional capital. An individual with more cleared land, with plows rather than hoes, or with a spinning wheel will be more productive than a person without such capital goods. As suggested above, the North American economy — or at least regional components of that economy — became more capital intensive during the eighteenth century. Technological progress — the more efficient use of resources — also lifts productivity. Such improvements can be thought of as advances in the *quality* of capital. Probably the most significant advances in colonial farming came in rice cultivation with the migration of the crop from dry upland soil, to lowland marshes, to the tidal marshes along the lower reaches of the great rivers.

Other concerns that boosted labor productivity in the nineteenth and twentieth centuries were relatively unimportant in the colonial era. Improvements in the labor force — reflecting increased education and training — would become crucial with the advent of commercial capitalism. But progress in this area had little impact on a society that worked with simple hand tools and adhered to traditional practices. Similarly, better management, so important

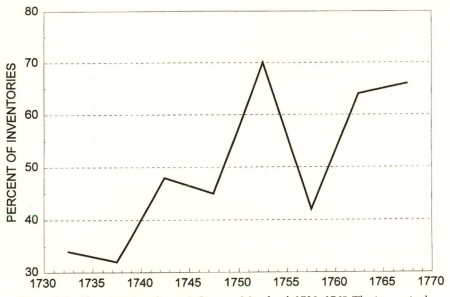

Figure 1.5. *Plows in Prince George's County, Maryland, 1730–1769.* The increasingly widespread use of plows suggests that southern agriculture was becoming more capital intensive. [*Source:* Allan Kulikoff, *Tobacco and Slaves: The Development of Southern Cultures in the Chesapeake, 1680–1800* (Chapel Hill, N.C., 1986), 409.]

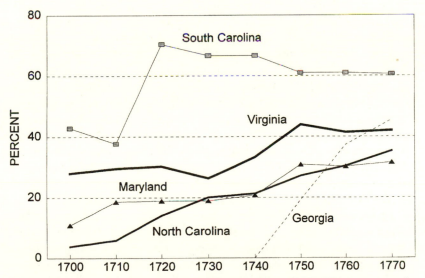

Figure 1.6. *Slaves as a proportion of southern population, 1700–1770.* In most southern colonies the proportion of slaves increased, suggesting that farming became more capital intensive. [*Source:* U.S. Bureau of the Census, *Historical Statistics of the United States, Colonial Times to 1970*, 2 vols. (Washington, D.C., 1975), 2: 1168.]

in the era of corporations, made little difference in an age of family farms and small-scale enterprises.[32]

In all, gains in labor productivity raised the standard of living only slightly in early North America. Most farmers, artisans, and traders conducted their affairs much as their parents had. The slow growth of labor productivity in the colonial era is thus a far cry from present-day society where such gains underlie rising levels of prosperity.[33]

THE IMPACT OF CULTURE

Short-run economic concerns were not the only impetus for growth. The deep-rooted outlook or "culture" of the several groups of colonists also influenced the course of development. A companion work, *Divergent Paths: How Culture and Institutions Shaped North American Growth*, explores these issues more fully. *Divergent Paths* argues that in the nineteenth century the impact of culture was far-reaching. It boosted the growth of the northern United States, while slowing the development of the South and French Canada. Before 1800, however, the impact of differing beliefs was less pronounced. Most settlers in North America were farmers and used the same rudimentary methods. Compared to the nineteenth century, there was less encouragement for the flowering of entrepreneurial skills.

In the seventeenth and eighteenth centuries ideologies had an effect on one significant area: immigration. The contrast between the movement to the French and English colonies is striking. Between 1606 and 1760 only 10,000 individuals settled in the St. Lawrence Valley. During a similar span (1630 to 1780) about 500,000 whites and 250,000 blacks became residents of the Thirteen Colonies.[34]

Particularly noteworthy is the contrast between the number of lay individuals who paid their own way to Canada and to the Thirteen Colonies. The vast majority of the 10,000 Canadian settlers were directed to come to the New World. Those "encouraged" to emigrate included soldiers, who received various inducements; indentured servants; women sent from poorhouses and orphanages; petty criminals exiled to Canada; clergy; slaves; and captured British subjects. Researchers agree that no more than 500, and probably closer to 250, lay individuals paid their own passage and made their lives in Canada. By comparison, perhaps a third of the 500,000 whites sailing to the British colonies were voluntary immigrants who financed their own passage.[35]

Patterns of belief, rather than economic motives, explain the reluctance of the French to move to the New World. Both the "pull" of favorable conditions in Canada and the "push" of misery in France were strong. Settlers in Canada lived far better than their Old World counterparts. There was abundant land in the St. Lawrence Valley, and it was granted with no fees. The population of France was far larger—and poorer—than that of England. But the communal values of French society discouraged emigration. Contemporaries expressed surprise at this behavior. Paul Le Jeune, a seventeenth-century French cleric, observed that "there are so many strong and robust peasants in

France who have no bread to put in their mouths; is it possible they are so afraid of losing sight of the village steeple, . . . that they would rather languish in their misery and poverty, than to place themselves some day at their ease among the inhabitants of New France?"[36] English men and women had fewer qualms about leaving their homes, and many more booked passage to the New World.

Differences in the flow of migration helped shape the course of North American development. In 1750 the Thirteen Colonies had 1,170,000 inhabitants, while Canada could claim only 50,000. The result was that Canada had fewer fighting men to defend the colony against the Indians and imperial enemies. And it had a smaller productive base to develop the range of activities a New World outpost needed. Despite a rise in the standard of living that paralleled the pace in the English colonies, Canadians remained more dependent for their prosperity—and even survival—on subsidies from the parent country.[37]

In sum, this chapter has presented a model of growth. The model emphasizes regions, sectors, and long swings as the framework for analysis, and it points to changes in the terms of trade and capital flows as the most important influences on the pattern of North American growth. Other influences—fluctuations in capital stock, gains in productivity, and culture—were of secondary importance in this era. This approach to the economy leads us back to the thesis that shapes the book: the colonies grew in a series of long swings that echoed the pace of development in the mother country. The chapters that follow explore this model, first for the Thirteen Colonies, and then for Canada.

PART I

The Thirteen Colonies

——✺——

TWO

Two Cycles of British Growth

The growth of the Thirteen Colonies was closely tied to the rhythms of British development, with two long swings shaping business activity on both sides of the Atlantic. The first, slower paced cycle lasted from 1713 to 1745, while the second, more vigorous wave of expansion stretched from 1745 to 1783. The intertwined colonial and metropolitan economies influenced each other's worldly progress. But Britain remained the team of horses, while the colonies were the high-wheeled wagon pulled down the path of development. A study of American growth necessarily begins with an investigation of the economy of the parent country. This chapter looks at several aspects of the British economy—population, agriculture, industry, and foreign trade—and shows that in each area the pace of growth quickened after 1745.

Population Growth

Economic historians agree that the growth of the British population accelerated after the 1740s. The shift from a slower rate, 1700–40, to a more rapid pace, 1740–80, is of fundamental importance. Even had there been no change in per capita income, the steeper rise in population meant that *total* output and consumption grew more rapidly after the 1740s than before.

A brief review of the data suggests the nature of this acceleration. Until recently, the accepted figures for eighteenth-century population growth came from the work of John Rickman. Rickman was a director of the British census

in the nineteenth century. He collected data on baptisms and burials for de-
cennial years from 1700 to 1780. Early in the twentieth century John Brownlee
reworked these data. He concluded that population grew 0.05 percent a year,
1701–40, and 0.73 percent a year, 1741–80.

Recent research confirms that this natural increase quickened, but mutes
the contrast between the two periods. Since 1964 the Cambridge Group for the
History of Population and Social Structure, assisted by hundreds of volunteers,
has compiled information from parishes throughout Britain. The estimates developed by the Cambridge Group show a growth rate of 0.3 percent per annum
for the period from 1701 to 1740, and 0.71 percent between 1741 and 1780.[1]

Why was growth relatively slow before the mid-1740s? Scholars point to
the impact of two demographic crises. One was in 1727–30, with mortality levels
fully 80 percent above normal. A second and less severe crisis came in 1740–
42. Unlike the situation in early eighteenth-century France, this surge in deaths
was not caused by famine. Rather various illnesses, such as chicken pox, smallpox, and whooping cough, were the culprits.

After the mid-1740s natural increase strengthened for several reasons. The
birth rate rose as the age of marriage for women fell from 27.0 years, 1740–49,
to 25.4 years, 1750–99. At the same time, medical advances—such as the spread
of midwifery, inoculation against smallpox, and perhaps an increase in natural immunity to typhus—helped lower the death rate. Improvements in transportation lessened the impact of local harvest failures, while the emergence of
new crops such as the potato improved nutrition. After the 1740s there were
no new demographic crises.

In short, the changes in the rate of population increase provide a solid
foundation for the two long swings of growth. The acceleration of agriculture
and industry after 1745 would be amplified by the rise in the number of Britons.[2]

Long Swings of Agricultural Growth

British agriculture was marked by a cycle of slow growth, 1713–45, and one
of more rapid development, 1745–83. The weight of evidence suggests hard
times for the farm sector before the mid-1740s. There were, to be sure, advances in agricultural productivity during the 1720s, 1730s, and early 1740s.
The spread of sown grasses (such as clover, lucerne, and sainfoin) and of root
vegetables (such as turnips) boosted soil fertility and made more advanced
crop rotations possible. The surplus of grain available for export grew (fig.
2.1). But relatively high levels of output did not translate into prosperity.
Because domestic demand was weak, agricultural prices and total farm income fell in this era, and the agricultural community suffered. Wheat quotations at Winchester slid from an average of 33.7 shillings a quarter in the
1720s, to 27.7 shillings in the 1730s, to 22.1 shillings between 1741 and 1745
(fig. 2.2). Signs of a rural depression, including arrears of rent and unten-
anted holdings, appeared in the 1730s and early 1740s. Several writers, including Phyllis Deane and W. A. Cole, authors of the landmark *British Eco-*

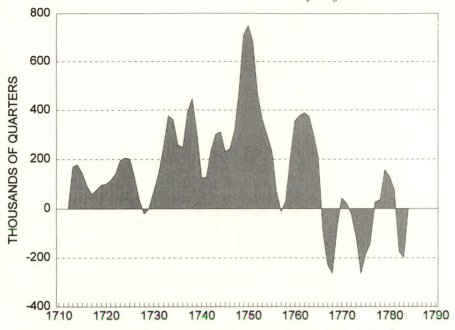

Figure 2.1. *Net exports of wheat and flour from Great Britain, 1713–1783: three-year moving average.* Up to mid-century Great Britain exported ever increasing quantities of grain. Then a rapidly growing population outraced the food supply, and Britain became a net importer of wheat. [*Source:* B. R. Mitchell and Phyllis Deane, *Abstract of British Historical Statistics* (Cambridge, Eng., 1962), 94–95.]

nomic Growth, 1688–1959: Trends and Structure, document the downturn in the countryside. And because of the importance of agriculture, the difficult conditions before 1745 slowed the entire economy. A depressed countryside meant less demand for industrial goods and a slower overall pace of growth.[3]

After 1745 the farm sector grew more prosperous. Population growth drove up farm prices and income. Quotations for grain rose from 27.1 shillings a quarter in the 1740s to 44.7 shillings in the 1770s. Continuing advances in productivity boosted output, which grew more rapidly than it had before 1745. So strong was the increase in domestic demand that, despite expanded production, the surplus available for export declined. By the 1760s Britain had become a net importer of wheat (fig. 2.1). Favorable conditions during this long swing stimulated investment in agriculture, and smaller farms were combined into larger ones. In most instances the land was brought together by agreement among the parties, but some combinations required an act of Parliament. The number of enclosure bills now climbed from a yearly average of 3.9 between 1725 and 1744 to 32.9 from 1745 to 1784. The upward trend in the size of individual holdings encouraged more efficient farming. Poor harvests in the late 1760s and early 1770s, however, notably slowed the growth of the agricultural sector.[4]

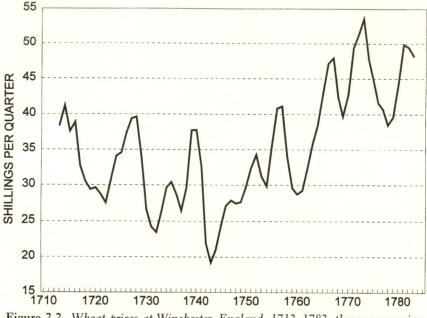

Figure 2.2. *Wheat prices at Winchester, England, 1713–1783: three-year moving average.* Wheat prices fell between 1713 and 1745 and rose from 1745 to 1783. The decline before 1745 reflected weak demand from a sluggish English economy, while soaring prices after 1745 testify to the quickening of business activity. [*Source:* Mitchell and Deane, *Abstract of British Historical Statistics*, 486–87.]

Two Cycles of Industrial Expansion

A variety of series and other testimony documents the two long swings in industrial output. The first long swing was marked by the gradual expansion of manufacturing during the 1710s and 1720s, and a decline in output between 1730 and 1745. The shape of this first, weak cycle emerges from the records of several industries, including woolens, the premier English manufacture. Weak growth in the farm sector underwrote the gradual expansion before 1730, just as agricultural depression in the 1730s and early 1740s brought the cycle to an end. European purchases, which quickened in the 1730s, provided a measure of relief for particular activities—including the production of copper, tin, and linen cloth. But they could not compensate for the enfeebled home market.

A second, and far stronger, cycle of industrial growth began in the 1740s. A broad range of enterprises commenced a sharp climb in output. Among these burgeoning activities were the production of woolens, the Scottish linen manufactory, silk weaving, and the mining of coal. The extraction and refining of copper, which at this time was more important than iron production, also "took off" in the late 1740s. In most instances, the pace of growth slowed noticeably in the 1760s or early 1770s. For example, the expansion of Scotland's linen industry weakened after 1763, while the fabrication of woolens slackened in the mid-1770s.[5]

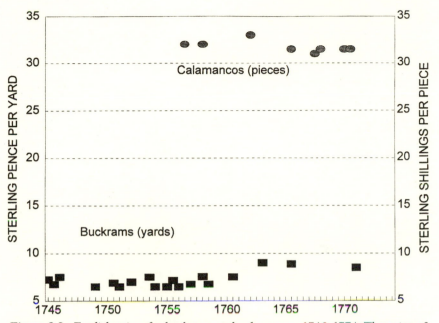

Figure 2.3. *English prices for buckrams and calamancos, 1746–1774.* The price of buckrams rose slightly, while that of calamancos remained the same. Farmers on both sides of the Atlantic benefited from the slow ascent of these British textile prices. [*Source:* Appendix B.]

An expanding population and rising farm incomes underwrote this broad rise in manufacturing. Significantly, after 1750 the "terms of trade" increasingly favored farmers over manufacturers. That is, one bushel of wheat could buy an increasing number of yards of cloth. Data for buckrams and calamancos (fig. 2.3) and for princess linens and red flannels (fig. 2.4) suggest that the price of textiles climbed less than 20 percent between 1745 and 1775. Manufacturers were able to hold the line on costs while increasing output. By contrast, the value of wheat rose more than 60 percent during this span (fig. 2.2). European prices for textiles, many of which Britain imported, followed the same pattern. Linen and cotton checks are an example of such wares, and here too price rises were modest (fig. 2.5). So there were more consumers in Britain with more wealth, and these individuals (or at least, the farmers) could buy finished goods on more favorable terms. All these developments benefited producers. And, as we shall see, purchasers in the colonies reinforced this surge of growth.[6]

Foreign Trade Mirrors the Domestic Economy

Two long swings also marked British foreign trade between 1713 and 1783. Commerce increased slowly between 1713 and the early 1730s, then declined until 1745. A second and more vigorous wave began in the mid-1740s, and weakened only after 1760. The parallels between the expansion of foreign trade

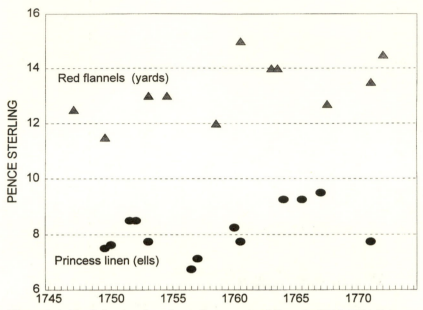

Figure 2.4. *English prices for princess linens and red flannels, 1746–1774.* Princess linen was imported from the continent; red flannels were made in Britain. The value of these two fabrics rose less than 20 percent during this period. [*Source:* Appendix B.]

and the rhythms of the domestic economy are more than coincidental. The demands of British consumers were the engine that drove the wheels of international commerce.[7]

Fluctuations in retained imports suggest the impact that Britain had on its trading partners (fig. 2.6). This set of statistics tabulates the difference between total imports and reexports. It tracks the value of goods brought into Britain and consumed there. The worth of these imports gradually rose, then fell, between 1713 and 1745. Then from the mid-1740s to 1783 the value of retained imports soared, reflecting the growing wealth of the nation. These purchases increased about 2.1 percent a year—a rate well above population growth, which was 0.7 percent annually. During the second long swing, British consumers were a powerful force, helping producers in both the New World and Old.

The strong tug of the British economy on the colonies bordering the Atlantic was felt within the framework of two grand triangles: Great Britain–West Indies–British North America, and Great Britain–West Indies–coast of Africa. British purchases of West Indian produce gently rose, then gradually declined, between 1713 and 1745. After the mid-1740s, however, imports of sugar skyrocketed, and this ascent slowed only in the 1770s. British exports to the sugar islands also followed the two cycles. But the trade between Britain and the sugar islands was characterized by a striking imbalance in favor of the Caribbean (fig. 2.7).

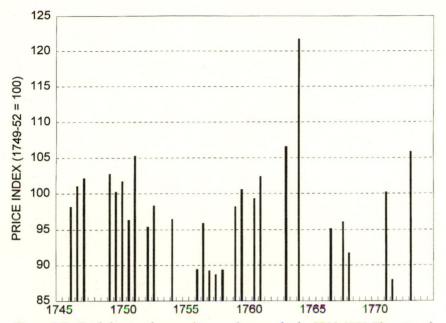

Figure 2.5. *English prices for seven linen and cotton checks, 1746–1774.* The price of checks, which Britain imported from the continent, showed no long-term rise. [*Source: Appendix B.*]

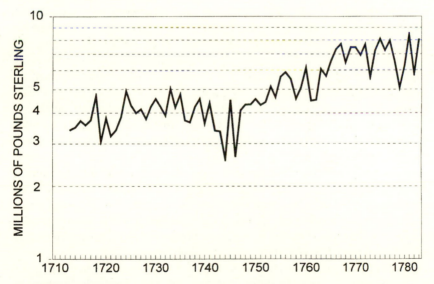

Figure 2.6. *Imports retained by Great Britain, 1713–1783.* This series tabulates the imports consumed in Britain, by measuring the difference between total imports and total reexports. Fluctuations in retained imports outline the two long swings of growth, 1713–45 and 1745–83. [*Source: Mitchell and Deane, Abstract of British Historical Statistics, 279–81.*]

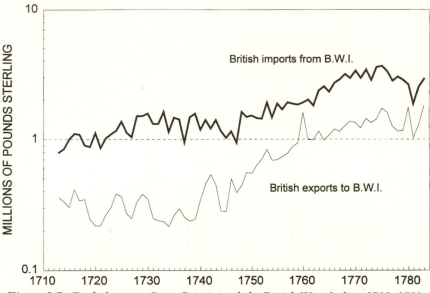

Figure 2.7. *Trade between Great Britain and the British West Indies, 1713–1783.*
British trade with the British West Indies reflected the two broad cycles of development, 1713–45 and 1745–83. [*Source:* Mitchell and Deane, *Abstract of British Historical Statistics,* 309–11.]

The British sugar islands, in turn, exerted a powerful influence on two
areas—the coast of Africa and the Thirteen Colonies—which supplied the
planters' needs. The west coast of Africa from Senegambia to Angola was the
source of slaves. England sent cloth, firearms, liquor, and other finished goods
to Africa, where the wares were bartered for laborers. Slave exports from Africa
to the British West Indies followed the pattern of two cycles. Growth was slow
before 1745. But when exports of West Indian sugar to Britain soared after 1745,
so did the number of slaves sent to the New World (fig. 2.8). Similarly, British
shipments to Africa kept pace with the rise and fall of the slave trade, and so
trace the two swings (fig. 2.9).[8]

The cycles of West Indian growth also helped shape the development of
British North America. Increased sales of sugar allowed island planters to buy
more produce from the Thirteen Colonies. Fluctuations in purchasing power
thus were transmitted from one leg of the triangular trade to the next. Shipments along the third leg of the triangle—North American imports from Britain—traced the familiar pattern of the two long swings.

The flow of credit from Britain to the New World reinforced the rhythms
of these cycles. The colonists bought more goods when British houses lengthened the credit period, or offered funds to marginal importers. Changes in credit
practices are discussed in subsequent chapters. But, broadly, expansion in the
movement of funds to the Thirteen Colonies came during the growth phase of
the long swings, and in particular from 1745 to 1760. Slower development in

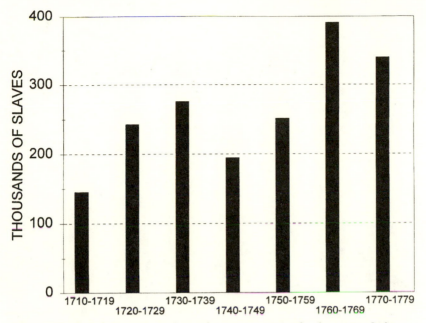

Figure 2.8. *British slave exports from Africa, 1710–1779.* The shipment of Africans to the British New World colonies broadly conformed to the two long swings of business activity. [*Source:* David Richardson, "The Eighteenth-Century British Slave Trade: Estimates of Its Volume and Coastal Distribution in Africa," *Research in Economic History* 12 (1989): 157.]

Britain (for example, from 1760 to 1775) was accompanied by a contraction of credit.

Exports from the Thirteen Colonies to Britain moved to the beat of a different consumer. This trade was not driven by West Indian purchasing power, and it did not soar after mid-century. The chief staples sent from North America to Britain — tobacco and rice — were reexported to Europe. And while European markets expanded, they did not exhibit the remarkable post-1745 wave of growth evident in Britain. Hence, after 1750 a gap opened between British exports to and imports from the Thirteen Colonies (fig. 2.10).

The rapid rise of the population of the Thirteen Colonies also affected the pattern of commerce. Between 1720 and 1770 the number of Africans and Europeans in the continental colonies rose more than four and a half times, from about 470,000 to 2,150,000. This remarkable increase in population helped underwrite the upsurge in shipments to the mainland colonies. Exports to the area that would become the United States rose more than five and a half times between 1720 and 1770. More broadly, the growth of population in the New World (and the stagnation of European commerce after mid-century) helped reorient the foreign trade of Great Britain. In 1700, 80 percent of British trade was with Europe, and 20 percent with the rest of the world. By 1800 these percentages were reversed.[9]

Figure 2.9. *Trade between Great Britain and Africa, 1713–1783.* British trade with Africa reflected the two long swings (1713–45, 1745–83) that shaped business activity in the Atlantic world. [*Source:* Mitchell and Deane, *Abstract of British Historical Statistics,* 309–11.]

The growth of colonial commerce had, in turn, a far-reaching impact on the economy of the mother country. Lacking established manufactures comparable to those in Europe, the burgeoning New World settlements relied on Britain for a staggering array of wares. English industry now moved away from its excessive reliance on woolen textiles, which had accounted for fully 85 percent of all manufactured exports at the beginning of the century. By the early 1770s these fabrics made up only 49 percent of finished wares sent overseas. The balance was a variegated collection of "other manufactures," a rubric embracing various linens, cottons, books, nails, clocks, coaches, buckets, buttons, tools, and sundry other dry goods and hardware. Colonial demand now lifted the fortunes of these industries.[10]

British trade with Europe also illustrates the impact of fluctuations in domestic growth (fig. 2.11). Imports from the continent broadly conformed to the cyclical pattern evident in the British economy. Imports rose and fell between 1713 and 1745 and then climbed strongly after 1745. But exports, which depended on continental consumers, traced a different path. These shipments moved upward between 1715 and 1740, an era of solid economic growth on the continent. They declined in the 1740s with the disruptions of war. Shipments recovered from their low point, but made little headway after mid-century because of strong protectionist sentiment.

Thanks to the rapid growth of the colonies, trade became an ever more important stimulus for the British economy. Deane and Cole's calculations suggest that the output of businesses oriented to foreign commerce expanded

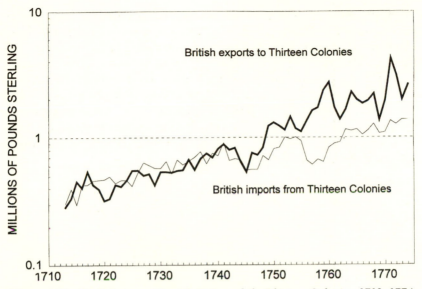

Figure 2.10. *Trade between Great Britain and the Thirteen Colonies, 1713–1774.* Exports to the Thirteen Colonies traced the two long cycles of growth, 1713–45 and 1745–83. Imports from the colonies followed a different pattern because the chief products—tobacco and rice—were reshipped to the continent. [*Source:* Mitchell and Deane, *Abstract of British Historical Statistics,* 309–11.]

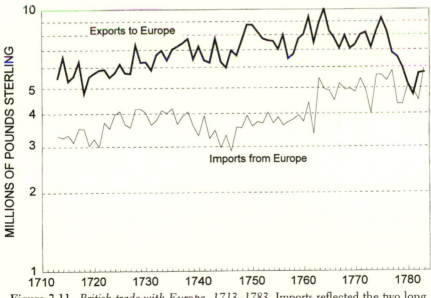

Figure 2.11. *British trade with Europe, 1713–1783.* Imports reflected the two long swings of British growth, 1713–45 and 1745–83. Exports, however, were influenced by the tug of continental markets and so did not follow these cycles. [*Source:* Mitchell and Deane, *Abstract of British Historical Statistics,* 309–11.]

by 444 percent during the eighteenth century. Those industries serving chiefly the domestic market increased their production by only 52 percent. The portion of industrial output exported climbed from about one-fifth in 1700 to one-third in 1800. The surging British economy shaped the patterns of overseas trade. However, in the process the prime mover was transformed.[11]

In sum, much evidence points to the existence of two long swings in British domestic growth: a cycle of gradual expansion, 1713–1745, and one of more rapid development, 1745–1783. Growth at home, in turn, shaped the overseas commerce of Great Britain. These two cycles help us understand business activity in the Thirteen Colonies.

━◦◦◦━

THREE

Thirteen Colonies

Portrait of an Aggregate

"What then is the American, this new man?" Hector St. John de Crèvecoeur asked in 1782. French-born Crèvecoeur had lived in the colony (later state) of New York since the 1760s. He answered his own question: "Americans are the western pilgrims, who are carrying along with them that great mass of arts, sciences, vigour, and industry which began long since in the east; they will finish the great circle. The Americans were once scattered all over Europe; here they are incorporated into one of the finest systems of population which has ever appeared, and which will hereafter become distinct by the power of the different climates they inhabit."[1]

Crèvecoeur may have rhapsodized the "Americans" as a single people. Before Independence, however, colony and region were far more important than any thought of a nation sweeping from north to south. Only occasionally in the years before 1776 did the inhabitants of the Thirteen Colonies consider what they had in common. Even then, the force behind such nationalism was more likely to be imperial conflict than a sense of interlocking economic interests.[2]

This chapter provides an overview of the Thirteen Colonies and underscores the importance of regions. It looks at separate societies that together comprised the Thirteen Colonies, examines the first signs of an emerging national economy, and discusses measures of growth and income. These pages serve as an introduction to the ensuing three chapters that focus on the northern colonies, Upper South, and Lower South.

The Regional Economies of the Colonial Era

Before there was a national economy known as the United States, there were the loosely connected regional economies of British North America. Like Gaul, the Thirteen Colonies can be divided into three parts. The three sections are the northern colonies, which include the eight provinces from New Hampshire to Delaware; the Upper South, that is, Maryland and Virginia; and the Lower South—the Carolinas and Georgia. Other groupings are possible, so we might ask why this threefold division, which helps organize the data in this book? It does not partition the land area or population equally. Rather it reflects functional units, defined by staples, patterns of trade, and methods of farming. The North exported foodstuffs, chiefly to the British West Indies, and secondarily to European markets. It was a region of small farms and noteworthy urban centers. The Upper South shipped tobacco to Britain, and less significantly, grain to Europe and the West Indies. Large plantations that relied on slave labor accounted for much of the staple production. The Lower South also depended on plantation agriculture. But instead of tobacco and wheat, its chief crops were rice, indigo, and naval stores—products that were sent primarily to Great Britain. Table 3.1 shows where the three regions directed their exports in the late colonial period.

By most measures the North was the leading section. During the sixty years before Independence, it had over one-half the total population of the Thirteen Colonies, with the Upper South a distant second. The Upper South, however, had most of the African-American population, while the Lower South stood second in that category (tab. 3.2). The North led in purchasing wares from Britain, well ahead of the Upper South (tab. 3.3). And while the North stood second to the Upper South in the value of commodity exports, it outdistanced all other regions in total earnings when returns from shipping are included (tab. 3.4). Gary Walton and James Shepherd suggest that shipping was a second "staple" for the Thirteen Colonies, trailing only tobacco in value. While this conclusion is probably overstated, there is no question that American, and particularly northern, traders directed a large merchant marine.[3] The Lower South—the Carolinas and Georgia—stood last in all categories except for slaveholding.

Table 3.1. *Distribution of Commodity Exports from the Thirteen Colonies, by Regions, 1768–1772*

Region	Great Britain	Ireland	Southern Europe	West Indies	Africa
North	15.6%	5.2%	24.3%	52.9%	2.0%
Upper South	76.0	5.2	9.4	9.4	0.0
Lower South	64.2	5.5	9.9	20.3	0.1

Source: James F. Shepherd and Gary M. Walton, *Shipping, Maritime Trade, and the Economic Development of Colonial North America* (Cambridge, Eng., 1972), 94–95.

Table 3.2. *Population of the Thirteen Colonies, by Regions, 1720 and 1770*

Region	White		Black		Total	
	1720	1770	1720	1770	1720	1770
North	65.2%	64.4%	21.5%	10.9%	58.8%	52.9%
Upper South	28.9	24.4	56.7	55.2	33.0	31.0
Lower South	5.9	11.3	21.8	33.8	8.2	16.1

Source: U.S. Bureau of the Census, *Historical Statistics of the United States, Colonial Times to 1970*, 2 vols. (Washington, D.C., 1975), 2: 1168.

Any understanding of the nature and pace of growth demands an analysis of the links between the regions and the British empire. Of the three sections, the North was most closely tied to the British economy. At first glance this assertion might seem surprising. The Upper and Lower South directed well over one-half their exports to Britain, while the northern colonies sent less than one-sixth of their shipments to the mother country (tab. 3.1). But the chief southern staples—Chesapeake tobacco and Carolina rice—were reexported by Britain. The ultimate customers were on the European continent. By contrast, most foodstuffs and lumber shipped by the northern colonies were directed to consumers in the British West Indies. These products remained within the confines of the empire. Southern Europe formed a secondary market for northern grain, and was significant only in the last decade of the colonial period.

As a result of these trade patterns, long swings in the North more closely reflected the fluctuations in England than did the cycles in the Upper or Lower South. Several graphs illuminate these similarities and differences. Figure 4.17, which shows per capita imports into the North, traces two long waves similar to those observed in England. But the graphs for per capita imports into the Upper South (fig. 5.6) and Lower South (fig. 6.8) display different contours. In the southern colonies, European consumers helped call the tune and the rhythms were no longer quite those of the British imperium. The overwhelming importance of the North helps explain why the oscillations of growth in the Thirteen Colonies so closely tracked the cycles of expansion in the mother country (fig. 3.1).

Table 3.3. *Imports into the Thirteen Colonies from Britain, 1718–1722 and 1768–1772*

Region	1718–22	1768–72
North	50.3%	52.8%
Upper South	44.5	32.7
Lower South	5.2	14.6

Source: *Historical Statistics of the U.S.*, 2: 1176–78.
Imports from Scotland before 1740 have been extrapolated.

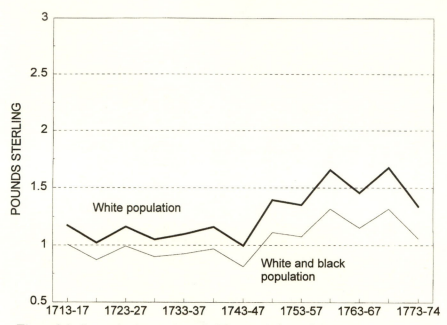

Figure 3.1. *Per capita imports into the Thirteen Colonies from Britain, 1713–1774.* Two cycles, 1713–45 and 1745–75, defined the development of the colonial economy. [*Source: Historical Statistics of the U.S.*, 2: 1168, 1176–78.]

Table 3.4. *Regional Shares of Sales of Goods and Services from the Thirteen Colonies, 1768–1772*

Region	Commodity Exports	Commodity Exports Plus Earnings from Shipping
North	37.0%	43.9%
Upper South	41.5	36.6
Lower South	21.5	19.6

Sources: Shepherd and Walton, *Shipping, Maritime Trade,* 94–95, 114–30. Shepherd and Walton's figures for earnings from shipping were reduced by 20 percent to account for those voyages where earnings failed to cover charges. See Marc Egnal, "The Pennsylvania Economy, 1748–1762: An Analysis of Short-Run Fluctuations in the Context of Long-Run Changes in the Atlantic Trading Community" (Ph.D. diss., Univ. of Wisconsin, 1974), 30–39, 273–90. Shipping earnings that Shepherd and Walton report for the South have been evenly distributed between the Upper and Lower South.

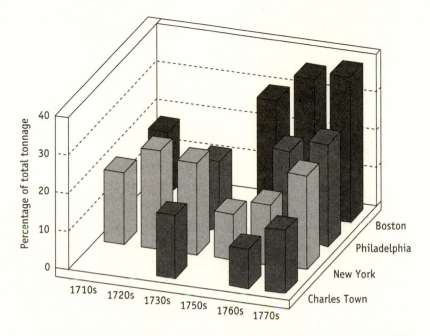

Figure 3.2. *Shipping from four colonial ports to the other Thirteen Colonies, 1710s to 1770s.* This figure addresses the question: did intercolonial trade increase more than other branches of commerce? The answer is a mixed one. For Boston and Philadelphia the proportion of tonnage going to the other colonies rose. But for New York and Charles Town it did not. [*Source: Historical Statistics of the U.S.,* 2: 1180–81. Note that for most decades this source provides information for only a few scattered years, and no figures at all for the 1740s. Tonnage figures for Philadelphia in the 1730s were estimated based on data for the number of ships. The graph combines data for the tonnage clearing and entering the four ports.]

Toward a National Economy: Intercolonial Trade and the West

Only at the end of the colonial era were there signs of an emerging national economy. Here we can focus on two sources of domestic growth — intercolonial trade and western lands — that had a noticeable if limited impact before Independence.

Intercolonial commerce gathered strength in the 1760s and 1770s, though never challenging the preeminence of international trade. For both Boston and Philadelphia, as figure 3.2 suggests, exchanges with other colonies became relatively more significant. In the 1710s less than 20 percent of the tonnage entering and clearing Boston was involved in intercolonial trade. By the 1770s more than 35 percent of Boston cargoes were directed to the other mainland colonies. Intercolonial trade also rose for Philadelphia, from 18 percent of tonnage in the 1730s to 27 percent in the 1770s. These exchanges stimulated both agriculture and manufacturing. New England ships brought rum to fill punch bowls in Philadelphia and Charles Town, and returned with grain to feed Bostonians. Philadelphia shipowners carried imported cloth to the southern colonies, and brought back South Carolina rice and North Carolina tar and turpentine.

However, the limitations of this commerce also must be underscored. The intercolonial trade handled by New York and Charles Town did not increase in relative importance. Moreover, much of this commerce was subordinate to overseas trade, and involved the distribution of imports or the gathering of goods for shipment overseas. Philadelphians collected grain from nearby colonies and directed these barrels to the West Indies and Europe. Bostonians forwarded English dry goods to the Carolinas. Intercolonial trade was not yet large enough or rich enough to sustain growth; each province still relied more heavily on earnings from foreign commerce.[4]

Similarly, while the lands beyond the Appalachians would become a tremendous source of national wealth, before 1776 this territory provided few returns to the colonists. In 1763 the British acquisition of the expanse between the Appalachians and the Mississippi seemed to guarantee future agricultural prosperity. Eventually western lands yielded rich profits to settlers, speculators, and the federal government. But during the late colonial period, the territory proved a troublesome asset for those seeking quick profits. Several companies, based for the most part in Virginia and Pennsylvania, projected schemes for the development of the West. These plans ran afoul of British regulations and the wiles of settlers. The Royal Proclamation of 1763 prohibited settlement west of the Appalachians. Although various treaties would modify this order, it still slowed efforts to patent and sell western lands. Moreover, relatively few settlers crossed the mountains—and among those who did venture west were many who preferred squatting to purchasing. Western lands were perhaps most important for the encouraging cast they gave to the future.[5]

Only after Independence would a national economy truly emerge. The Revolutionary War, the Constitution, and Alexander Hamilton's program (with its national bank and national debt) helped pull together the diverse regions of the young country and establish a foundation for growth. But before 1776 that rising republic remained a far-off and uncertain vision.

Estimates of Growth Rates and Income Levels

No overview of economic growth in the Thirteen Colonies would be complete without estimates of the pace of development and the size of colonial incomes. We begin with an analysis of changes in the standard of living. And here we must provide two sets of figures because of the size and distinct nature of the African-American population. In 1720 fully 15 percent of the colonists were black and unfree; by 1770 this proportion had risen to 21 percent. Indices measuring the changing national product for each white inhabitant provide only part of the picture, because such data ignore the poor living conditions and lack of gains registered by blacks. Statistics that cover the total population,

Table 3.5. *Rate of Annual Growth of Per Capita Income in the Thirteen Colonies, Computed for White Population, 1713–1775*

Region	1713–35	1735–45	1745–60	1760–75	1713–75
North	0	−2.0 to 0	+3.0 to +4.0	−1.0 to +1.0	+0.6
Upper South	−2.5 to −1.0	+1.0	+0.5 to +1.2	−0.5 to +0.5	+0.2
Lower South	+3.0 to +4.0	−3.0	+1.0 to +2.5	−0.5 to +0.5	+1.2
Thirteen Colonies	+0.1 to −0.3	−1.5 to 0	+2.0 to +3.0	−0.5 to +0.5	+0.6

Sources: These figures are estimates based on several time series. Initial approximations were derived from data on per capita imports. These estimates were then checked against data for long-term changes in probate wealth and value of exports. Statistics for per capita imports from *Historical Statistics of the U.S.*, 2: 1168, 1176–78. For data on the decedent wealth and exports, see materials presented in chaps. 4–6.

however, create a misleading aggregate and minimize the rapid advances made by white settlers.

The colonial growth rates presented in tables 3.5 and 3.6 are estimates that reflect the congruence of a variety of time series. Per capita purchases of British textiles and hardware provide one benchmark. Judged against the growth of the white population, shipments from England and Scotland increased at roughly 0.6 percent a year between 1713–17 and 1773–74. They climbed at a somewhat slower pace, 0.5 percent a year, when measured against the expansion of the total population. However, imports of British wares represent only one proxy for economic growth and are questionable guides for short spans. The ensuing chapters present other data—including changes in probated wealth and fluctuations in the value of exports—that help corroborate and modify the fluctuations traced by the influx of wares from Britain.

The estimates for growth rates make clear that between 1715 and 1775 the pace of development—roughly 0.6 percent per annum for the white popu-

Table 3.6. *Rate of Annual Growth of Per Capita Income in the Thirteen Colonies, Computed for Total Population, 1713–1775*

Region	1713–35	1735–45	1745–60	1760–75	1713–75
North	0	−2.0 to 0	+3.0 to +4.0	−1.0 to +1.0	+0.6
Upper South	−2.5 to −1.0	+0.2	+0.5	−0.5 to +0.5	+0.1
Lower South	+2.0	−2.0	+1.0 to +2.5	−0.5 to +0.5	+0.9
Thirteen Colonies	0 to −0.5	−1.5 to 0	+2.0 to +3.0	−0.5 to +1.0	+0.5

Sources: These figures are estimates based on several time series. Initial approximations were derived from data on per capita imports. These estimates were then checked against data for long-term changes in probate wealth and value of exports. Statistics for per capita imports from *Historical Statistics of the U.S.*, 2: 1168, 1176–78. For data on the decedent wealth and exports, see materials presented in chaps. 4–6.

lation, or 0.5 percent for all inhabitants—was well below the rates characterizing the rise of the American standard of living in later years. Between 1840 and 1960, for example, per capita income climbed at an estimated 1.56 percent each year.[6] Small differences in rates compound. Incomes rising at an annual rate of 1.5 percent a year more than double in a half century; those increasing 0.5 percent climb less than a third during that span. Colonists witnessed far less change within their lifetimes than their descendants would observe in the nineteenth and twentieth centuries.[7]

Next, drawing upon the work of Alice Hanson Jones, we can suggest the size of colonial incomes. Using probate inventories as her chief source, Jones presents figures for 1774. For the Thirteen Colonies she estimates that annual income per capita stood somewhere between £10.7 and £12.5 sterling. Her regional breakdown is shown in table 3.7, and suggests comparable earnings in the North and South. It is important to emphasize that these figures are conjectural. Jones derives income figures from wealth data. (And her findings for wealth are themselves tentative.) She translates data for wealth into income levels by assuming a wealth/income ratio of 3.5 to 1. But that ratio is only a guess; observations of other societies produce multiples ranging from 10:1 to 2.5:1. Jones admits: "The income estimates are tenuous because of inadequate knowledge from which to determine the correct capital–output ratio."[8]

Still, Jones's estimates of per capita income are probably of the right magnitude, if a bit low. Thomas Weiss calculates that per capita Gross National Product—equivalent to per capita income—was $59 in 1793 and $66 in 1800. (These figures are in 1840 dollars and so adjusted for inflation.)[9] Translating Jones's 1774 sterling figures into the same 1840 dollars indicates an income between $50.90 and $59.50. Since most economic historians suggest little or no economic growth between 1774 and 1793, Jones's top figure is a plausible one.[10]

We might well ask: what is the significance of an average income of £12 sterling? The figure can be taken simply as a benchmark, a point of comparison with earlier and later numbers. But average income is also a measure of colonial well-being, so it is useful to indicate what £12 sterling would buy. Table

Table 3.7. *Per Capita Income in the Thirteen Colonies, 1774*

Region	Income (in pounds sterling)
Thirteen Colonies	10.7–12.5
New England	10.4–12.1
Middle Colonies	11.5–13.4
South	10.4–12.1

Source: Alice Hanson Jones, *Wealth of a Nation to Be: The American Colonies on the Eve of the Revolution* (New York, 1980), 63.

Table 3.8. *Widow's Allotment, Pennsylvania, 1774*

Item	Quantity for Annual Subsistence	Value
Wheat	13.2 bu.	2.7
Pork	102 lbs.	0.9
Beef	51 lbs.	0.4
Rye	5.4 bu.	0.7
Apples	unspecified	0.3
Wool	6.0 lbs.	0.3
Money		4.5
Total Value		9.8

Sources: James T. Lemon, *The Best Poor Man's Country: A Geographical Study of Early Southeastern Pennsylvania* (New York, 1972), 155. Included here are only the items cited most frequently (fifty times or more) in Lemon's sample of Lancaster and Chester County wills. For price data see Anne Bezanson et al., *Prices in Colonial Pennsylvania* (Philadelphia, 1935); Jones, *Wealth of a Nation to Be*. Values for apples and raw wool are conjectural. All values are in pounds sterling.

3.8 shows a typical "widow's allotment" in Pennsylvania in the late colonial period. This is the amount of food, clothing, and cash that would allow a single, older woman to live comfortably, though not lavishly. The total worth of the most frequently mentioned entries amounted to £9.8 sterling. (But almost all wills would have included several other items, such as Indian corn, butter, liquor, and garden vegetables.) This tabulation suggests that by the eve of Independence the colonial economy was producing enough wealth, on the average, to provide most individuals with a reasonable level of subsistence.[11]

To conclude, the economy of the Thirteen Colonies was the sum of its regional components: the North, the Upper South, and the Lower South. Growth was unmistakable but slow, while the emergence of a national economy was no more than a faint light on a far horizon. The real focus of analysis must be on the regions. The next three chapters will look at these areas in more detail.

———✦✦✦———

FOUR

Northern Colonies

Solid long-term growth marked the northern colonies in the eighteenth century. But the pace of development was uneven, and not all individuals viewed the future with optimism. When Benjamin Franklin opened his printing shop in Philadelphia in the late 1720s, some in the city felt the local economy would not support such an enterprise. One dour individual, Samuel Mickle, told the young printer (as Franklin reported) that "he was sorry for me because it was an expensive undertaking and the expense would be lost, for Philadelphia was a sinking place." However, Franklin and Philadelphia grew steadily wealthier, and the printer had the last laugh. Mickle, Franklin observed, refused "for many years to buy a house there because all was going to destruction, and at last I had the pleasure of seeing him give five times as much for one as he might have bought it for when he first began his croaking."[1]

The economic development that Franklin celebrated took place in the context of two long swings. These cycles, stretching from 1713 to 1745 and from 1745 to 1775, mirrored the pattern of expansion in the mother country. Like the course of development in Britain, the ascent of the northern colonies was brisker after 1745 than in the earlier decades.

A Cycle of Slow Growth, 1713–1745

The first wave of growth in the northern colonies was characterized by a slow rise in the standard of living between 1713 and 1730 and a gradual retreat during

Figure 4.1. *Sugar exported from the British West Indies to England and Wales, 1713–1775.* Production rose little during the first long swing, 1713–1745, but soared after 1745. [*Source:* Richard B. Sheridan, *Sugar and Slavery: An Economic History of the British West Indies, 1623–1775* (St. Lawrence, Barbados, 1974), 487–89.]

the next decade and a half. This weak expansion was evident in the activities of both farmers and townfolk.

HARD TIMES FOR STAPLE PRODUCERS

Lackluster sales of flour, bread, and other exports slowed northern growth. At the heart of the problem was the downturn in the British West Indies. The sugar colonies connected the northern provinces to the British economy—and before 1745 both the mother country and its Caribbean possessions grew at a snail's pace. While the quantity of sugar sent to Britain climbed after 1713, this rise was checked by 1730, and shipments gradually declined over the next fifteen years (fig. 4.1). Sugar prices slid to new lows, sounding bottom in the mid-1730s. They did not regain the levels of 1713–15 until the mid-1740s (fig. 4.2).

Contemporary testimony corroborates the gloomy statistics on West Indian growth. Comments on the hard times filled the packets of official documents sent home and the letterbooks of West Indian houses. In 1735 the council and assembly of Jamaica observed: "It is very apparent that the [British] sugar colonys have been long declining and very much want the assistance of the legislature [Parliament] to put them upon an equal footing with their neighbors, the French."[2] The hard-pressed islanders purchased less from Britain as well as from the mainland colonies. The downturn, the governor of Antigua explained,

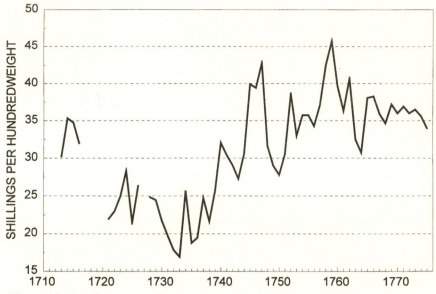

Figure 4.2. *London muscovado sugar prices, 1713–1775.* Prices for muscovado (raw) sugar illustrate the two broad swings, even though these data suggest renewed growth began in the 1730s rather than the 1740s. [*Source:* Sheridan, *Sugar and Slavery,* 496–97.]

has "brought among us an oeconomy that calls for fewer supplies from home for our pleasures than heretofore."[3] Lamented a Barbados house: "At present every branch of trade is here in a withering state."[4]

Initiatives undertaken by the island governments and Parliament to revive the sugar trade were unavailing. An attempt in the late 1720s to establish a port on the north side of Jamaica failed because weak demand for sugar undercut plans to expand cane cultivation. In 1733 the West India interest in Britain secured the Molasses Act, which interdicted the shipment of French molasses to the American colonies. But the measure proved unenforceable, and efforts at implementation were quietly abandoned.[5] Rising sugar prices after 1736 provided some relief for the British West Indies, but full recovery would come only once the British economy rebounded in the mid-1740s.[6]

Other markets for northern produce could not compensate for shortfalls in demand from the British West Indies. The French sugar islands grew briskly during these years, but remained a secondary destination for northern shippers. The French Antilles had become of the chief source of molasses for the rum distilleries of the North. However, these islands received most of their foodstuffs from France and purchased only limited quantities of northern grain. After 1730 shippers in the Thirteen Colonies had to contend with another significant competitor: New France. Flour from Canada and fish from Louisbourg supplemented the produce sent directly from France.[7]

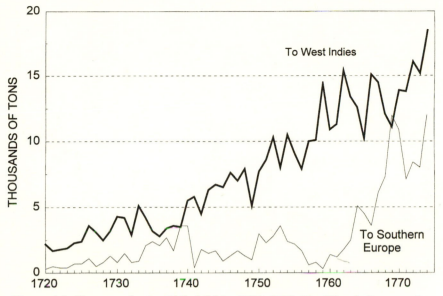

Figure 4.3. *Tonnage clearing Philadelphia, 1720–1774.* The West Indies were the most important market for Pennsylvania produce, while southern Europe stood second. [*Sources*: For 1720–39, James G. Lydon, "Philadelphia's Commercial Expansion, 1720–1739," *Pennsylvania Magazine of History and Biography* 91 (1967): 410, 412– 13; for 1740–54, *Pennsylvania Gazette*, clearances; for 1755–74, William S. Sachs, "The Business Outlook in the Northern Colonies" (Ph.D. diss., Columbia Univ., 1957), 104, 271, 272, 276. In some instances clearances were converted into tonnage with the assumption that the average tonnage of vessels engaged in trade with southern Europe increased from 65 tons in 1735–36 to 94 tons in 1768–72, and the displacement of vessels trading with the West Indies rose from 38 tons in 1720–29 to 61 tons in 1768–72. See pages cited in Lydon and Sachs, and also John J. McCusker, "Sources of Investment Capital in the Colonial Philadelphia Shipping Industry," *JEH* 33 (1972): 146–57.]

Northerners also sent goods to southern Europe and Britain, but in most years these markets consumed only limited quantities of northern foodstuffs. Crop failures in Europe in the late 1730s and in 1740 produced a sudden surge in shipments to Lisbon, Cadiz, and the Mediterranean ports. But these calls were short-lived and focused chiefly on Philadelphia, which had stronger ties with the entrepôts of Iberia than Boston or New York had (fig. 4.3).[8] Shipments to England were low—generally less than £100,000 in most years—and rose and fell with the rhythms of this long swing (fig 4.4).

Hard times in the British Caribbean, and weak markets elsewhere, translated into slow growth for the North. The trade in grain—the most important regional export—slumped. Per capita flour shipments from Pennsylvania fell from 0.84 barrels in 1728–32 to 0.60 in 1733–37, and recovered only slightly to 0.63 in 1738–42 (fig. 4.5). Prices for bread, flour, and wheat also declined during these years (figs. 4.6 and 4.7). No information is available before 1750

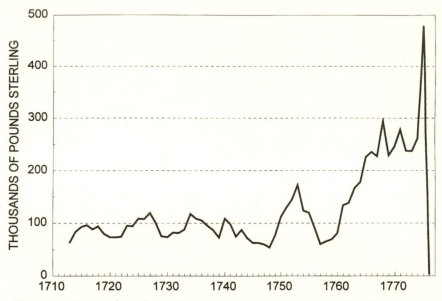

Figure 4.4 *Exports from the northern colonies to England, 1713–1776.* England was the third market (after the West Indies and southern Europe) for northern exports. Shipments to the mother country followed the contours of the two long swings, although growth was interrupted by the Seven Years' War. [*Source:* U.S. Bureau of the Census, *Historical Statistics of the United States, Colonial Times to 1970,* 2 vols. (Washington, D.C., 1975), 2: 1176–78.]

on the amount or value of fish exported, although rising quotations for other minor staples, including lumber, beef, and pork, suggest that a few producers received good news. The price of these exports began their ascent in the late 1730s. However, scattered data indicate that the quantities laded did not increase until after 1745.[9]

Low productivity compounded the farmer's problems. Landowners recorded few advances in agricultural techniques. Fragmentary evidence suggests some increase in horsepower as well as improvements in the design of hand tools. Robert Livingston of New York reported in 1724: "The Dutch as well as the English on Long Island do not reap any more with the sickle, but with the scythe and cradle."[10] Duane Ball and Gary Walton's study of Chester County, Pennsylvania, suggests that the value of farm implements on an average farm rose from 1714–31 to 1734–35. But basic methods of cultivation remained unchanged. Farmers depleted rich soils, made little use of fertilizers, and implemented only rudimentary schemes of crop rotation. And Ball and Walton calculate that the land planted with crops declined from an index of 100 in the period 1714–31 to an index of 85 during the span 1734–45 (fig. 1.3).[11]

The result of poor markets and stagnant productivity was a lack of growth in the rural North. Data for Massachusetts underscore these difficult conditions. Daniel Vickers's study of Essex County shows that the wages paid farm workers

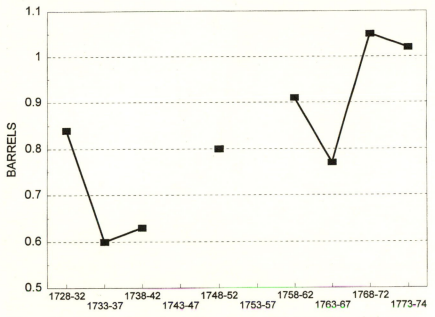

Figure 4.5. *Per capita Pennsylvania flour exports, 1728–1774.* Although there were
no gains in output during the first long swing of slow growth, flour production per
person increased after 1750. [*Source: Historical Statistics of the U.S.*, 2: 1168; Helen
L. Klopfer, "Statistics of Foreign Trade of Philadelphia, 1700–1860" (Ph.D. diss., Univ.
of Pennsylvania, 1936), 173.]

dropped sharply from 1716–25 to 1736–45 (tab. 4.1). Gloria Main's analysis of
probate wealth in three Massachusetts counties depicts a similar trend. Main's
series examines individuals at the same point in their life cycle, and indicates
that the wealth recorded when "young fathers" died reached a peak in the mid-
1720s and declined until the mid-1740s (fig. 4.8).[12] Terry Anderson's study of
Hampshire County, Massachusetts, shows a similar absence of secular growth,
mapping out a gentle rise and fall between 1715 and 1745 (fig. 4.9).[13]

COMMERCIAL AND ARTISANAL ACTIVITIES

Reflecting the leisurely pace of development in the countryside and, more
generally, in the English Atlantic, the northern towns grew slowly before 1745.

Weakness in the sale of staples hurt the cities, as did the lack of noteworthy progress in craft production. Shipping and shipbuilding were probably the
most important industries centered in the towns. These activities employed
hundreds of sailors, carpenters, and kindred laborers. The data available suggest no upsurge in the tonnage coming off the stocks or improvements in the
way vessels were built. Some gains, however, were recorded in the productivity of shipping because of the introduction of larger vessels and the reduction
of the time spent in the port.[14]

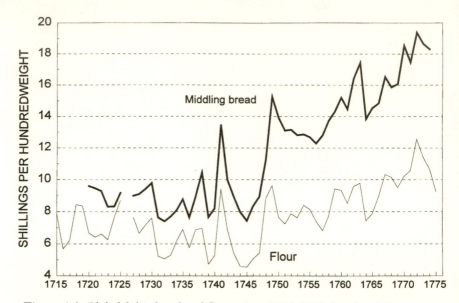

Figure 4.6. *Philadelphia bread and flour prices, 1715–1775.* Bread and flour prices illustrate (1) the long swing of slow growth, 1713–45; (2) the resurgence of the northern economy because of rising West Indian demand, 1745–60; and (3) the impact of mounting demand from Britain and southern Europe after 1760. [*Sources: Historical Statistics of the U.S.*, 2: 1197, 1198; Arthur H. Cole, *Wholesale Commodity Prices in the United States, 1700–1861*, 2 vols. (Cambridge, Mass., 1938), 2: appendix; John J. McCusker, *Money and Exchange in Europe and America, 1600–1775: A Handbook* (Chapel Hill, N.C., 1978), 185–86.]

Table 4.1. *Summer Wages for Farm Workers in Essex County, Massachusetts, 1716–1775*

Year	Wages (Shillings Sterling/Day)
1716–25	1.39
1726–35	1.17
1736–45	1.01
1746–55	1.21
1756–65	1.66
1766–75	1.57

Source: Daniel Vickers, *Farmers & Fishermen: Two Centuries of Work in Essex County, Massachusetts, 1630–1850* (Chapel Hill, N.C., 1994), 248.

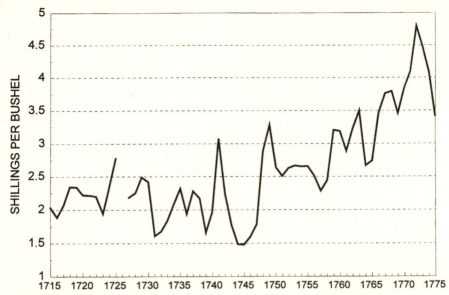

Figure 4.7. *Philadelphia wheat prices, 1715–1775*. Wheat prices illustrate the same trends as quotations for bread and flour: slow growth until 1745 and a rapid ascent after that date. [*Sources: Historical Statistics of the U.S.*, 2:1197, 1198; Cole, *Wholesale Commodity Prices*, 2: appendix; McCusker, *Money and Exchange*, 185–86.]

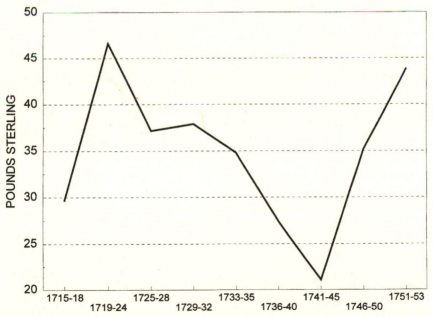

Figure 4.8. *Value of consumption goods in estates of young fathers in rural Massachusetts, 1715–1753*. This series, which compares individuals at the same point in their life cycle, illustrates the first long swing of growth and part of the second one. [*Source*: Gloria L. Main, "The Standard of Living in Colonial Massachusetts," *JEH* 43 (1983): 105.]

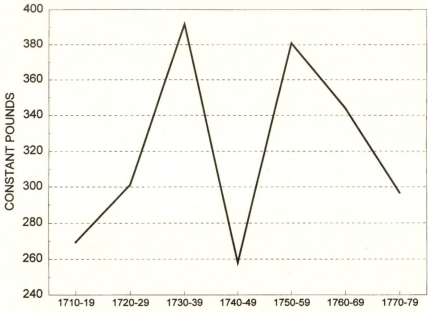

Figure 4.9. *Wealth in Hampshire County, Massachusetts, 1710–1779.* Fluctuations in the wealth of decedents illustrate the two long swings of growth. [*Source:* Terry L. Anderson, "Economic Growth in Colonial New England: 'Statistical Renaissance'," *JEH* 29 (1979): 250.]

Nor were advances recorded in the manufacture of textiles, the leading industrial activity outside the cities. Household production of cloth was widespread. A British official in New England noted in 1719: "There is scarce a Country man comes to town or woman but are clothed with their own Spinning."[15] In the 1730s the Board of Trade summarized the reports it had received from the colonies: "In New England, New York, Connecticut, Rhode-island, Pennsylvania, and in the county of Somerset, in Maryland, they have fallen into the manufacture of woolen cloth and linen cloth, for the use of their own families only." Techniques of production, however, based on spinning wheels and hand looms, remained unchanged.[16]

Hard times in the commercial sector were reflected in the slow growth of the towns. The number of urbanites climbed during this long swing, but the rate of increase was well below the pace evident after mid-century. In the 1740s, for example, city population rose only 15 percent, compared to a heady 55 percent in the 1750s (fig. 4.10). Overall, townsfolk comprised a declining portion of the northern population during this cycle (fig. 4.11).

Data for earnings and wealth depict an era during which few in the cities recorded significant gains. Wages for seamen in Boston (fig. 4.12) and Philadelphia (fig. 4.13) and laborers in Philadelphia (fig. 4.14) did not rise until mid-century. The value of probated wealth in Boston, even for the top 10 percent, shows no upward trend before 1750 (fig. 4.15). The only exception to

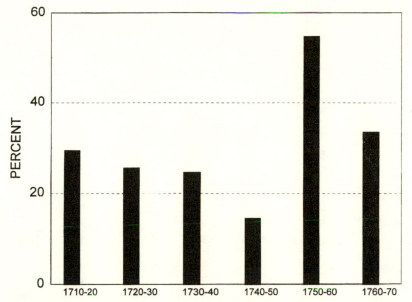

Figure 4.10. *Percentage increase in urban population of the northern colonies, 1700– 1770.*
Urban growth followed the contours of the two long swings, with modest growth before
mid-century and more vigorous expansion during the second long swing. [*Sources:* Gary
B. Nash, *The Urban Crucible: Social Change, Political Consciousness, and the Origins of
the American Revolution* (Cambridge, Mass., 1979): 407–8; Lester J. Cappon et al., eds.,
Atlas of Early American History: The Revolutionary Era (Princeton, N.J., 1976), 97.]

emerge from the data is the gains made by the upper strata in Philadelphia.
These citizens grew richer during this period. But there was no improvement
for the bottom 60 percent in the Quaker City (fig. 4.16).

ENGLISH FUNDS

The weak expansion of capital imports reinforced the pattern of slow growth
in both the countryside and towns. Most money came to the northern colonies as credit to facilitate the sale of dry goods. Wares were forwarded to America
with a six- or nine-month grace period before repayment or interest was demanded.[17] Hence the figures for per capita imports, which were low and
declining between 1713 and 1745, provide a first approximation of the sums
extended to the colonists (fig. 4.17). The slow pace of growth of the British
economy during this period also suggests no marked expansion of credit flows
before 1745. Jackson Turner Main's study of Connecticut shows that the net
indebtedness of the colony was minimal during this long swing, a sharp contrast to the large balance owed outsiders in the 1760s.[18]

In sum, lackluster sales of northern staples and the slow growth of other
activities made for a cycle with no overall gains between 1713 and 1745. A

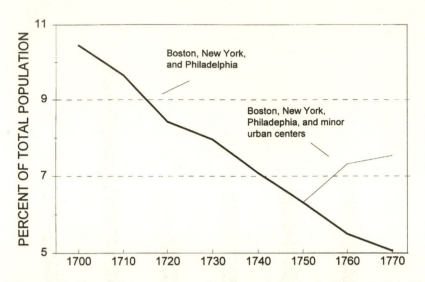

Figure 4.11. *Townsfolk as percentage of total population in the North, 1700–1770.*
Towns declined in importance during the first half of the century as northerners lessened their dependence on the fur trade and expanded their farms. Strong growth of
the cities, particularly the smaller centers, reversed this trend after mid-century. [*Sources:
Historical Statistics of the U.S.,* 2: 1168; Nash, *Urban Crucible,* 407–8; *Atlas of Early
American History,* 97. The sources are silent about the population of the smaller towns
before 1760. It is very possible that additional data for Marblehead and Salem, Mass.
and Newport, R.I., would place the upturn in urban growth earlier.]

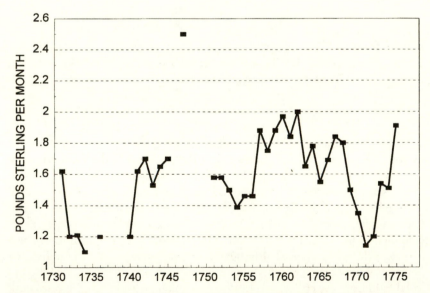

Figure 4.12. *Boston wages for sailors, 1731–1774.* Wages followed the contours of
the two long swings. Despite fluctuations they showed no overall growth before 1745.
Then they rose during the 1750s and declined after 1760. Unusual demand from the
royal navy sent wages soaring in 1747. [*Source:* Nash, *Urban Crucible,* 392–94.]

56

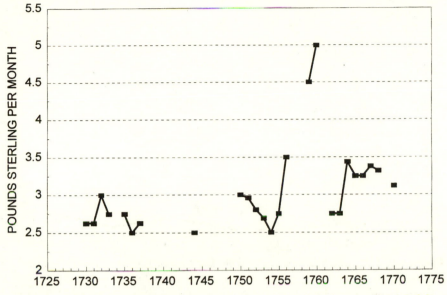

Figure 4.13. *Philadelphia wages for sailors, 1730–1770.* Sailor's wages in Philadelphia, much like the pay in Boston, reflected the economic rhythms of the two long swings. [*Source:* Nash, *Urban Crucible*, 392–94.]

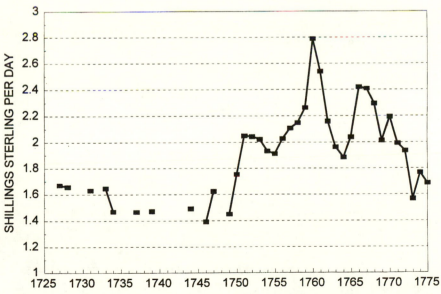

Figure 4.14. *Philadelphia wages for laborers, 1727–1775.* Wages for laborers mirrored the patterns of the two long cycles. [*Source:* Nash, *Urban Crucible*, 392–94.]

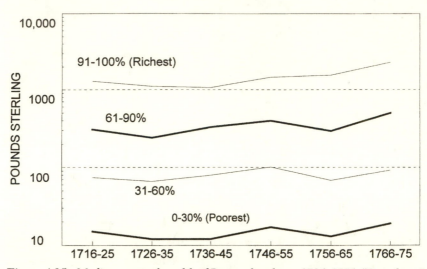

Figure 4.15. *Median personal wealth of Boston decedents, 1716–1775.* "Decedents" were individuals who died and had their estates probated. For the bottom 60 percent there was only slight improvement during the six decades from 1716 to 1775. The wealthiest Bostonians recorded some gains—chiefly because of higher real estate values. [*Source:* Nash, *Urban Crucible,* 399.]

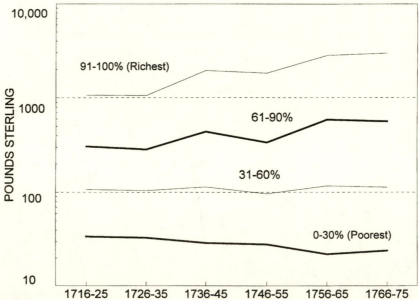

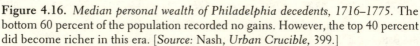

Figure 4.16. *Median personal wealth of Philadelphia decedents, 1716–1775.* The bottom 60 percent of the population recorded no gains. However, the top 40 percent did become richer in this era. [*Source:* Nash, *Urban Crucible,* 399.]

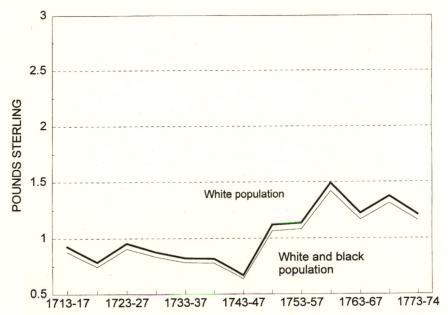

Figure 4.17. *Per capita imports into the northern colonies from Britain, 1713–1774.* This key series shows both the era of slow development, 1713–45, and the cycle of stronger growth, 1745–75. [*Source: Historical Statistics of the U.S.,* 2: 1168, 1176–78.

gloomy picture emerges when we bring together the data for per capita imports to the northern colonies (fig. 4.17) with the series for rural Massachusetts: farm workers' wages (table 4.1) and probate wealth (figs. 4.8 and 4.9). For many northerners the standard of living did not rise during this long swing.

The North Enjoys a Cycle of Strong Growth, 1745–1775

Like a crowded field of race horses breaking from the gate, a broad range of activities leaped forward after 1745. The years from the mid-1740s to the early 1760s were a period of remarkable growth in the North, with most indices slowing in the 1760s. The decline after 1760 was not as steep as the ascent and, broadly viewed, this long swing was characterized by a rise in the standard of living. Strong growth was evident in both the agricultural and commercial sectors.

FAVORABLE MARKETS FOR NORTHERN COMMODITIES

Vigorous demand for northern goods fostered growth in the colonies from Delaware to New Hampshire. We can study this export-led boom by looking at markets, the changes in prices and quantities shipped, and the impact of these developments on northern prosperity.

The British West Indies remained the leading destination for northern shippers, although southern Europe and England grew relatively more important during this cycle. Between 1768 and 1772, fully 53 percent of northern exports went to the sugar islands, while southern Europe stood next with 24 percent, and Great Britain was third with 16 percent (tab. 3.4). The most important northern exports—bread, flour, and dried fish—were sent primarily to the islands. (Figure 4.18 shows the leading northern products in the period from 1768 to 1772.) Among the other staples sent chiefly to the Caribbean were horses, cattle, barrel staves and headings, beef, pork, and spermaceti candles.

The island economies boomed between 1745 and 1760 then gradually weakened in step with the slowdown in the mother country. Several indices demonstrate the strong growth in the British Caribbean between 1745 and 1760. Sugar prices soared, continuing the rise first evident in the late 1730s. Between 1749–51 and 1759–61 the value of a hundredweight of muscovado (unrefined) sugar rose 40 percent from 29.1 shillings to 40.6 shillings (fig. 4.2). The quantity of the sweetener exported to the mother country also skyrocketed after 1745; these shipments had languished during the first long swing (fig. 4.1). Estimates for the profitability of cane culture, calculated by J. R. Ward, point to a vigorous expansion in the 1750s. Ward used the records of various plantations in the British sugar islands to arrive at his overall figures (tab. 4.2). The pace of population growth in the English Caribbean also quickened in the years before 1760 (tab. 4.3).

Not all the British sugar plantations participated in this era of rapid development. The soils of Barbados, southeastern Jamaica, and the Leeward Islands—Antigua, Nevis, Montserrat, and St. Christopher—permitted no increase in output after mid-century. Much of the upsurge in production came from plantations in the northern and western reaches of Jamaica. In 1758 British Customs established three new ports of entry on Jamaica to serve these districts and to supplement Kingston, which handled sugar from the estates of the south and east.

After 1760 growth in the West Indies gradually slowed. Sugar prices, which had risen so strongly, now declined (fig. 4.2). The profits earned by the sugar planters slipped, as did the pace of population growth (tabs. 4.2 and 4.3). The

Table 4.2. *Average Rates of Profit for Sugar Plantations in the British West Indies, 1749–1782*

Year	Profit
1749–55	10.1%
1756–62	13.5
1763–75	9.3
1776–82	3.4

Source: J. R. Ward, "The Profitability of Sugar Planting in the British West Indies, 1650–1834," *Economic History Review*, 2d ser., 31 (1978): 207.

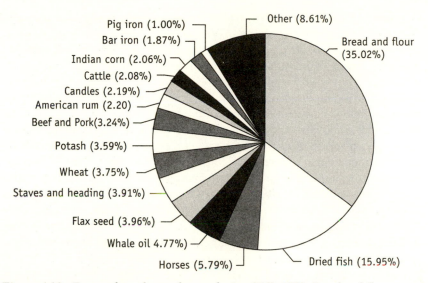

Figure 4.18. *Exports from the northern colonies, 1768–1772.* Bread and flour were the most important exports from the northern colonies, while dried fish stood second in importance. Also striking is the diversity of products exported by these provinces. The average annual value of total shipments from the northern colonies during these five years was £964,764 sterling. [*Source:* James F. Shepherd and Gary M. Walton, *Shipping, Maritime Trade, and the Economic Development of Colonial North America* (Cambridge, Eng., 1972), 211–24.]

Table 4.3. *Percentage Increase in the Population of the British West Indies, 1740–1780*

Period	White	Black	Total
1740–50	3	18	16
1750–60	17	24	23
1760–70	10	19	18
1770–80	7	13	12

Sources: John J. McCusker, "The Rum Trade and the Balance of Payments of the Thirteen Continental Colonies, 1650–1775" (Ph.D. diss., University of Pittsburgh, 1970), 712; note the correction in John J. McCusker and Russell R. Menard, *The Economy of British America, 1607–1789: Needs and Opportunities for Study* (Chapel Hill, N.C., 1985), 154.

only favorable index for the British sugar islands was the steady rise in exports. Britain gained Tobago, Dominica, St. Vincent, and Grenada in the 1763 peace treaty. the expansion of production in these possessions allowed shipments home to grow at a fairly constant rate until the disruptions of war in the mid-1770s (fig. 4.1).[19]

Rising demand from southern Europe, the second market for northern produce, helped cushion the impact of the post-1760 downturn in the West Indies. The increase in colonial wheat sales to Iberia after 1765 was a by-product of British growth. England had long been an exporter of wheat and flour, with shipments rising to record heights in the 1740s and 1750s. But soaring domestic consumption in Great Britain changed this picture. Britain became a net importer in the 1760s, and southern Europe — which had long relied on British supplies — now turned to the New World (fig. 2.1). By the late 1760s Portugal and Spain were the chief destinations for northern shipments of wheat and Indian corn, and were an important market for bread, flour, and fish. The impact of this expanded trade, however, was greater for Pennsylvania, the bread-basket of the North, than for the other colonies. Compare figure 4.3, which focuses on Philadelphia, and figure 4.19, which charts the total tonnage clearing four northern ports (Salem, Boston, New York, and Philadelphia).

Calls from Great Britain, the third market for northern exports, also soared in the late colonial era. English purchases of northern goods had risen after 1745, in step with the expansion phase of the long swing. The Seven Years' War temporarily checked this growth. Significantly, demand did not slacken in the 1760s when the British economy slowed. Shortages of grain led the home government to open the ports (in particular years) to colonial flour, bread, and wheat (fig. 4.4). British purchases of a variety of semifinished goods — whale oil, bar and pig iron, and potash — also remained strong. The demand for these secondary products contributed to the diversification that marked the northern colonies (fig. 4.18).[20]

Favorable markets, particularly before 1760, drove up prices and encouraged northerners to plant more grain and catch more fish. Between 1744–46 and 1759–61 there were increases of 92, 85, and 103 percent, respectively, in the price of flour, bread, and wheat (figs. 4.6 and 4.7). The value of fish — the second most important northern export — also climbed (fig. 4.20), as did quotations for beef, pork, and staves.[21] The quantity of flour shipped by Pennsylvanians jumped both in absolute and in per person terms (fig. 4.5). The number of barrels of beef and pork forwarded from Philadelphia soared between 1745 and 1760.[22]

After 1760 bad news was mixed with good. Reflecting weaker Caribbean markets, the price of many northern wares and the quantities exported slumped. The value of fish declined slightly, while quotations for beef, pork, and staves retreated from the high levels achieved during the Seven Years' War. Data for amounts shipped suggest the same pattern. Exports of beef and pork from Philadelphia made no further gains after 1760.

However, the price and volume of grain shipped did *not* decline after 1760. Between 1759–61 and 1772–74, flour, bread and wheat prices climbed by an additional 27, 28, and 44 percent, respectively (figs. 4.6 and 4.7).[23] This con-

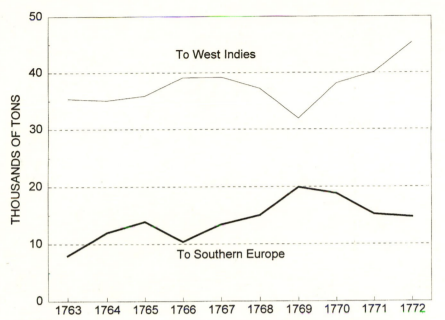

Figure 4.19. *Tonnage clearing northern ports for the West Indies and southern Europe, 1763–1773.* This graph presents data for Philadelphia, New York, Boston, and Salem. A comparison with figure 4.3 suggests that while the growth of southern European demand was crucial for Philadelphia (the center of the grain trade), it had less of an impact on the northern colonies as a whole. [*Source:* Sachs, "Business Outlook," 170, 181, 182.]

tinuing ascent reflected the impact of markets in southern Europe and, to a lesser extent, purchases by the mother country. Philadelphian William Pollard explained in 1772: "Our produce has advanced for several years past and is now really very high. This I conceive is chiefly occasioned by the demands from Lisbon and Cadiz and some other parts of Europe, who formerly had their supplies chiefly from Europe."[24]

The broad rise in staple prices before 1760, and the increases in grain quotations throughout this long swing, boosted the standard of living. As figures 4.21, 4.22, 4.23, and 4.24 indicate, the cost of textiles—which made up well over one-half the goods purchased from the mother country—did not climb between 1750 and 1775. So a hundredweight of flour bought more. Where this measure commanded four yards of calamancos in the late 1740s, the same hundredweight could be traded for eight yards in 1760 and for more than twelve yards in the 1770s (fig. 4.25). The result? Per capita imports of goods from Britain rose from 1745 to 1760, and remained at high levels despite a contraction in the flow of credit (fig. 4.17).

The changing value of northern staples after 1760 had a different impact on the middle colonies and New England. Rising flour and bread prices boosted the well-being of the middle provinces. Although some Pennsylvanians and

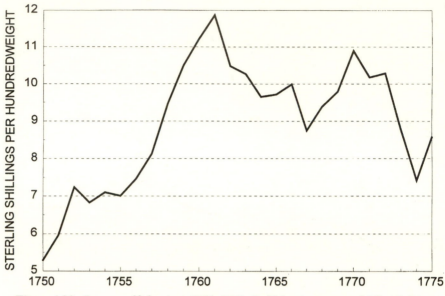

Figure 4.20. *Boston codfish prices, 1750–1775.* Codfish prices rose and fell with West Indian demand and so trace the outlines of this long swing. [*Source:* Cole, *Wholesale Commodity Prices,* 2: appendix.]

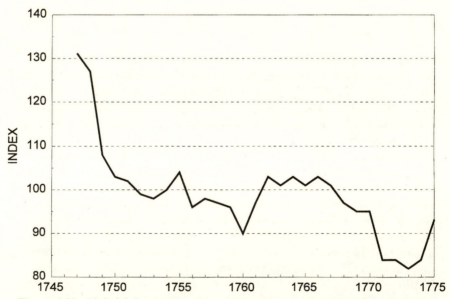

Figure 4.21. *Philadelphia textile prices—linen and cotton checks, 1747–1775.* Prices for these European fabrics declined during this long swing, helping to boost the standard of living in the colonies. [*Source:* Appendix A. Note that 100 = annual average, 1750–54.]

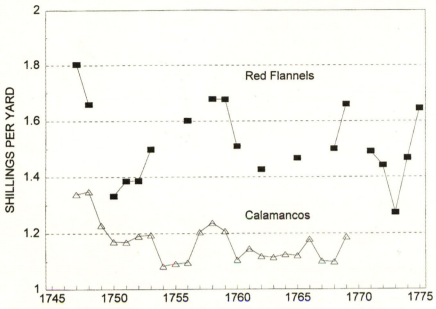

Figure 4.22. *Philadelphia textile prices—flannels and calamancos, 1747–1775.* Long-term prices for these British textiles showed no rise, allowing Pennsylvanians to improve their standard of living. [*Source:* Appendix A.]

New Yorkers struggled to reduce their indebtedness during these years, many farmers celebrated the high prices and bought unprecedented quantities of dry goods. Conditions were gloomier in New England. Falling or level quotations for fish, lumber, and meat and the soaring cost of wheat hurt the Puritan colonies. Hard times in the New England countryside are reflected in two series. Anderson's study of Hampshire County, Massachusetts, shows a sharp decline in probated wealth after 1760 (fig 4.9).[25] Vickers's tabulation of farm wages in Essex County, Massachusetts, presents a similar pattern. Payments rose in this area of mixed farming between 1736–45 and 1756–65 and then declined during the last decade of the colonial era (tab. 4.1).[26]

Finally, northern farmers were helped during this long swing by rising agricultural productivity. It helped lift the standard of living during the years of expansion, 1745–1760, and it slowed the decline after 1760. Ball and Walton's study indicates that the physical output of individual homesteads in Chester County, Pennsylvania, rose. The index of land under cultivation, which had dropped from 100 for 1714–31 to 85 for 1734–45, now climbed to 106 for 1750–70 (fig. 1.3). Total output also increased. Richard Bushman suggests that around mid-century farmers moved toward a more intensive approach to cultivation. But probably the greatest gains came simply from bringing more land under the plow. On most homesteads methods of cultivation confirmed Jedidiah Morse's observation: "The common husbandmen in the country generally choose to continue in the old track of their forefathers."[27]

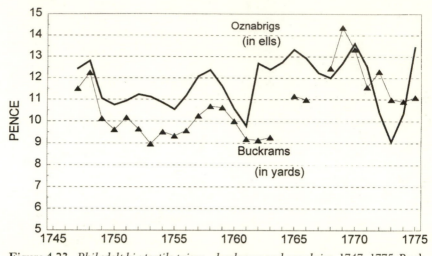

Figure 4.23. *Philadelphia textile prices—buckrams and oznabrigs, 1747–1775.* Buckrams were made in Britain, while oznabrigs came from the European continent. Prices for these fabrics showed little increase. [*Source:* Appendix A.]

Figure 4.24. *Boston textile prices—Russia duck, 1753–1774.* Despite significant fluctuations, there was little long-term increase in the price of this durable cotton cloth. [*Source:* Cole, *Wholesale Commodity Prices*, 2: appendix.]

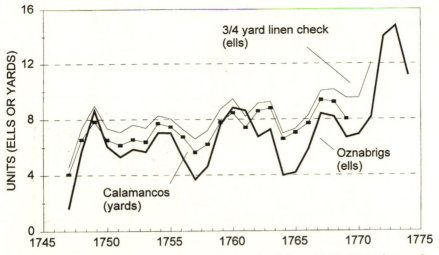

Figure 4.25. *Purchasing power of a hundredweight of flour, 1747–1774.* This graph illustrates conditions in the Philadelphia market where a hundredweight of flour bought increasing quantities of cloth. Consumers in the grain-growing colonies of New York and Pennsylvania benefited from the combination of rising wheat prices and stable quotations for dry goods. [*Sources:* Appendix A; *Historical Statistics of the U.S.,* 2: 1197.]

COMMERCIAL AND INDUSTRIAL ACTIVITIES

The prosperity of the nonagricultural sector also rose and fell in step with this growth cycle. Most of this activity was focused in the towns of Boston, New York, and Philadelphia. These centers accounted for about 5 percent of the northern population in 1760 and for a far larger proportion of regional wealth. The following sections examine commercial and industrial activities by focusing on mercantile profits, manufacturing, and the well-being of the townsfolk.

Mercantile Profits. Merchant income was probably the most important determinant of the prosperity of the nonagricultural sector. Colonial importers provided the majority of funds for local investments and directly or indirectly employed many individuals. The earnings of these traders, in turn, came largely from two activities: the dry goods trade and West Indian commerce. Profits from these enterprises increased during the late 1740s and 1750s and then fell in the 1760s and early 1770s.

Returns from the sale of manufactures tracked the larger cycle. The margin of profit in this branch of commerce can be calculated from data on the cost of dry goods in England and the selling price in the colonies, as well as freight, insurance, and exchange rates. As figure 4.26 shows, net earnings on the sale of dry goods remained high between 1745 and 1760. But such favorable returns yielded to losses in the prolonged slump following the French and Indian War. During these lean years, merchants may have covered the costs of the fabric, freight, and insurance (hence *gross* profits were usually positive). But they did

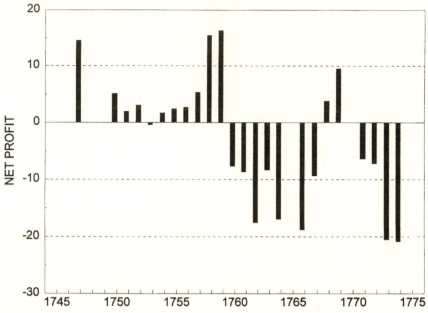

Figure 4.26. *Net profits on Philadelphia dry goods, 1747–1774.* Profits were higher during the growth phase of this long swing than during the period of contraction that followed 1760. This series brings together data for eleven fabrics. [*Sources:* This series is calculated according to the following formulas:

net profit = .75 × gross profit

gross profit as % = (sterling receipts– total sterling costs) / (total sterling cost × .01)

total sterling cost = (Eng. sterling unit price) × (1 + freight + insurance + commission + charges)

sterling receipts = Pa. currency unit price / (0.01 × exchange rate)

Appendix A presents data on colonial textile prices, Appendix B provides English prices, and Appendix D gives insurance rates. Exchange rates are found in McCusker, *Money and Exchange,* 185–86. Commissions were typically 2.5 percent of value, while sundry charges added another 1 percent. Computations are based on half years, with the English costs drawn from the *preceding* half year. For more information on this computation, see Marc Egnal, *A Mighty Empire: The Origins of the American Revolution* (Ithaca, N.Y., 1988), 134–36.]

not make enough to compensate themselves for salaries, overhead, bad debts, and other expenses. It is these *net* profits that are shown in figure 4.26.[28]

Analysis of West Indian commerce also suggests that northern merchants had higher earnings before 1760 than between 1760 and 1775. Before 1760 traders typically sent goods to the British sugar islands as "ventures." In these speculative undertakings, the northern exporter assumed the risk and reaped most of the profit or loss. The merchant purchased foodstuffs and lumber, and directed these staples to a factor resident in the islands. On the return voyage, rum or sugar was sent to the northern colonies. Data for flour, rum, and ex-

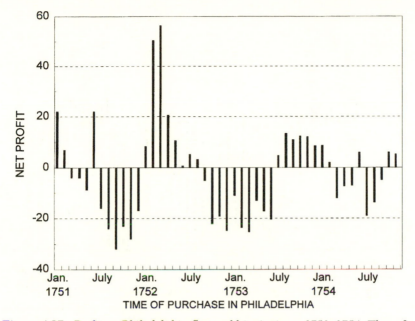

Figure 4.27. *Profit on Philadelphia flour sold in Antigua, 1751–1754.* These figures illustrate the possibility of substantial profits for the shipper with good market information — or luck. [*Sources:* This series is calculated according to the following formulas:

profit as percentage = (100 × net profits)/Phila. costs

net profit = remittance to Phila. − Phila. costs

remittance to Phila. = Receipts in Antigua − (wharfage + cooperage + freight + commission)

Phila. costs = price of flour − (nailing & searching + insurance)

The calculations are based on Philadelphia flour prices and Antigua quotations three months later to take into account the time needed for shipping and sale. For Philadelphia flour prices, Anne Bezanson et al., *Prices in Colonial Pennsylvania* (Phila., 1935), appendix; for Antigua prices, see Appendix E. For data on wharfage, etc., see Marc Egnal, "The Changing Structure of Philadelphia's Trade With the British West Indies, 1750–1775," *Pennsylvania Magazine of History and Biography* 99 (1975): 158–63.]

change rates in Antigua and Philadelphia in the 1750s allow an assessment of returns on these ventures, and suggest that with care the trade could be a profitable one. As figures 4.27 (for Philadelphia flour) and 4.28 (for Antigua rum) indicate, market conditions, favorable and unfavorable, tended to persist for several months. A Philadelphia exporter could, with justifiable hope, respond to the advice of his Antiguan correspondent even though the shipment would not arrive at the island until six weeks or more after a request was made.

After 1760 the returns from venturing declined, and merchants turned more and more to dealing on commission. Speculative voyages suffered as cane

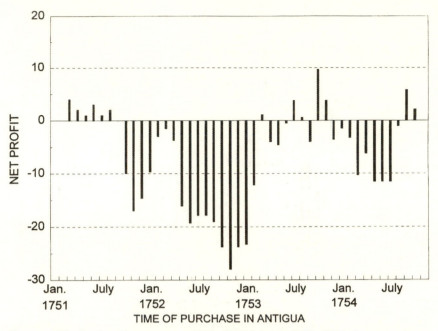

Figure 4.28. *Profit on Antigua rum sold in Philadelphia, 1751–1754.* Compare these figures with those for flour shipments to Antigua. Rum, it seems, was more of a means of remittance than a profitable investment. [*Sources:* This series is calculated according to the following formulas:

profit as percentage = (100 × net profit)/ Antigua costs

net profit = net receipts – Antigua costs

Antigua costs = cost of rum + duty + cooperage + wharfage + commission + insurance

Net receipts = earnings from sale of rum in Phila. – freight

These calculations are based on Antigua rum prices and Philadelphia quotations three months later to take into account the time needed for shipping and sale. For Antigua rum prices, see Appendix E; for Philadelphia prices, Bezanson, *Prices in Colonial Pennsylvania*, appendix. For data on wharfage, cooperage, etc., and more information on these calculations, see Egnal, "Changing Structure of Philadelphia's Trade," 158–63.]

cultivation became less profitable. The soaring price of flour and bread in the 1760s, coupled with the level trend in the value of West Indian produce, lessened the islanders' ability to recompense northern traders. Merchants responded by venturing cargoes less often and expanding their commission business. They now forwarded produce in response to firm orders from houses in the Caribbean or England, and willingly accepted a fixed percentage (usually 5 percent) of the outlay for foodstuffs. These changing practices were evident in each of the northern ports. For example, in the 1750s Thomas Hancock of Boston had ventured cargoes to the sugar islands. But his nephew, John

Hancock, who took over his uncle's business in 1764, limited his dealings with the West Indies to a commission trade, directed from London.[29] The letter books of Philadelphia merchants also testify to the increased importance of such transactions. Commission business may have provided adequate returns to a few houses, but it limited the number of firms that dealt with the Caribbean. On balance, it lessened the earnings northern traders received from these exchanges.[30]

Manufacturing. The activities of artisans and other manufacturers expanded in the late colonial period. The growth of these enterprises helped moderate the post-1760 slump, although the value added by these crafts was less significant than the earnings from commerce.

The production of finished goods strengthened after 1760 for several reasons. First, the boycotts of British manufacturers in 1765–66, 1768–70, and 1774–76 widened the market for local producers. These agreements reflected a mix of self-interested and patriotic motives, and in each instance they began with broad support. Craftspeople backed the agreements, recognizing that the pacts boosted sales of their wares. Merchants saw the embargoes as a means of reducing indebtedness.[31] And revolutionaries applauded the pacts as a blow against Britain. In 1766 Benjamin Franklin told the House of Commons of the colonists' patriotic resolve:

[Question:] What used to be the pride of the Americans?
[Franklin:] To indulge in the fashions and manufactures of Great Britain.
[Question:] What is now their pride?
[Franklin:] To wear their old clothes over again, till they can make new ones.[32]

Second, manufacturing expanded because civic leaders felt such activities could (as a Boston committee remarked) "employ the great numbers of poor." Boston, New York, and Philadelphia established manufactories in the 1760s to assist the unemployed, and reduce the unprecedented burden of public relief (fig. 4.29). Typically, these enterprises coordinated the work of several hundred spinners and many weavers.

Third, production jumped as the ratio between settlers and land lengthened in the long-settled areas of the North. Philadelphian William Pollard explained in 1773 that "many thousands, rather than go far back into the country where lands are cheap or undertake the arduous task of clearing new lands, turn to manufacturing, and live upon a small farm, as in many parts of England."[33] The burgeoning cities, which accounted for an increasing portion of the population, were also a source of craftspeople. Master artisans had no difficulty recruiting apprentices from among the literate townsfolk.

The strides the North made in craft production were unmatched by the Upper or Lower South. This industrial activity, as table 4.4 suggests, included shipyards, potteries, paper mills, sugar refineries, rum distilleries, and the silversmith shops. In most of these enterprises, the northern share of colonial output far exceeded the 53 percent of the total population (or 64 percent of the

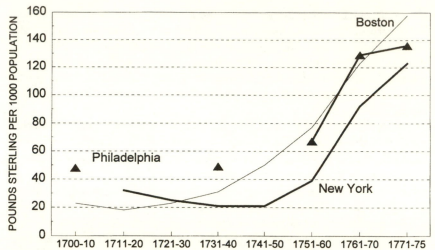

Figure 4.29. *Poor relief expenditures in three cities, 1700–1775.* Conditions worsened for the poor citizens in Boston, New York, and Philadelphia, particularly during the second long swing. Unlike farmers, city dwellers were punished by the soaring grain prices in the years after 1745. [*Source:* Nash, *Urban Crucible*, 402.]

Table 4.4. *Industrial and Commercial Activities in the Thirteen Colonies, by Region, 1760–1775*

Region	Potteries, 1760–75		Paper Mills, 1760–75		Marine Insur. Offices, c. 1763	
	Number	%	Number	%	Number	%
North	27	87	29	94	14	100
Upper South	0	0	2	6	0	0
Lower South	4	13	0	0	0	0

Region	Ironworks, 1760–75		Shipbuilding, 1769–71		Silversmiths, 1775	
	Number	%	Tonnage	%	Number	%
North	114	66	17,690	86	310	81
Upper South	56	32	1,862	9	42	11
Lower South	4	2	1,008	5	30	8

Region	Sugar Refineries, 1770		Rum Distilleries, 1770	
	Number	%	Number	%
North	24	96	141	92
Upper South	0	0	7	5
Lower South	1	4	4	3

Source: Atlas of Early American History, 26–30. In computing the number of silversmiths, the following assumptions were made: towns with three to ten smiths had six; towns with eleven to twenty-two had fifteen; towns with twenty-three to fifty-two had thirty-five.

white population) this commercial section claimed. The South kept pace only in iron production. Northerners also dominated the manufacture of shoes, with Massachusetts, and particularly the town of Lynn, emerging as a center of production. Lynn craftspeople produced 80,000 pairs in 1768. American-made shoes not only predominated in the rural areas of New England, but gradually replaced shoes of British manufacture in trading towns such as Worcester and Boston.[34]

Northern entrepreneurs could point to some noteworthy gains in productivity. By 1775 the flour mills in Pennsylvania and Delaware were among the most advanced in the world. Innovations such as the mechanical elevation of wheat and new methods of cleaning grain increased the capacity of mills and reduced the labor required. The output of sawmills rose. Such labor-saving techniques as mechanical log carriers were American in origin. These diverse activities laid the basis for the subsequent industrialization of the North.[35]

Urban Prosperity—and Misery. The well-being of the townspeople rose and fell with the long swing. There was mounting prosperity before 1760, but hardship for many after that date. The broad pattern was reflected in the pace of population growth. In hard times fewer newcomers arrived, and fewer individuals, it seems, were encouraged to expand their families. During the 1750s the number of town dwellers rose a remarkable 55 percent, well above the increases recorded during the first long swing. The jump in population was markedly less, 34 percent, between 1760 and 1770 (fig. 4.10).

The common folk in the towns were lifted by the rising tide of prosperity during the 1750s. Wages for Philadelphia seamen and laborers soared. Measured in sterling, the amount paid to a sailor for a day's labor increased 73 percent between 1749–51 and 1759–61, while the income of workers rose 44 percent (figs. 4.13 and 4.14). The rates for Boston sailors also climbed (fig. 4.12). Generous credit practices made dry goods more available and provided funds that allowed craftspeople to expand their enterprises. To be sure, higher food prices reduced some of these benefits. And rising expenditures for poor relief suggest some fared poorly even during these years (fig. 4.29). But on balance the decade was a favorable one for those who worked with their hands.

For many ordinary citizens, however, these gains were short-lived. The last fifteen years of the colonial era were difficult ones for the less wealthy. Wages for Philadelphia sailors and laborers fell despite higher food costs (figs. 4.13 and 4.14). Payments to Boston seamen also dropped (fig. 4.12). Merchants and shopkeepers pressed their debtors as the contraction deepened. And while some artisans were buoyed by the demand for local manufactures, others who had gone too heavily in debt were forced into bankruptcy. Per person expenditures on poor relief skyrocketed in the three northern ports (fig. 4.29). And probate records indicate that the poorest 60 percent of the citizenry in the major towns made few gains (figs. 4.15 and 4.16). Indeed, the spread of urban poverty was a bitter note during an era where the larger theme was a rising standard of living.

Conditions were more favorable for the urban elite, who had more resources to fall back upon during the troubled years after 1760. Many traders had diversified their activities and could pursue investments and lines of commerce that remained buoyant, such as the shipment of grain to Europe. Probate data suggest that the wealth of the top 10 percent of decedents climbed in the late colonial era in both Philadelphia and Boston (figs. 4.15 and 4.16). However, not all merchants were lucky or so quick-footed. During the 1760s each city was rocked by the failure of several prominent trading houses.[36]

MOVEMENT OF FUNDS

The flow of British funds helped shape this cycle of strong growth in both the countryside and towns. Like a languid brook broadening into a torrent, the flow of credit to the northern colonies quickened as the British economy grew between 1745 and 1760. After 1760 this swollen stream gradually constricted as growth slowed in the parent country.

Data drawn from various sources detail the movement of these funds.[37] Because credit accompanied the shipment of goods to the colonies, figures for per capita imports offer one proxy for undulations in the flow of this money. These statistics suggest a strong expansion in the 1750s and a slowdown after 1760 (fig. 4.17).

Fluctuations in the length of the credit period also reflect the contours of this long swing. During the 1750s the repayment period increased from less than a year to a year. A London merchant explained in 1754: "The credit I usually give is nine, not exceeding twelve months."[38] The credit period gradually expanded as the British economy grew. When Barlow Trecothick, a prominent London exporter, testified before Parliament in 1766, he could observe matter-of-factly: "The credit is 12 months on average."[39] As hard times hit Britain after 1760, several exporters, including the large London house of David & John Barclay, sought to return to a shorter period. But the difficulty collecting funds kept traders from carrying out such plans.[40]

The rise and fall of credit flows was also evident in the generosity of English houses in the 1750s and in the insistent demands for repayment heard in the 1760s and 1770s. Between the late 1740s and 1760 London houses seemed only too eager to extend funds to marginal importers. One Philadelphian remarked in 1750 that Londoners Neate & Neave "have been very fond of proposing to our retailers to import their own goods."[41] The charge was echoed by others.[42] The drumbeat of offers from British firms reached a crescendo in the late 1750s, when a single London house might be extending credit to well over 100 individuals in a northern city, with many of these "importers" little more than ambitious shopkeepers.[43] By contrast, in the 1760s the transatlantic commerce is filled with insistent requests for repayment, and pleas from the colonists for leniency. Several English firms appointed or sent representatives to help them with their collections.

The impact of the fluctuations on the flow of funds was unmistakable in the countryside. Farmers benefited from the strong expansion of credit beginning in 1745. They bought more goods and patented more land. This growth culminated during the French and Indian War, which was the North American counterpart of the Seven Years' War (1756–1763) in Europe. Farmers benefited from lavish British military spending as well as generous offers of credit

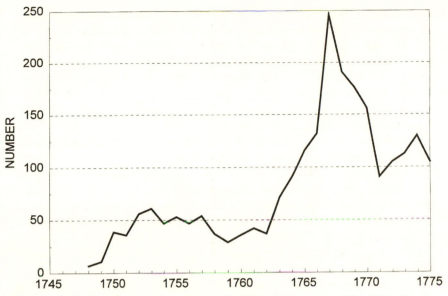

Figure 4.30. *Forced sales of property in the Philadelphia area, 1747–1774.* Court-ordered sales of property were low in the prosperous 1750s, but soared after 1762, as the economy weakened. [*Source:* Series tabulated from the *Pennsylvania Gazette*. Each advertisement was counted only at its first appearance.]

from local firms. In 1760 a Philadelphia firm noted the result: a soaring demand for imported wares. "The war has occasioned such a plentiful circulation of cash in this and the neighboring provinces," observed James & Drinker, "that the demand of its inhabitants for European and India goods [is] beyond what any person not fully acquainted therewith can conceive."[44]

The contraction of the 1760s was also felt in the countryside, particularly as conditions worsened in the second half of the 1760s. Foreclosures soared in the Philadelphia area (fig. 4.30), while New York Governor Henry Moore reported in 1768 that there were "numberless instances of Suits against Farmers whose Estates have been sold upon Execution."[45] The amount of new land taken up in Lancaster and Cumberland counties in Pennsylvania plummeted after 1766, and rural shopkeepers increasingly complained of financial stringency. "The scarcity of money is the reason that I cannot send you the balance just now," a Lancaster trader told his Philadelphia correspondent.[46] And an Albany shopkeeper explained to New Yorker James Beekman, "The declining Condition of trade and the Scarsety of Money here is not to be Exsprest."[47] Worsening conditions in the early 1770s also had an impact on the rural North.

However, the downturn did not hit all farmers with equal severity. Those who had just begun farming or had borrowed heavily found their survival threatened. These farmers barely held onto their lands or saw their estates sold at sheriff's auctions. But other landowners had few outstanding debts and profited handsomely from rising grain prices. The credit contraction hurt the farming community. But for most individuals it was a storm they could weather.[48]

The fluctuations in the movement of British funds were felt still more immediately and sharply in the trading towns. While the expansion of credit in the 1750s reinforced the favorable conditions in the cities, the contraction of the 1760s proved a sharp check. Some traders were forced into bankruptcy, and most complained about the "scarcity of money"—merchant shorthand for the difficulty traders found collecting debts. In 1764 New Yorker John Watts observed that "commerce is so stagnated here that little or nothing sells, and payment for what does sell keeps the same dull pace."[49] The next year Philadelphian Thomas Clifford reported, "Money is much scarcer here at present than it hath been some years past"; Daniel Roberdeau, another Philadelphian, observed: "I have no more expectation of raising the money than I have of drawing blood out of a flint."[50] Bostonian John Hancock spoke for many when he observed in 1767: "The situation of our trade and the scarcity of money is such that I have almost come to a resolution to suspend the importation of goods for a year or two."[51]

The credit contraction temporarily eased between 1768 and 1771, reducing the pressure on merchants and shopkeepers. This brief upturn reflected more favorable conditions in England as well as the impact of the non-importation agreements. Traders had entered these pacts in part for patriotic reasons and in part because the press of creditors made this step necessary. But hard times returned by 1772 and the colonial era closed with British firms once again dunning northern importers.[52] The problems of northern merchants, like those of the farmers, must be kept in perspective. Colonial traders pursued many roads to success, and such diversity helped most importers remain liquid—and allowed some to prosper even in tough years.

OVERVIEW

Despite the slowdown after 1760, the northern colonies enjoyed strong overall growth during the second long swing. Contemporary observers in the North underscored the permanent gains in their standard of living. The comments of Cadwallader Colden, made in 1764, open chapter 1. Connecticut minister and essayist Jared Eliot observed that his colony was "Improving and Advancing very much." He added that there was "a great deal of Silver and Gold in the Country," and that people had "better Houses, Publick and Private, richer Furniture, better Food and Cloathing; better Bridges and Highways, fatter Cattle and finer Horses, and Lands bear a higher Price."[53] Connecticut Governor Roger Wolcott contrasted life in the late 1750s with conditions early in the century. "Their buildings were good to what they had been," he declared, "but mean to what they are now; their dress and diet mean and coarse to what is now."[54]

Of course, any optimistic portrayal of the northern colonies during this cycle must be carefully qualified. Growth slowed after 1760, even if all gains were not erased. Some groups, such as New England farmers and the less wealthy townsfolk, undoubtedly lost ground in the late colonial period. But in much of the countryside there was significant long-term progress, and broadly viewed, the long swing from 1745 to 1775 was one of solid growth. It contrasted sharply with the era of slower expansion, 1713 to 1745. Independence and the disruptions of the War of the American Revolution brought an end to the second cycle. Not until the 1780s would the northern economy enter upon a new wave of development.

FIVE

—⟨ℛℓℛ⟩—

Upper South

The two cycles that characterized growth in the North and in the Thirteen Colonies as a whole were barely visible in the Upper South. The Chesapeake economy marched to a different drummer. Its rhythms were those of the tobacco trade and the markets of continental Europe. To be sure, the sale of grain and the influx of British funds helped shape the course of development. But above all else the Chesapeake economy was tied to what the colonists called "sot-weed." Ebenezer Cooke, who inherited property in Maryland, knew he had arrived in a world of tobacco planters as soon as he got off the boat in Piscataway Bay:

> With neither Stockings, Hat, nor Shooe,
> These *Sot-weed* Planters Crowd the Shoar,
> In Hue as tawny as a Moor.[1]

Virtually all tobacco was sent to Britain, but most of it did not stay there. Typically, over 70 percent was reshipped to Europe. So the Chesapeake economy was linked to the bourses of Amsterdam and Paris and the decisions of consumers in Holland, France, and Germany. Fluctuations in European purchases help demarcate two periods for the economy of the Upper South. Between 1713 and 1731 the economy recorded few gains; from 1732 to 1775 the Chesapeake experienced a steady but moderate rise in the standard of living.

Weak European Demand Hurts the Chesapeake, 1713–1731

The period from 1713 to 1731 were ones of fitful recovery from the ravages of imperial war. (In Europe these conflicts were known as the War of the League

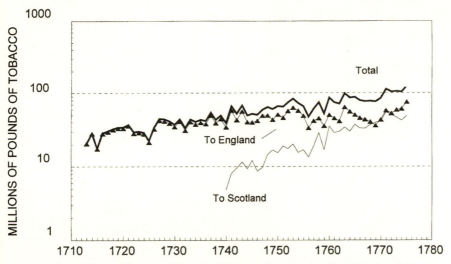

Figure 5.1. *Tobacco shipments from the Chesapeake to England and Scotland, 1713–1775. The most dramatic change in the tobacco trade was the expansion of shipments to Scotland after 1745. Exports to England exhibited less growth.* [*Source:* U.S. Bureau of the Census, *Historical Statistics of the United States, Colonial Times to 1970,* 2 vols. (Washington, D.C., 1975), 2: 1190. Some data for Scotland are estimated.]

of Augsburg, 1689–1697, and the War of the Spanish Succession, 1702–1713. In the British colonies they were called King William's War and Queen Anne's War.) At the heart of the problems besetting the Upper South in the 1710s and 1720s were faltering sales of tobacco. By contrast, the commerce in grain was relatively unimportant during this era, and the contribution fo the commercial sector was negligible.

Troubles in the tobacco trade made this a difficult time for Virginia and Maryland. Soon after peace returned in 1713, continental demand for the weed strengthened and exports from the Chesapeake rose. However, a prolonged downturn that began in 1720 checked this upsurge in shipments. The slump was triggered by the bursting of speculative "bubbles" in France and England. Joint-stock companies, which had been launched with great fanfare in both countries, collapsed amidst widespread financial panic. Many branches of commerce, including trade with the Chesapeake, suffered (fig. 5.1). Virginian Robert Carter informed his son: "Mr. Perry tells me many a melancholy story of the ruinous effects of the South Sea stock and other bubbles, and what is worse, the fatal consequences to trade and particularly tobacco, which looks with but a dark aspect." The crisis in France forced the Indies Company, which purchased tobacco for the kingdom, into bankruptcy. Only in the early 1730s were signs of recovery evident.[2]

The steady decline of Amsterdam prices compounded the planter's problems (fig. 5.2). The Dutch were the chief customers for British tobacco, and the steep slide in quotations was soon felt in Britain and the Upper South.

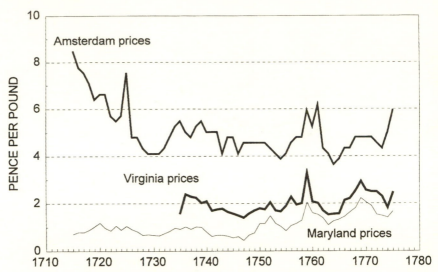

Figure 5.2. *Tobacco prices in Amsterdam and the Upper South, 1715–1775.* These figures illustrate (1) the hard times in the 1720s, (2) the stability of European prices after 1730, and (3) the convergence of Amsterdam and Chesapeake prices between the 1730s and 1770s. [*Sources: Historical Statistics of the U.S.,* 2: 1198; N. W. Posthumus, *Inquiry into the History of Prices in Holland,* 2 vols. (Leiden, 1946–1964), 1: 202–3, 597–602; Allan Kulikoff, *Tobacco and Slaves: The Development of Southern Cultures in the Chesapeake, 1680–1800* (Chapel Hill, N.C., 1986), 80; Jacob M. Price, *France and the Chesapeake: A History of the French Tobacco Monopoly, 1674–1791, and of Its Relationship to the British and American Tobacco Trades,* 2 vols. (Ann Arbor, Mich., 1973), 2: 852; Carville V. Earle, *The Evolution of a Tidewater Settlement System: All Hallow's Parish, Maryland, 1650–1781* (Chicago, 1975), 228–29; John J. McCusker, *Money and Exchange in Europe and America, 1600–1775: A Handbook* (Chapel Hill, N.C., 1978).]

Growers complained loudly. "You are too well acquainted with Virginia not to know that we cannot live and maintain our families at these prices," Robert Carter told a London correspondent in 1727.[3] The total value of tobacco shipments declined by 27 percent from 1718–20 to 1730–32 (fig. 5.3).[4]

Because of their heavy dependence on tobacco sales, landowners suffered more during this downturn than they would during subsequent slumps. In later years planters cushioned such blows with their wealth, their involvement with other crops, and their growing commitment to local manufacturing. But those developments lay in the future. During the early 1730s Governor William Gooch could complain: "Negroes go naked all the winter, have not proper tools to work with, and their quarters for want of nails are tumbling down."[5] Home production of textiles remained no more than a desirable goal. John Randolph observed in 1729: "The price of the planter's labor is fallen below what they are able to bear, and unless they can be relieved, they must be driven to a necessity of employing themselves more usefully in manufacturing of woolen and linen."[6]

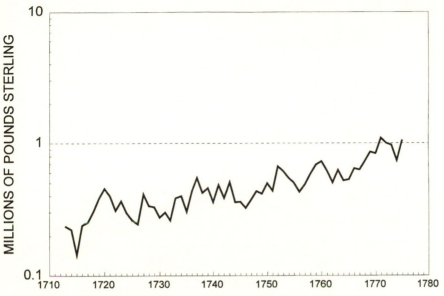

Figure 5.3. *Value of tobacco shipped to Great Britain, 1713–1775.* This figure shows the steady rise in the value of shipments to Great Britain. It is based on the total quantity shipped multiplied by Virginia prices. [*Sources: Historical Statistics of the U.S.,* 2: 1190; see the price data cited in the notes to figure 5.2. Missing data are interpolated.]

Grain sales provided little relief: the Upper South grew relatively little corn or wheat. The combined value of these two crops in the inventories of six Chesapeake counties was less than half that of tobacco. (In contrast, in the late colonial era, the two together would be worth more than tobacco.) And the inventoried value of grain fell between 1710–22 to 1723–32 (fig. 5.4).

The statistical evidence paints a picture of dark clouds pierced by only a few rays of light. The evidence of hard times is unmistakable. Measured on a per person basis the worth of tobacco exports declined between 1713–17 and 1728–32 (fig. 5.5),[7] as did purchases of British wares. Per capita imports from the mother country would not fall so low again until the very end of the colonial period (fig. 5.6). Land prices in two Maryland counties — Prince George's and Anne Arundel — slid during the 1720s and did not rebound until after 1730 (fig. 5.7). Inventoried wealth in St. Mary's County, Maryland, touched a low point in 1730 (fig. 5.8). Planters also bought fewer slaves. In the 1720s the African-American population in the Upper South declined as a percentage of the total population (fig. 1.6). And the number of slaves showed the smallest percentage increase for any decade between 1700 and 1770.[8]

Despite this litany of bad news, there were some favorable signs. This slump was not as bad as that oppressing the Upper South during the war years, 1689 to 1713 — an era when prices for the weed reached historic lows and sales stagnated. Although there was a decline in per capita figures, the total

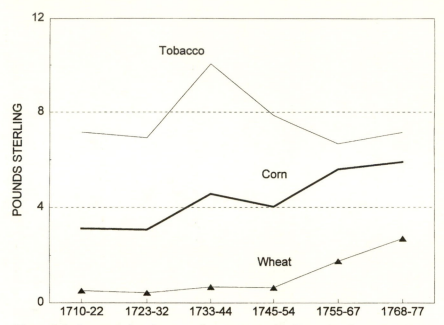

Figure 5.4. *Average value of crops in the inventories of six Upper South counties, 1710–1777.* Tobacco remained the most valuable crop in the Upper South, even though corn and wheat rose in importance. The counties in this tabulation are Somerset, rural Anne Arundel, Talbot, St. Mary's, and Price George's (all in Maryland) and rural York (in Virginia). [*Source:* Lois Green Carr, "Diversification in the Colonial Chesapeake: Somerset County, Maryland, in Comparative Perspective," in *Colonial Chesapeake Society*, ed. Lois Green Carr, Philip D. Morgan, and Jean B. Russo (Chapel Hill, N.C., 1988), 358–59.]

value of tobacco shipments rose between 1713 and 1732 (fig. 5.3). And developments on both sides of the Atlantic laid the foundation for subsequent growth. In Virginia, the Inspection Act of 1730 placed commerce on a more solid footing. This legislation designated a series of sites where all tobacco was to be inspected and the poor quality weed destroyed. In Britain, the government removed all duties from reexported tobacco. In France, the Indies Company rose like a phoenix from the ashes of bankruptcy, and in 1730 the firm leased its monopoly to the United General Farms. The new body would prove to be an effective agency for acquiring and distributing tobacco. The growing use of snuff in Europe boosted consumption. The stage was set for better times.[9]

An Era of Steady Growth, 1732–1775

Beginning in the early 1730s the economy of the Upper South entered an era of growth. The rise in the standard of living, however, was more steady than spectacular, and the pace of development never rivalled the growth that trans-

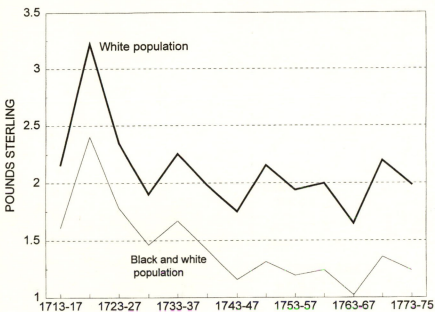

Figure 5.5. *Tobacco exports per capita, 1713–1775.* Shipments per person showed no growth, even though total exports of tobacco climbed steadily (see figs. 5.1 and 5.3). [*Source: Historical Statistics of the U.S.,* 2: 1168, 1190.]

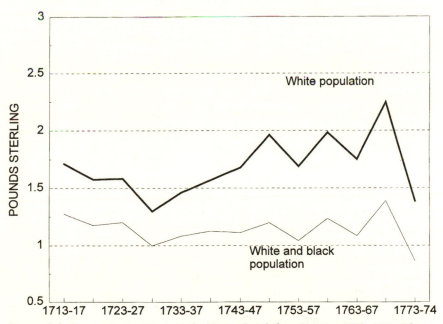

Figure 5.6. *Per capita imports into the Upper South from Britain, 1713–1774.* This key series shows hard times, from 1713 to 1731, followed by a long period of slow, steady growth from 1732 to 1775. [*Source: Historical Statistics of the U.S.,* 2: 1168, 1176–78.]

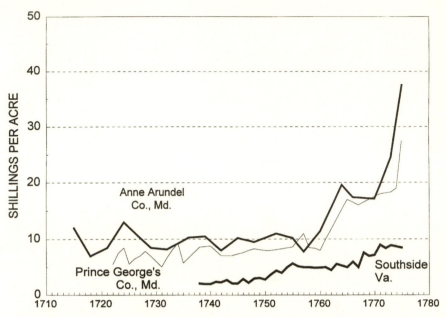

Figure 5.7. *Land prices in the Upper South, 1715–1775.* These series show strongly rising land prices in the long-settled areas during the late colonial period. But any conclusions about prosperity must be tempered by the fact that much of the population was landless, and foreclosures were soaring during these years. [*Sources:* Kulikoff, *Tobacco and Slaves,* 133; Earle, *Evolution of a Tidewater Settlement,* 211. Missing data in these series have been interpolated.]

formed the North after 1745. The gradual expansion of the tobacco trade provided a basis for this ascent. These earnings were supplemented by returns from the sale of wheat. Two other impetuses for growth — the cultivation of new crops and the expansion of commerce and manufacturing — made only a slight contribution to regional prosperity. The widening influx of British funds boosted agriculture as well as the small commercial sector.

TOBACCO TRADE

The slow, steady climb in the value of tobacco exports after 1732 shaped the growth of the Upper South. Thanks to the expansion of European consumption and rising Chesapeake prices, the worth of shipments increased steadily in this period. Considered in relation to the white population of Virginia and Maryland, however, these exports remained level. And judged against the total number of inhabitants, the value of tobacco sold per capita actually declined (fig. 5.5). We can scrutinize the trade more closely by looking at the quantity shipped, the prices received, and the productivity of the labor force.

Between 1730 and 1775 the quantity of tobacco sent to Britain rose by 20 percent a decade (fig. 5.1). This seemingly steady growth in consumption masks

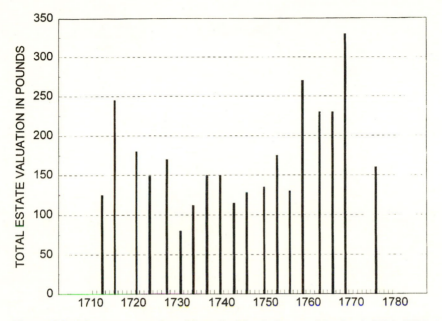

Figure 5.8. *Mean inventoried wealth in St. Mary's County, Maryland, 1714–1776.*
These data show the hard times in the 1720s, and the gradual improvement after 1730.
This series is adjusted for the age of those inventoried, since older individuals tended
to die wealthier. [*Source:* Lois G. Carr and Lorena S. Walsh, "Changing Life Styles
in Colonial St. Mary's County," Regional Economic History Research Center, *Working Papers,* 1, no. 3 (1978): 99.]

a series of shifts in demand. Britain comprised a secondary market, retaining
between 6 and 26 percent of Chesapeake shipments each year. Home consumption followed the familiar pattern of the two long swings discussed in Chapter 2.
From 1730 to 1742 British purchases slumped. The next cycle began with an
era of strong growth, 1745–1760. Tobacco sales in the home market reached a
peak in the early 1760s, and then declined until the early 1770s (fig. 5.9).

Fortunately for the planters, purchases by traders on the European continent usually compensated for the slack times in Britain. The strong expansion
of the French economy in the 1730s and early 1740s underwrote an upsurge
in sales just as the British market weakened. During these years, France temporarily surpassed Holland as the leading purchaser of British tobacco.[10] After
1745 the growth of European consumption slowed. The disruptions that accompanied the War of the Austrian Succession (which stretched from 1740 to
1748 and was called King George's War in the British colonies) and slower
growth on the European continent hurt tobacco sales. British demand now
helped keep the growth in shipments steady. In the 1760s, for once, hard times
in the continent reinforced the slowdown in the mother country. But during
the first half of the 1770s, renewed European calls for tobacco helped send
Chesapeake exports to record heights (fig. 5.1).

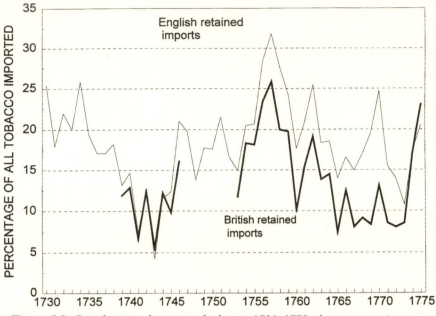

Figure 5.9. *British retained imports of tobacco, 1730–1775: three-year moving average.* British tobacco consumption reflected the long swings of growth. [*Source: Historical Statistics of the U.S.*, 2: 1190.]

Not only did the quantities shipped rise, but so did the prices the planters received. The upward trend of Chesapeake tobacco prices is, at first glance, puzzling. The long-term trend of European prices for the leaf was downward. Quotations in Amsterdam, the chief entrepôt for tobacco on the continent, declined slowly between 1731 and the eve of Independence. Prices spurted only during the Seven Years' War (fig. 5.2). The disparity in price movements between Europe and the Upper South is striking, and demands an explanation. As table 5.1 indicates, Chesapeake prices became a steadily larger percentage of Amsterdam quotations.

What explains this narrowing price gap? To begin with, quotations in Virginia and Maryland exhibited different trends. Between 1735 and 1747 Maryland prices averaged only 41 percent of those received by Virginia. As Maryland Governor Thomas Bladen acknowledged, the price differential reflected the superior quality of Virginia tobacco. Maryland planters, Bladen explained in 1744, were "under no kind of restraint" and "put all manner of trash, though unfit for anything but manure" in their hogsheads. Bladen praised the Virginia Inspection Act of 1730 and urged the legislature to frame a comparable measure.[11] Despite opposition from the Eastern Shore counties, which produced a low grade of tobacco, Maryland adopted an Inspection Act in 1747. The result was that Maryland prices now climbed more rapidly than those in Virginia. Between 1747 and 1774 they averaged 67 percent of prices in the Old Dominion (tab. 5.1).

The impact of the Maryland Inspection Act sheds light on the unusually swift rise of prices in one colony, but not on the convergence of quotations in Amsterdam and the Upper South. Much of the explanation for that development lies with the initiatives of the Scots, who brought new efficiencies to the tobacco trade. The remarkable rise of Scotland in the middle decades of the eighteenth century resembles, in some respects, the ascent of the Japan in the 1970s and 1980s. Both began as relatively poor countries, with limited natural resources. Both focused on a narrow but lucrative range of activities. Both offered goods and services that were highly competitive and increased their market share at the expense of older, less innovative countries. For Japan the ticket to success was cars and electronics; for Scotland it was textiles and the tobacco trade.

The Scots brought Chesapeake prices closer to those in Europe by trading aggressively and reducing the charges that burdened this commerce. Traditionally, London houses had dominated the tobacco trade. They dealt only with the large planters, who consigned them tobacco for sale in the London market. The less wealthy landowners in Virginia and Maryland had to rely on their affluent neighbors for the shipment of tobacco. The Scots changed all that. They established chains of stores along the river valleys of the Chesapeake and traded directly with the small planters. The Scots provided credit to these middling landowners, bid for their crops, and often pushed prices above the levels offered by the Londoners. George Washington complained bitterly in

Table 5.1. *Maryland and Virginia Tobacco Prices as a Percentage of Amsterdam Prices, 1715–1774*

Year	Maryland	Virginia
1715–19	11.4	
1720–24	16.5	
1725–29	16.2	
1730–34	17.1	
1735–39	18.8	40.6
1740–44	14.1	37.4
1745–49	13.5	34.2
1750–54	27.9	41.7
1755–59	26.5	47.2
1760–64	29.3	37.8
1765–69	38.1	51.5
1770–74	35.7	49.7

Sources: Historical Statistics of the U.S., 2: 1198, presents Maryland prices; for Virginia, see Allan Kulikoff, *Tobacco and Slaves*, 80; for Amsterdam, Price, *France and the Chesapeake*, 2: 852.

1768: "I have lost (at least) four years out of five by my consignments having better prices offered in the Country than my Tobo. has sold for in England."[12] These aggressive tactics not only elevated Chesapeake prices, but also enlarged the Scottish tobacco trade. Between 1740–42 and 1770–72 annual shipments of tobacco from the Chesapeake to Scotland soared from 8 million to 44 million pounds, while exports to England increased only slightly, from 46 to 49 million pounds (fig. 5.1).[13]

Scottish efficiency also helped lower freight rates. These traders cut the amount of time that a ship spent loading tobacco in Virginia and Maryland, from 100 days at the beginning of the century to one-half that time in the 1760s. Resident Scots storekeepers filled their warehouses with hogsheads and so speeded the turnaround time. No such advances were recorded by English vessels, which depended on the labors of large planters to bring together the tobacco for shipping.[14]

Improvements in transatlantic shipping reduced costs—and so also helped narrow the gap between European and colonial tobacco prices. Steady improvements in vessel design allowed fewer individuals to crew larger ships. The number of tons per sailor on the Chesapeake–London route climbed from less than nine in the 1720s to almost fourteen in the 1760s. And there were noteworthy gains in packing tobacco. During most of the eighteenth century the peacetime charge for shipping tobacco was £7 a ton, with four hogsheads judged equal to one ton. While this fee remained stable, the size of the hogsheads increased. In the 1730s about 700 pounds could be packed into each container; by the early 1770s, about 1,100 pounds. More tobacco shipped for the same charge meant a drop in freight rates of over 50 percent. Other lesser fees, such as the amounts paid to brokers, coopers, and porters, also were typically charged by the hogshead, rather than by weight, and so these fees declined as well.[15]

Finally, along with changes in the quantity shipped and the price received, fluctuations in productivity affected the prosperity of tobacco planters. The long-term trend in this period, however, suggests no dramatic rise or decline in output per worker. On the one hand, soil exhaustion lowered the quantity each individual harvested. In the late seventeenth century, a worker—servant or slave—might produce more than 2,000 pounds of tobacco a year. Yields of more than 1,000 pounds were common. By the middle years of the eighteenth century harvests of more than 1,000 pounds per hand were recorded only in the newer lands of the Piedmont, the Southside (Virginia south of the James River), and the Shenandoah Valley.

On the other hand, tobacco planters took steps to increase output and so lessen the impact of exhausted soils. Landowners switched from servants to slaves—a change that allowed them to keep a work force in the field more hours each day and more days a week. They now penned their livestock and used the manure on the crops. Many individuals moved from a cultivation based on the hoe to one that relied on the plow (fig. 1.5). On hoed land a worker could plant about 320 "hills" of tobacco or corn in one day. On plowed land the same individual could plant 450 hills. Finally, planters migrated with their slaves to newer soils where the yields were higher. We can summarize these changes in productivity with a cautious statement: in the forty-five years after 1730 tobacco planters were not injured by any sharp fall in output.[16]

WHEAT AND CORN, AND OTHER CROPS

He was a tall man, with gray-blue eyes, and a face marked by smallpox. His neighbors knew him as an outstanding horseman, a soldier, and a gentleman. But George Washington was also an concerned planter and estate manager, who took great pains in running the plantations he had inherited or acquired through marriage. In the 1760s Washington instructed his overseers to plant more wheat and less tobacco. "Having discontinued the growth of Tobo. myself," he told a London house in 1768, "except at a plantation or two upon York River, I make no more of that Article than barely serves to furnish me with Goods."[17]

Like Washington, landowners in Virginia and Maryland grew an increasing quantity of wheat and corn in the late colonial period. Typically, older lands were given over to grain, or a mix of grain and tobacco, while tobacco planters migrated to new soils. Income from these food crops provided an all-important supplement to tobacco revenues. The amount of wheat harvested soared, increasing a remarkable fourfold in the inventories of six Chesapeake counties between the 1730s and 1770s. The value of the corn produced rose by 30 percent, while tobacco output showed no rise. Despite these trends, farmers produced more tobacco than corn at the end of the colonial era, and raised twice as much corn as wheat (fig. 5.4).

Particularly striking was the rise in wheat exports. Between the 1730s and 1770s the worth of wheat, flour, and bread shipped from Virginia increased twentyfold (tab. 5.2). By comparison, white population rose only 2.2 times, and total population expanded 2.5 times. Shipments of Indian corn grew more slowly. In 1737–42 the corn sent from Virginia was worth about £7,700, almost twice the value of the exports of wheat, flour and bread. By 1768–1772 corn shipments from the Upper South totalled about £75,000, but this was less than one-half the worth of wheat products. (Figure 5.10 shows the relative importance of Virginia exports, 1768–72, but excludes products entering the coastal trade.)[18] The sharpest rise in wheat shipments came in the 1760s. The upsurge in exports reflected developments in the international grain trade.[19] After 1760 Britain, pressed by the requirements of its own growing population, was no longer able to satisfy southern European demand. So Iberia and the Mediterranean ports now turned to the New World. Between 1768 and 1772 more than half the grain the Upper South sent overseas was shipped to Lisbon and the Mediterranean.[20]

Grain had an importance in the economic development of the Upper South that went beyond its second-place standing among exports. The worth of tobacco exports was perhaps three times that of corn and wheat shipments. However, the total value of the corn and wheat raised approximated the worth of the tobacco crop. These statistics reflect the fact that most foodstuffs were consumed domestically, while all but a few percent of tobacco grown was shipped overseas. Of course, much of this grain never entered the market and hence was a weak force for growth. But the extensive production of wheat and corn encouraged the development of milling centers, towns, roads, and artisanal activity.[21]

Although the production of grain flourished, other attempts to diversify agriculture in the Upper South were less successful. A few planters, noted British traveller Andrew Burnaby, "have endeavoured to improve their estates by raising indigo, and other schemes: but whether it has been owing to the climate, to their inexperience in these matters, or their want of perseverance, I am unable to determine, but their success has not answered their expectations."[22] In the 1760s a bounty boosted the planting of hemp. But Virginia Governor Francis Fauquier noted, "the inhabitants seem contented with their Staple Tobacco, and cannot *as yet* be brought to cultivate those articles for which the Society for the Encouragement of Arts and Manufactures in London offers so large Premiums."[23] Unlike the diversified northern economy, the Upper South had few exports apart from its chief staples: tobacco and grain (compare figs. 5.10 and 4.18).

COMMERCE AND MANUFACTURING

The commercial sector was far less important in the Upper South than in the North. Toward the end of the colonial period, however, these activities made an appreciable contribution to regional income.

Table 5.2. *Exports from Virginia, 1737–1742, and the Upper South, 1768–1772*

Virginia Exports, 1737–42	Annual Average (Values in Pounds Sterling)		
Tobacco	£165,000		
Wheat, flour, & bread	£4,000		
Ratio: tobacco to grain	41.3:1		

	Annual Average (Values in Pounds Sterling)		
Upper South Exports, 1768–1772	Virginia	Maryland	Total
Tobacco	£515,000	£253,000	£768,000
Wheat, flour, & bread	£80,000	£98,000	£178,000
Ratio: tobacco to grain	6.4:1	2.6:1	4.3:1

Sources: James F. Shepherd and Gary M. Walton, *Shipping, Maritime Trade, and the Economic Development of Colonial North America* (Cambridge, Eng., 1972), 214–24; David Klingaman, "The Significance of Grain in the Development of the Tobacco Colonies," *JEH* 29 (1969): 272–73; Lester J. Cappon et al., eds., *Atlas of Early American History: The Revolutionary Era, 1760–1790* (Princeton, N.J., 1976), 26–27. Klingaman provides data for 1737–42; all three sources offer statistics for 1768–72. And although all three are based on Customs 16/1, totals and averages differ (usually by less than 10 percent). Such discrepancies were averaged. Grain exports include amounts sent in coastal trade; Maryland coastwise exports computed by analogy with Virginia.

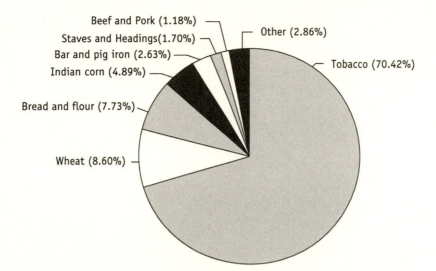

Figure 5.10. *Exports from the Upper South, 1768–1772.* Tobacco was the most important export from Maryland and Virginia. Wheat, flour, and bread stood a distant second. The average annual value of total shipments from the Upper South during these five years was £1,046,883 sterling. [*Source:* Shepherd and Walton, *Shipping, Maritime Trade,* 213–225. This graph is based on Customs 16/1 data tabulated in Shepherd and Walton. It differs from the figures presented in Table 5.2, which takes into account the coastal trade. When coastal shipments are included, tobacco exports are somewhat less important. Tobacco then amounts to 69 percent of the total, and the percentage for grain is increased.]

During most of this long swing (and earlier), the Upper South had no towns worthy of the name. The administrative centers of Williamsburg, Virginia, and Annapolis, Maryland, were for many years the most significant urban places in the two colonies. In the late colonial period the booming trade in grain fostered the rise of Baltimore and Norfolk. Neither town had been more than a small settlement in 1760, but by 1775 Baltimore had 6,700 inhabitants and Norfolk 6,000. Merchants in these towns oversaw the export of flour and wheat to southern Europe and the West Indies. Various artisans, from coopers to shipwrights, supported this commerce.[24]

The region also had noteworthy manufacturing activity—much of it taking place outside the towns. With fifty-six ironworks in the 1770s, the Chesapeake region boasted about a third of the foundries in the Thirteen Colonies (tab. 4.3). Between 1732 and Independence, the Upper South shipped far more pig iron to England than did the northern colonies. These exports, however, averaged only £18,600 between 1768 and 1772, far below the worth of the agricultural staples. The region also had several productive shipyards, with yards in Maryland producing an average of 1,500 tons between 1769 and 1772, and those in Virginia producing 1,350 tons. These figures place output in the two

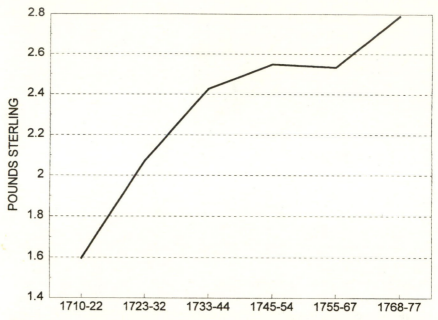

Figure 5.11. *Average value of craft tools and materials in inventories of six Upper South counties, 1710–1777.* Artisanal activity increased in the Upper South during this period. For a list of the six counties included in this series, see the notes to figure 5.4. [*Source:* Carr, "Diversification in the Colonial Chesapeake," 359.]

colonies on a level with northern colonies such as Pennsylvania, New York, and Connecticut—though well below the great shipbuilding provinces of Massachusetts and New Hampshire.

Craft production also contributed to regional wealth, though here too output remained below northern levels. The work of Lois Green Carr, Lorena S. Walsh, Alan Kulikoff, and Jean Russo documents the spread of artisanal activities in the Upper South. During the course of the eighteenth century spinning wheels, looms, hammers, saws, and the tools of craftspeople such as shoemakers appeared with increasing frequency in Chesapeake inventories (fig. 5.11). But only in those districts where mixed farming rivaled tobacco planting (such as Somerset and Talbot counties in Maryland) did the number of these implements compare to that in the North. The Virginians, remarked English traveler Burnaby in 1760, "make a kind of cotton cloth, with which they clothe themselves in common . . . and some inconsiderable quantities of linen, hose, and other trifling articles: but nothing to deserve attention."[25] The Upper South also trailed far behind the North in the number of potteries, paper mills, and silversmiths (tab. 4.4).[26]

THE EXPANSION OF BRITISH CREDIT

The influx of British funds lifted the standard of living in the Upper South. The fluctuations in the movement of credit paralleled the growth of the Brit-

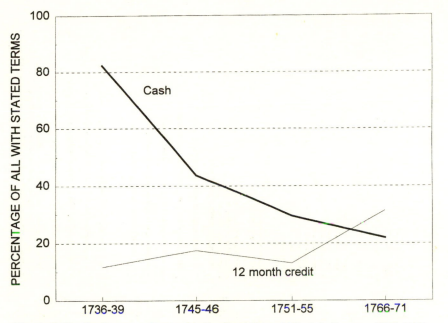

Figure 5.12. *Credit terms advertised in Purdie & Dixon's* Virginia Gazette, *1736–1771.* Credit grew more important in the Chesapeake economy. Reflecting this trend, fewer advertisements demanded cash, and a growing number announced a willingness to provide long-term (twelve month) credit. [*Source:* Compiled from Purdie & Dixon's *Virginia Gazette.*]

ish economy, with a strong expansion between the 1740s and 1760, and a contraction from 1760 to 1775.

Statistical series and planter correspondence illustrate the strong growth of credit after the 1740s. An analysis of advertisements in the *Virginia Gazette* suggests the growing importance of these funds. In the 1730s the typical advertisement for land or slaves demanded payment in cash. By the 1760s, long credit—a year or more—had become more common than the demand for "ready money" (fig. 5.12). As in other regions, per capita imports from Britain serve as an approximation for the flow of funds, because credit accompanied the shipment of dry goods. Here too solid growth was evident (fig. 5.6). The records of William Prentis & Co, a leading Williamsburg store, also depict the expansion of credit after 1745. The amount lent by the company (and its successor firms) took off in 1745 and climbed until the mid-1760s (fig. 5.13).

The testimony of two knowledgeable Virginians sheds light on the expansion of loans between the 1740s and 1760s. In 1764 Jerman Baker expressed his wish that "Virginia may again see the Halcyon days she knew 20 Years ago, when they lived in peace & plenty, & feared a Debt in England as the worst of calamitys."[27] John Wayles, who was Thomas Jefferson's father-in-law, provided a still fuller account in 1766. "Within these 25 years £1000 due to a merchant was looked upon as a sum immense and never to be got over," he observed. "Ten times that sum is now spoke of with Indifference & thought no great

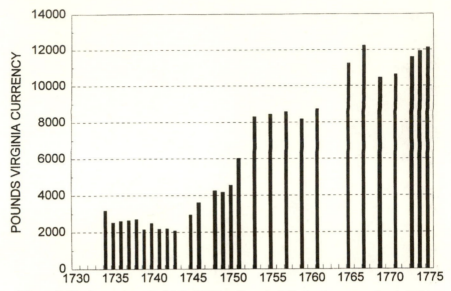

Figure 5.13. *Accounts receivable for William Prentis & Co. (and successor firms), 1734–1775.* The records of this one firm suggest the strong expansion of credit after 1745. [*Source:* James H. Soltow, *The Economic Role of Williamsburg* (Williamsburg, Va., 1965), following p. 132.]

burthen on some Estates. Indeed, in that series of time Property is become more Valuable, & many Estates have increased more then tenfold, But then Luxury & expensive living have gone hand in hand with the increase of wealth. In 1740 I don't remember to have seen such a thing as a turkey Carpet in the Country except a small thing in a bed chamber, Now nothing are so common as Turkey or Wilton Carpetts, the whole Furniture of the Rooms Elegant & every appearance of Opulence. All this is in great measure owing to the Credit which the Planters have had from England, & which has enabled them to Improve their Estates to the pitch they are Arrivd at."[28]

In large part, the increased value of funds offered during the late 1740s and the 1750s reflected the generosity of Scottish firms. These traders gained business by providing credit to the smaller landowners. The pattern of indebtedness makes clear the division of business between the Scots, who dealt with the less wealthy planters, and the English, who focused on the large landowners. According to Richard Sheridan's analysis, the average sum owed two Glasgow houses was £29. No obligation was more than £1,000. By contrast, the amounts outstanding to five London and one Bristol merchant in the consignment trade averaged £664. More than one-third of these debts were above £1,000. "A substantial proportion" of these short-term loans, according to Sheridan, was converted into long-term obligations—bonds, notes, mortgages and deeds.[29]

This bountiful era of credit expansion came to an end in the early 1760s. Planters and the local merchants who served them now complained about the "scarcity of money" and the near impossibility of collecting debts. "I find difficulty in carrying on business at this time," a Maryland importer commented in 1764, "as money is not to be got in here."[30] "Poor Virginia," remarked another trader, is "held in scorn and derision by the merchants of Great Britain and torn to pieces by their and our country law suits."[31] In 1766 a Virginia planter reported: "I have several thousand due me for the great part of which I have brought suits above two years ago . . . but have not yet got judgements. Others I have not sued but entreated and persuaded but to no purpose as money was so scarce it could not be got by them. Nay, if they sold their estates (as some offered to do) they could not expect above half price."[32] A Caroline County storekeeper observed in 1768: "The slow payments here with the necessity there appears to be for quick remittances . . . gives me great uneasiness."[33]

Just how severe was the contraction of the 1760s in the Upper South? The evidence is contradictory. Correspondence suggests that planters were hard pressed by creditors, while storekeepers were forced to draw in their affairs and struggled to satisfy the demands of British houses. Merchant account books, however, tell a different story. They indicate that many local traders expanded the amount of credit extended to their customers. For example, the debts owed William Allason, a merchant of Falmouth, Virginia, climbed from £2,691 in 1761 to £5,770 in 1764. Similarly, at the Glassford store in Colchester, Virginia, accounts outstanding jumped from £975 in 1760 to £5,000 in 1764, to £8,550 in 1769.[34] Debts also rose for the Williamsburg firm of William Prentis & Company, with unpaid balances reaching a peak in 1767 (fig. 5.13). Perhaps many Chesapeake firms sought to contract their affairs in the 1760s but found that the hard times demanded leniency—and more not less credit. Contemporaries reported that in the mid-1760s the Upper South labored under an enormous burden of debt, estimated at between one and two million pounds sterling.[35]

The last years of the colonial era were marked by a brief period of leniency (in 1770 and 1771) and then by a harsh renewal of the credit contraction (beginning in 1772). During the late 1760s the British economy temporarily recovered from the postwar slump, and the flow of funds to the planters enlarged once more. For example, the obligations of the London consignment house, John Norton & Sons, in Virginia soared from £11,000 in 1769 to £18,500 in 1770, and by 1773 had reached £41,000.[36]

The collapse of a Scottish bank in June 1772 ignited a panic that spread through Britain, shook traders on the European continent, and brought new pressures to the Upper South. A Virginia merchant noted in June 1773: "The late bankruptcies have made prodigious alterations within these 9 months. The factors for the Scotch merchants in Glasgow are forbid to draw, and a great number of bills come back protested."[37] Debt cases now climbed to record heights in the Chesapeake. For many planters, conditions in the mid-1770s were even more difficult than those in the 1760s.[38] The indebtedness of the Upper South remained substantial. According to Jacob Price's computations, obligations to British merchants in 1774 stood at "something over two million sterling."[39]

The impact of fluctuations in the movement of funds was evident not only in the countryside but also in the towns. The records of William Prentis & Co., a leading Williamsburg store, illuminate both the expansion and contraction. The amount lent by the company (and its successor firms) took off in the mid-1740s and climbed until the mid-1760s, when it leveled off again (fig. 5.13). And the rigors of the post-1760 downturn were evident even in the growing towns of Baltimore and Norfolk. William Lux, a Baltimore grain merchant, told an English house in 1764: "I cannot send you any orders, as it is impossible in the present uncertain state of our trade to be punctual." Still, favorable conditions rather than complaints characterized the economic climate in these two cities. Lux boasted to a correspondent in 1767, "Our town increases in its trade daily and the importation of European goods [is] much enlarged." For those in Baltimore and Norfolk the rising demand for Chesapeake wheat was more significant than tightening credit.[40]

OVERVIEW

Any analysis of the development of the Chesapeake between the 1730s and Independence must focus on the countryside, which claimed most of the population and wealth. And it must underscore the growth of the region. But how steady or spectacular was that expansion? Who were the winners and losers? This section reviews the evidence, and argues that the pace of development was moderate. It emphasizes the need for balance in interpreting diverse data.

For some planters and artisans in the Upper South these were golden years. The sound of hammers and saws echoed through the tidewater and piedmont. Craftspeople erected the magnificent Georgian mansions that have come to characterize colonial Virginia and parts of Maryland. Land values ascended steeply, particularly in such tidewater counties as Anne Arundel and Prince George's (fig. 5.7). Because real estate formed a major component of total wealth, some commentators argue that overall prosperity climbed strongly in the third quarter of the century.[41]

However, many were excluded from these gains. Blacks made up 39 percent of the population and held little real property. Even many white households owned no land. In Prince George's County, for example, more than one-half the free families were tenants in the 1770s.[42] The personal economies of the middling and lower classes too often stood becalmed while favorable breezes aided the affluent.

More broadly, several series sketch in a moderate pace of development for the white population. Data for per capita imports map out a pattern of slow growth (fig. 5.6). Such a picture is reinforced by the very gradual rise in the total value of consumer goods, such as table linen, beds, dishes, cutlery, and books, registered in the probate records of four tidewater counties (fig. 1.1).[43] The value of estate inventories in St. Mary's County, Maryland, climbed steadily after 1730. But the peak reached in the late 1760s was little above the value attained earlier in the century, and the sharp fall in the 1770s undercuts any long-term climb (fig. 5.8).[44]

A full evaluation of changes in Chesapeake wealth must balance evidence of improvement among the "haves" against indications that conditions were worsening in the late colonial period for many "have-nots." Everywhere in the Upper South the number of poor increased after 1760. Nearly one in seven households in Anne Arundel County, Maryland, depended on charity in the late 1760s. Throughout both Maryland and Virginia, counties built poorhouses and filled them (according to the wording of a 1768 Maryland law) with "rogues, vagrants, vagabonds, beggars and other dissolute and disorderly" persons.[45] Tenantry rose and the number of debt cases soared. In Pittsylvania County, on the Virginia frontier, actions brought by irate creditors climbed in the early 1770s. In some years, more than 30 percent of all householders were dragged into court (tab. 5.3).[46]

Hence the good news of rising land and estate values must be tempered by the grim tidings of mounting numbers of individuals harried into the ranks of the landless and poor. Figures for household wealth in three of four Chesapeake counties turn down in the 1770s, suggesting the pressure of the continuing contraction on many property holders. The economy of the Upper South grew between 1732 and 1775, but its ascent was plodding rather than breathtaking, and the benefits of this increasing wealth were unequally shared.

To sum up, the pattern of development in the Upper South—decline or stagnation between 1713 and 1732 and a slow ascent from 1732 to 1775—stood apart from the two long swings that defined growth in the North and in the

Table 5.3. *Cases Per 1,000 Taxables Brought to Court in Pittsylvania County, Virginia, 1767–1774*

Year	Number of Cases
1768	167
1769	157
1770	254
1771	162
1772	304
1773	314
1774	357

Sources: Michael Nicholls, "Credit Crisis and Court Closures: Judgement Debt and Collection in Pittsylvania County, Virginia, 1767–1775" (paper presented at American Historical Association, West Coast Branch 1978), table 3; Nicholls's data are also discussed in Kulikoff, *Tobacco and Slaves*, 130.

Thirteen Colonies taken as a whole. Instead, Virginia and Maryland adhered to rhythms shaped by the tobacco trade and, to a lesser extent, by the fluctuations in the sale of grain and the movement of British funds. After the Revolution, the Chesapeake economy would continue to diversify. The region would become less dependent on tobacco and would draw more of its income from the production of foodstuffs.

~oⁿⁿ~

Lower South

The Lower South grew at a pace that bore only a slight resemblance to the long swings of British expansion. Rice was the leading export, and most of the crop was consumed on the continent of Europe. So, more than any other single influence, the tug of markets in Holland, Germany, and Spain shaped the cycles of prosperity and depression in the Lower South. There were, to be sure, economic ties with Britain. Indigo, the second most valuable regional product, was directed to British cloth makers. That purple dye and the flow of credit linked the Carolinas and Georgia to the economy of the mother country. But these concerns were less important than fluctuations in the rice trade.

Together these influences helped demarcate two long cycles between 1713 and 1775. The first was an era of spectacular growth that gathered strength by 1720, peaked in 1740, and ended in the soul-wrenching downturn of the 1740s. The next cycle was marked by a long era of steady expansion that began in the late 1740s, quickened in the mid-1760s, and ended with the Revolutionary War.

Any analysis of the Lower South must also confront the striking dissimilarity between North Carolina, on the one hand, and South Carolina and Georgia, on the other. North Carolina, it is true, could claim most of the regional population. In 1770 it had 57 percent of the inhabitants of the Lower South, compared to 36 percent for South Carolina and 7 percent for Georgia. But South Carolina and (by the late 1760s) Georgia were far wealthier and far more involved in international trade. Between 1768 and 1772 the three chief products of South Carolina and Georgia—rice, indigo, and deerskins—accounted for almost 82 percent of Lower South exports. The leading wares of North Carolina — naval stores, lumber products, and tobacco — totaled only 12 percent of regional shipments (fig. 6.1). The difference in these staple economies made for striking disparities in the standard of living. In none of the other regions of North America was the geographical distribution of wealth so unequal.[1]

The Flourishing Rice and Indigo Economy of South Carolina and Georgia

South Carolina and Georgia dominated the economy of the Lower South. Rice accounted for most of the exports of the two provinces (and of the region) and shaped the long swings of growth. Indigo emerged as the second staple after 1745. Other products, such as deerskins, naval stores, and wheat, had only a minor impact on the well-being of the two colonies. Commercial and artisanal activities also contributed to the wealth of the region, particularly during the second long swing. Credit flows affected both the rural and urban sectors.

RICE SALES SHAPE THE PATTERN OF GROWTH

Rice sales defined two long swings of economic development: 1713–45 and 1745–75. These two periods may be considered in turn.[2]

The first cycle was marked by the rapid expansion of the rice trade in the 1720s and 1730s and soaring prosperity in South Carolina. The quantity of rice exported skyrocketed to new heights in these years (fig. 6.2), as did quotations for this grain (fig. 6.3). Between 1726 and the early 1740s the value of exports remained well above the trend line of long-term growth (fig. 6.4).

This era of expansion, 1713–40, reflected strong demand from Holland, Germany, and southern Europe. In 1704 rice had been enumerated, which meant that any barrels of the grain sent to Europe had to be landed first in Britain. So the calls from Holland and Germany were indirect ones. But together these two northern European countries frequently purchased more than one-half the Carolina crop (fig. 6.5). Trade with southern Europe took off only in the 1730s. In the 1710s and 1720s colonists complained that enumeration made it difficult for them to respond to the seasonal demands for rice in Spain and Portugal. South Carolina's London agent, Francis Yonge, remarked in 1722 that since "the aforesaid act [enumeration] obliged all [rice] to be brought to Great-Britain, the Spaniards and Portugeze, who consume very great quantities, especially during their Lent season, are almost wholly supply'd by the Italians, with rice much inferior to that of Carolina, which is esteemed the best in the world by those nations." In 1730 Parliament allowed direct exportations to Spain and Portugal, and this commerce boomed. By 1731–35 southern Europe purchased roughly one-fourth of South Carolina rice exports (fig. 6.6).[3]

During this era of prosperity the number of slaves brought into Charles Town soared (fig. 6.7), as did purchases of British wares. Imports per person

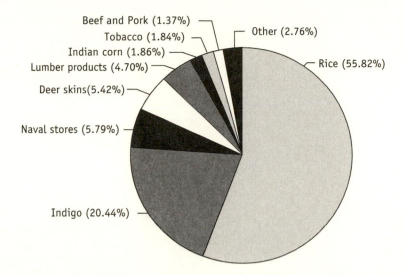

Figure 6.1. *Exports from the Lower South, 1768–1772.* Rice and indigo, which were grown in South Carolina and Georgia, were the leading staples of the region. North Carolina products — naval stores and lumber — were much less important. The average annual value of total shipments from the Lower South during these five years was £543,234 sterling. [*Source:* James F. Shepherd and Gary M. Walton, *Shipping, Maritime Trade, and the Economic Development of Colonial North America* (Cambridge, Eng., 1972), 213–27.]

for the Lower South climbed from £0.9 sterling for each white inhabitant in 1718–22 to £2.5 in 1738–42. This peak was well above the levels reached in the northern colonies and the Upper South (fig. 6.8).

The years of bountiful growth came to an abrupt end in the early 1740s when the War of the Austrian Succession disrupted transatlantic trade and rice exports plummeted (fig. 6.2). South Carolinians complained bitterly about the hard times. In 1745 the governor, council, and assembly petitioned the King for more naval protection and the privilege of sending rice directly to Europe. The lawmakers lamented "That the Calamitys of this Province are exceedingly increased by the entire decay of our Rice Trade, which must soon impoverish the Inhabitants since that Grain is now become not worth the labor and expence of making and bringing to the Market of Charles Town."[4] Prices for this staple fell (fig. 6.3) and as did the value of shipments (fig. 6.4). Purchases of slaves and per capita imports also declined (figs. 6.7 and 6.8). Rice sales fell throughout Europe, with the sharpest drop recorded in Holland — the single most important market for this staple (fig. 6.5).

Recovery was evident by the late 1740s, as the rice colonies embarked upon another cycle of growth. In the fall of 1748 Governor James Glen of South Carolina noted the economic upturn. He explained to the Board of Trade that he had earlier approved an act helping debtors, because "For a considerable

Figure 6.2. *Rice exports from South Carolina and Georgia, 1710–1774.* Rice exports rose strongly, although the War of the Austrian Succession (1740–48) and the Seven Years' War (1756–1763) temporarily checked this ascent. [*Source:* U.S. Bureau of the Census, *Historical Statistics of the United States, Colonial Times to 1970,* 2 vols. (Washington, D.C., 1975), 2: 1192.]

time before and at the time of my passing this Act the circumstances of many of our Planters was unspeakably bad." But now he had changed his mind about the measure: "As since that time the Province has surprizingly emerged, it now appears to be less necessary."[5] The era of growth that began in the 1740s was long-lived but less spectacular than the expansion of the 1720s and 1730s. And unlike the long swing that defined the growth of the British economy and the northern colonies, the cycle in the Lower South was marked by stronger growth after 1765 than before. Broadly viewed, the prices (fig. 6.2), quantity (fig. 6.3), and value (fig. 6.4) of rice exports rose throughout this period. But a close examination of these series suggests a particular surge between the mid-1760s and 1774. Marked growth in the late colonial era is also evident in the data for the number of blacks brought into Charles Town (fig. 6.7).

Increased demand from several important customers—the Dutch, West Indian planters, and the English home market—fueled the upsurge in rice sales after 1765. Purchases by Dutch houses provided the underpinnings for this expansion and reflected the strength of the northern European economy during these years.[6] Sales to the West Indies and English market expanded as wheat prices soared, and consumers searched for an alternative to costly flour and bread. Parliament aided this commerce by removing the duties that had restricted the home market for rice (fig. 6.5).[7]

Finally, on the supply side, Georgia provided more and more of the ballooning rice exports of the late colonial era. Georgia had exported some rice

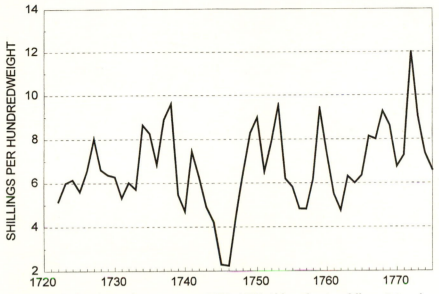

Figure 6.3. *South Carolina rice prices, 1722–1775.* Although prices fell precipitously during the 1740s, the long-term trend was toward higher quotations. [*Source:* Peter A. Coclanis, *The Shadow of a Dream: Economic Life and Death in the South Carolina Low Country, 1670–1920* (New York, 1989), 106.]

since the 1730s, but as late as 1759–61 the colony accounted for only five percent of shipments from the Lower South. By 1770–72 Georgia supplied 16 percent of a much larger total.[8]

PRODUCTIVITY GAINS FOR RICE GROWERS

"The culture of rice in Carolina," historian and revolutionary David Ramsay observed, "has been in a state of constant improvement."[9] Unlike most farmers in eighteenth-century North America, rice planters enjoyed significant gains in productivity. For the most part, these advances reflected the relocation of rice cultivation into areas that were better suited to this staple.

Rice was a cash crop in South Carolina by the 1690s, and initially planters grew this grain on dry, upland soil and relied on rainfall for irrigation. Rice flourished in the warm South Carolina climate, but harvests were comparatively small. During these early years rice remained a second staple, with shipments worth less than the value of deerskin exports.

Growers soon recognized the advantages of swampy, lowcountry land, and by the 1720s they had shifted the crop to these areas, where irrigation was far easier. Planters learned to dam freshwater streams and create reservoirs, which allowed them periodically to flood the crop. This practice controlled weeds and grass, and made slaves more productive. Such arrangements—low lying

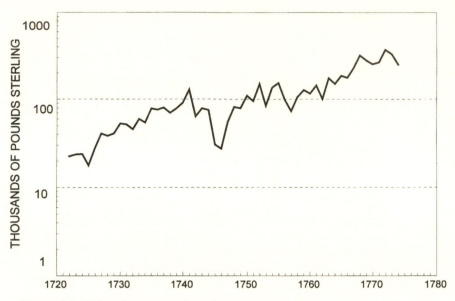

Figure 6.4. *Value of rice exports from the Lower South, 1722–1775.* The value of rice shipments increased strongly during the eighteenth century. The most rapid ascent came before 1740 and was checked by the severe depression of the 1740s. [*Sources:* Coclanis, *Shadow of a Dream,* 106; *Historical Statistics of the U.S.,* 2: 1192.]

estates irrigated by reservoirs and fresh water streams—typified rice production from the first decades of the century down to the Revolution.[10]

But there were problems with the combination of swampy lands and streams. The supply of water was too uneven. Droughts dried up creeks and reservoirs, while heavy rains swelled rivers and ruined fields. Gabriel Manigault complained in 1766 that South Carolina had "such incipient Rains that all the Rice Lands are under Water and numbers of people will not be able to plant this year."[11]

As early as the 1730s planters discovered a still better location for rice growing: tidal swamps. These were the lands that lay along lower reaches of the major rivers, stretching perhaps thirty or thirty-five miles from the river mouth. Each day the force of the tide raised and lowered the fresh water level in these rivers some six to eight inches. Using tidal currents, landowners could regularize the flooding of their rice fields. This approach improved the cultivation of rice, and allowed each worker to tend more plants. But tidal estates required major outlays: planters had to construct and maintain an elaborate set of dikes, and not until the 1780s, it seems, was there a major shift to the river marshes. Still an increasing proportion of rice was grown in these areas, while many estates used a mix of reservoirs and tidal irrigation.[12]

These changes boosted the productivity of the rice plantations. Early in the eighteenth century, planters calculated that an acre of rice land would produce 1,000 pounds of clean rice. By the Revolution, landowners expected

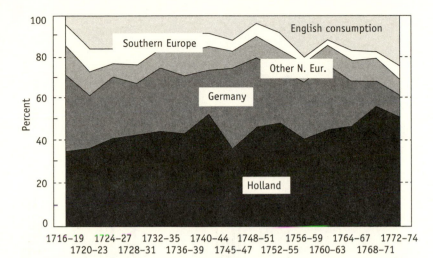

Figure 6.5. *Final destination of rice sent to England from the Lower South, 1716–1774.* Most rice was exported to England but did not remain there. Holland was the chief destination on the continent. [*Source:* R. C. Nash, "South Carolina and the Atlantic Economy in the Late Seventeenth and Eighteenth Centuries," *Economic History Review* 45 (1992): 688.]

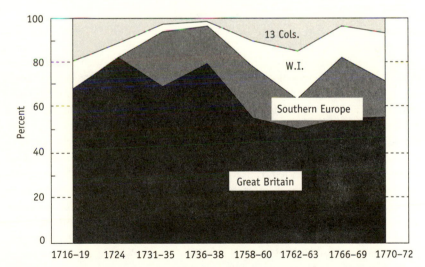

Figure 6.6. *Rice exports from Charles Town by region, selected dates, 1717–1772.* Most rice was shipped to Great Britain. But other markets—the Thirteen Colonies, West Indies, and southern Europe—increased in importance. [*Source:* Nash, "South Carolina and the Atlantic Economy," 692.]

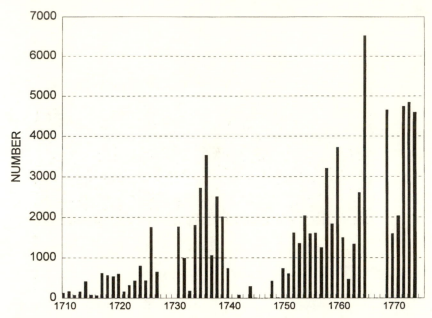

Figure 6.7. *Slave imports into Charles Town, 1710–1775.* Slave imports mirrored the pattern of growth in the Lower South. They rose during the first long swing, plummeted in the 1740s, and climbed again after 1750. The dip during the 1760s reflected the prohibitive tax in effect from 1766 to 1768. [*Source: Historical Statistics of the U.S.*, 2: 1173–74.]

each acre to yield 1,500 pounds. Also striking were the gains in output for each worker. Unlike the gangs of slaves who toiled in the tobacco fields of the Chesapeake, the African Americans growing rice worked individually—an approach called the "task system." A typical daily task might be cleaning the weeds out of a quarter acre rice field. Once that work was completed the balance of the day belonged to the slave. As cultivation moved from upcountry estates to lowland marshes to tidal swamps, planters were able to increase the "task." This allotment of work expanded from a quarter acre on lowland marshes to a half acre on tidal swamps. Production for each hand rose as well. Where an average field hand might raise 2,000 pounds of rice a year in 1750, such a worker produced 3,000 to 3,600 pounds during the second half of the century.[13]

Improvements in machinery and ocean transport also expanded rice production. Fans to winnow the rice appeared early in the century and were in widespread use by the late colonial period. Large-scale pounding machines, which removed the outer husk from the rice, also became more common. Like tobacco planters, rice growers benefited from gains in shipping bulky goods long distances. Freight charges fell as the average size of a barrel increased. Taken together, improvements in rice planting, machinery, and shipping helped planters achieve strong gains in productivity whether measured in output per worker or per acre. Figure 6.9, which combines rice and indigo ex-

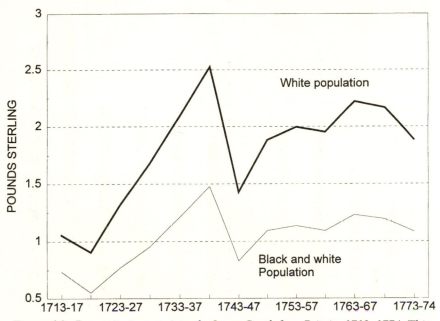

Figure 6.8. *Per capita imports into the Lower South from Britain, 1713–1774.* This series provides an overview of regional prosperity. It shows the strong growth between 1720 and 1740, the hard times in the 1740s, and the steady expansion that began just . before mid-century. [*Source: Historical Statistics of the U.S.*, 2: 1168, 1176–78.]

ports, suggests productivity gains per worker. Such advances spurred output and allowed planters to serve expanding markets in continental Europe, England, and the West Indies.[14]

THE EMERGENCE OF INDIGO

Eliza Lucas was a remarkable young woman. In 1738 she came with her family from Antigua to South Carolina. Early in the century her grandfather, John Lucas, had purchased three estates in South Carolina. Her father, Major George Lucas, now took these over, but left at once to rejoin the English forces on Antigua. With her mother ailing, Eliza managed the family holdings. In 1740 the seventeen-year-old Eliza told a friend in England: "I have the business of 3 plantations to transact, which requires much writing and more business and fatigue of other sorts than you can imagine. But least you should imagine it too burthensom to a girl at my early time of life, give me leave to answer you: I assure you I think myself happy that I can be useful to so good a father."[15]

Eliza not only ran the estates, but she experimented with a variety of crops— and particularly indigo. In her "coppy book of letters to my Papa" for 1740 she observed: "I wrote my Father a very long letter on his plantation affairs. . . . On the pains I had taken to bring the Indigo, Ginger, Cotton and Lucerne and Casada to perfection, and had greater hopes from the Indigo (if I could have

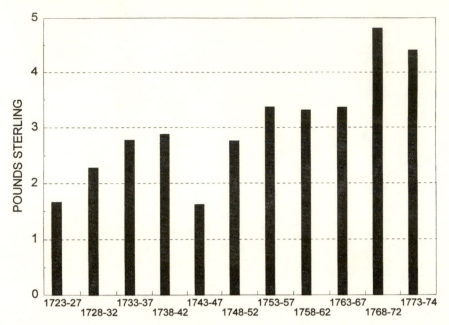

Figure 6.9. *Value of rice and indigo exports from South Carolina and Georgia per slave, 1723–1774.* The output of the average laborer increased during this period. [*Sources: Historical Statistics of the U.S.*, 2: 1168, 1189, 1192; Coclanis, *Shadow of a Dream*, 106–7.]

the seed earlier next year from the West India's) than any of the rest of the things I had tryd."[16] Lucas persevered through a series of poor crops, and by 1742 had a large enough indigo harvest to consider processing and marketing the dye. Her father then sent her a dyemaker, Nicholas Cromwell, from the island of Montserrat. Cromwell grumbled ("He said he repented coming as he should ruin his own country by it") but built the vats needed to reduce the blue flowers to dyestuff.[17]

Eliza Lucas's efforts helped establish indigo as an important South Carolina staple by the mid-1740s. She encouraged the cultivation of indigo not only on her family's plantations but also throughout the colony. Lucas and Charles Pinckney, whom she wed in 1744, distributed seeds and information to many individuals. By 1745 South Carolina was beginning to export the dye to Great Britain. Growers received a further boost in 1748 when Parliament placed a bounty on the product. The vigorous efforts of James Crokatt, who became the London agent for South Carolina in 1749, also encouraged sales of the dye.[18]

Fluctuations in the shipment of indigo generally reflected the long swings in the British economy. Although indigo growers fared poorly in the early 1750s, the years from 1755 to 1760 were marked by a great surge of growth. Planters prospered during the Seven Years' War both because cloth manufacturers expanded their output and because the conflict severed British ties with the French West Indies, which had been the chief source of the dye. Growth

Figure 6.10. *Value of indigo sent to Great Britain, 1748–1775.* Despite broad fluctuations, the value of indigo exports climbed between the late 1740s and Independence. [*Sources: Historical Statistics of the U.S.*, 2: 1189; Coclanis, *Shadow of a Dream*, 107.]

in the value of exports after 1763 was less striking (fig. 6.10). Quantity figures tell a similar story. There was, however, a notable surge in the early 1770s once the English textile industry recovered from the depression of the 1760s (fig. 6.11). Indigo prices show less evidence of the cycles of British growth (fig. 6.12).[19]

The sale of indigo helped modify, if only slightly, the patterns established by the rice economy. It buoyed South Carolina during the Seven Years' War, a period when rice shipments faltered. Processed indigo was more compact than rice, so a few ships could transport the production of an entire year. Hence it was more economical to ship during wartime when freight and insurance rates were high and cargo vessels were scarce. Indeed, during 1757–59 the value of indigo shipments exceeded the worth of rice exports. The surge in indigo sales during the early 1770s gave a further boost to the South Carolina economy.

Did the spread of indigo make plantations more productive? Indigo and rice complemented each other, and the combination seemed to offer planters a new strategy for using land and labor more efficiently. A large plantation might assign the high, dry ground to indigo, while rice was planted in the marshes. The work schedules for the two crops were distinct, so slaves could be moved between these staples. Some landowners, such as Eliza Lucas, raised both crops. A 1755 essay on the cost of establishing a plantation assumed an estate with "two acres of indigo and one of rice to each hand." However, some research-

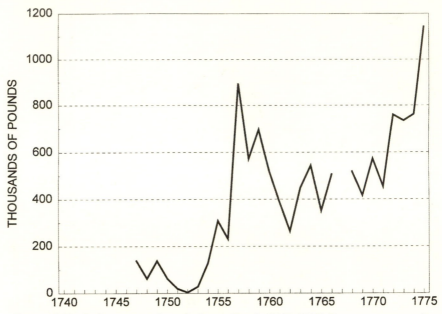

Figure 6.11. *Indigo exports from the Lower South, 1747–1775.* Exports rose strongly during the Seven Years' War and again in the 1770s. [*Source: Historical Statistics of the U.S.*, 2: 1189.]

ers now question how common such hybrid plantations were. A study of the loyalist claims suggests that estates growing rice and indigo were rare.[20]

Even if crops were not combined on individual plantations, indigo was an important addition to the economy of the Lower South. Figure 6.9 indicates that when rice and indigo are considered together the output for each slave in South Carolina and Georgia rose substantially between 1723 and 1774.

These two lucrative staples helped create in the lowcountry the richest group of landholders in British America. "Few countries," historian David Ramsay remarked in 1809, "have at any time exhibited so striking an instance of public and private prosperity as appeared in South-Carolina between the years 1725 and 1775." Alice Hanson Jones's study of probate records makes clear the extraordinary wealth of these individuals.[21]

DEERSKINS, NAVAL STORES, AND OTHER PRODUCTS

Three other staples—deerskins, naval stores, and grain—played a secondary role in the economic life of the rice colonies.

Deerskins provided valuable earnings, although the relative importance of these hides steadily diminished during the eighteenth century. These skins were the leading South Carolina export until about 1705 when their worth was surpassed by rice. Deerskins then remained the second most important South Carolina product until the mid-1750s, when indigo sales climbed. Shipments

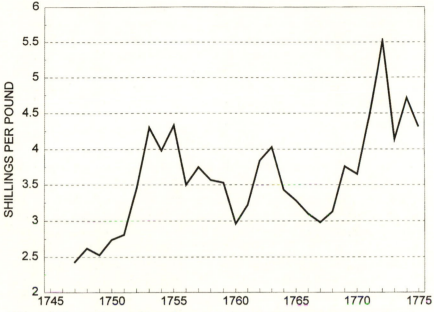

Figure 6.12. *South Carolina indigo prices, 1747–1775.* Prices climbed in the mid-1750s with the expansion of the British economy. Quotations increased again in the early 1770s as textile production recovered from the downturn of the 1760s. [*Source:* Coclanis, *Shadow of a Dream,* 107.]

of hides averaged perhaps £20,000 sterling at the beginning of the century, £25,000 in the 1720s, £36,000 at mid-century, and about the same in the period 1768–72. Britain was the chief market for the hides.[22]

Like deerskins, naval stores — tar, pitch, and turpentine — were far more important for South Carolina at the beginning of the century than in the late colonial period. Parliament encouraged production in 1704 with a bounty on pitch and tar. The renewal of this law in 1714 was the signal for a strong expansion of output. In some years between 1717 and 1724 the value of shipments was over £30,000 sterling, though a total around £20,000 seems more typical. The bounty led to an oversupply in England as well as to loud complaints about the quality of the pitch and tar produced in South Carolina. In 1724 Parliament canceled this incentive, and then reintroduced payments in 1729 at a much lower level. These policy changes dealt a harsh blow to the naval stores industry in South Carolina. Production in the late 1720s amounted to only £5,000 sterling, and by mid-century shipments were worth less than £4,000.[23]

Some of the Indian corn, wheat, and livestock raised in the backcountry also was exported. By 1770 this rapidly growing section could claim 30,000 of South Carolina's 49,000 white inhabitants. A portion of the harvest was shipped to the other colonies and the West Indies. The *Boston Chronicle* noted in 1768, "the produce of good wheat has been so great this year that we may soon expect, from Camden [South Carolina] alone, 2000 barrels of flour and 1500 of ship bread." These foodstuffs also helped feed the lowcountry. By 1770 more than 3,000 wagons, loaded with provisions, as well as some indigo and tobacco, traveled to Charles Town each year. But the value of these exchanges was limited, and backcountry settlers remained on the fringes of the commercial economy. Peter Coclanis estimates that only 5 percent of the goods imported into Charles Town were consumed in the backcountry.[24]

COMMERCIAL AND ARTISANAL ACTIVITIES

Commercial and artisanal activities also contributed to the rising prosperity of the rice colonies, particularly after mid-century.

Charles Town was always the most important metropolis in the rice colonies, but it played a more noteworthy role in the local economy after midcentury than before. Before 1750 local traders typically were individuals of modest means. Often they had no holdings outside of town. And those who sold dry goods were forced to compete with the representatives of British firms. A Charles Town merchant observed in 1726: "Here is so many Scott's pedlers, West Country, Bristoll men with cargoes this year and which is no small halp to the prejudice and sale of goods." Resident slave importers typically acted as commission agents for English houses. They sold the blacks, collected the payments, and remitted the proceeds, keeping a percentage for themselves.[25]

Craft production was inconsequential during this long swing. The artisan community in Charles Town remained small, and the planters produced few goods. Governor Robert Johnson reported in 1720: "Severall usefull manufacteris might begen upon in this province to good advantage but our planters applying them selves almost wholly to makeing rice, pitch and tarr they do not think thereof."[26]

During the second long swing Charles Town grew in relative importance, as did its merchant and artisan communities. By the 1750s and 1760s the capital boasted an affluent, independent set of importers. Slave traders now purchased blacks on their own account and provided credit to the planters. And Charlestonians (led by the merchant class) acquired much of the improved rural land and over one-fourth of the slaves working outside the capital. By 1760 the city had 8,000 individuals, making it fourth among the towns in the Thirteen Colonies. Charles Town had about 8.5 percent of the population of South Carolina and undoubtedly contributed more than twice that percent to the domestic product of the colony.[27]

Between 1760 and Independence, the rapid ascent of Charles Town continued, reflecting the flourishing rice economy. The prosperity of the capital contrasted sharply with the hard times in the northern cities. A Rhode Island merchant visiting the South Carolina capital in 1764 was impressed by the high standard of living. "The city . . . has increased with sumptuous brick houses in very great number," Moses Lopez observed. "One cannot go anywhere where one does not see new buildings and large and small houses started, half finished, and almost finished. To me who comes from poor, humble Rhode Island, it seems to be a new world. In spite of so much new building, I never knew the rent of houses so high."[28] Between 1760 and 1775 the population almost doubled, a pace that easily surpassed the rate of growth in the other large towns. On the eve of Independence, Charles Town, with 15,000 inhabitants, was now nearly as large as Boston.[29]

To be sure, such prosperity did not extend to the slaves or to some of the whites who worked with their hands. During the 1760s the workhouse and hospital became overcrowded, and the town was forced to lodge the indigent in an army barracks. In 1768 the assembly voted funds for a new almshouse. Still, many of the common folk benefited, as did the affluent traders, from the rice boom of the late colonial era.[30]

Manufacturing also flourished in the bustling capital. By the early 1770s Charles Town had more than ten silversmiths, as well as several sugar refineries, rum distilleries, printing houses, and potteries. There was some shipbuilding. But the annual average of 467 tons built in South Carolina, 1769–1771, was not in the same league as the 7,664 tons that came off the stocks in Massachusetts.[31]

BRITISH FUNDS

The influx of funds also contributed to the development of the countryside and towns. During the first long swing the rice colonies appear to be one of the few places where British traders were willing to increase sharply the loans they granted to correspondents. Because credit accompanied the goods arriving in America, the figures for per capita imports suggest a strong expansion during the 1720s and 1730s in the funds offered the rice colonies (fig. 6.8).

British credit also helped underwrite growth during the second long swing. According to claims made after the Revolutionary War, South Carolinians owed British houses approximately £347,000 sterling on the eve of Independence. Internal indebtedness was also high. The South Carolina assembly taxed "money at interest," and in 1768 these loans amounted to £550,593 sterling, a figure that was twice the 1760 total. Typically these funds were extended to assist the purchase of dry goods and slaves.[32]

It seems likely—though hard evidence is lacking—that credit expanded between 1745 and 1760, mirroring the growth of the British economy. But in the period 1760–75 there are clear signs of the contraction that marked the British commercial world. Charles Town traders frequently noted the difficulty they met in collecting funds.[33] Backcountry settlers complained loudly about the press of lowcountry creditors. Indeed, this grievance was one reason that small farmers joined together in the Regulator movement during the 1760s. Many wealthy South Carolinians struggled during these years to pay for the slaves they required—a problem that was compounded by the soaring price of bondspeople (figs. 6.7 and 6.13). The collapse of Middleton, Liston, & Hope, a Charles Town house involved in the slave trade, suggests the risks that came with slow payments. To reduce their indebtedness, South Carolinians adopted a three-year ban on slave importations, commencing January 1, 1766.[34]

Figure 6.13. *North American slave prices, 1703–1775.* Slave prices in North America began to rise by the 1740s. This increase probably reflected growing demand from the West Indies. [*Source: Historical Statistics of the U.S.*, 2: 1174.]

However, unlike the situation in the North, in the Lower South prosperity muted the rigors of contraction. In anticipation of the ban on slave imports, merchants brought in record numbers of blacks. Governor William Bull complained in December 1765 that this action had "in great measure defeated the salutary end proposed, as above 8000 [blacks] have been imported this year, being nearly equal to three years' importations." Despite the efforts of some firms to contract their affairs, the amount of "money at interest" increased sharply during the 1760s. And in these years South Carolinians were more likely to rejoice in the favorable conditions than complain about the "scarcity of money."[35]

The Slow Growing Economy of North Carolina

North Carolina made a contribution, if a minor one, to the economic development of the Lower South. The tarheel colony was less affluent than its neighbors to the south, and less oriented to export markets. But there are clear indications that after mid-century North Carolina grew in wealth as well as in population.

The expansion of the North Carolina economy must be set in the context of its relative poverty. The statistical record is less complete for the tarheel colony than for South Carolina and Georgia. But the adverse conditions that characterized North Carolina are well documented. In the 1720s a Virginian compared the Old Dominion to its neighbor and noted that North Carolina "is vastly inferior, its trade is smaller, and its inhabitants thinner, and for the most part poorer." Historian Roger Ekirch has calculated that for the period from 1768 to 1772, North Carolina exported through its own ports or through those of neighboring colonies goods worth £1.2 sterling for each white inhabitant. By contrast South Carolina shipped produce valued at £9.1 sterling.[36]

Perhaps the most important reason for the low standard of living in North Carolina was the poor quality of its ports. "Within the whole province," remarked one observer, "there is not one good harbour, being all obstructed with bars, and fluctuating sand-banks." A planter summed up the plight of the colony: "The badness of our Navigation makes our Land and Slaves of very little profit to us." Wilmington, at the mouth of the Cape Fear, was the most accessible of the ports, but even here a sandbar limited the size of vessels that could enter the harbor. In an era when it was far easier to move bulky goods by water than by land, the lack of facilities for large ships seriously hampered economic development. Despite these problems, North Carolina recorded noteworthy growth between 1750 and Independence.[37]

STAPLE PRODUCTION

Staple production gradually lifted incomes in North Carolina. However, these gains reflected the buoyancy of "secondary" crops, rather than the success of the leading export—naval stores. The worth of naval stores—tar, pitch, and turpentine—increased but slowly and totaled perhaps £30,000 sterling between 1768 and 1772. The center of the industry was in the Cape Fear River valley, where forests of long-leaf pine provided abundant raw material. Because of the importance of this industry, which depended on slave labor, the Cape Fear region had the highest concentration of blacks in the colony and contained the only two counties where slaves made up more than one-half the population in the 1760s. Available data depict the slow rise in the quantity and the value of shipments. Exports climbed from 84,012 barrels in 1753 to 127,697 barrels in 1768. In per capita terms, however, this was a decline from 1 barrel per person to 0.7 barrels. Nor, it seems, were price trends as favorable as they were for other colonial staples. If Philadelphia quotations can serve as a proxy, the worth of pitch and tar remained level between the 1720s and 1770s.[38]

Shipments of other goods—particularly lumber, tobacco, and grain—expanded more rapidly. In the period 1768–72 annual exports of wood products amounted to between £15,000 and £25,000 sterling. Moreover (again relying on Philadelphia data), lumber prices rose strongly. The value of barrel staves, largely sent to the sugar islands, jumped in the late 1750s as the West Indian economy soared, and it remained high in the 1760s. Quotations for pine boards, which were also destined for the Caribbean market, may well have followed the same trend.[39]

Tobacco exports also increased during the third quarter of the century. This rise was the beginning of a long-term trend that would make North Carolina the leading producer of the weed in the United States. Exports through North Carolina ports climbed from about 100,000 pounds in the early 1750s to over two million pounds in the early 1770s. Predictably, the area devoted to tobacco broadened. Initially production was concentrated in the northeast corner of the colony near Albemarle Sound, but cultivation of the crop soon expanded to the west and south. Growers also benefited from a gradual increase in prices (fig. 5.2). In the period 1768–72 exports through local ports averaged £10,000 sterling, and in some years shipments were worth nearly double that figure. In addition, significant (but unmeasured) quantities were carted overland to Virginia.[40]

North Carolinians also exported increasing amounts of Indian corn and wheat. These grains became more important as small farmers swelled the population of the backcountry. Most of the harvest was consumed locally. But in the last decade of the colonial period, North Carolinians annually laded Indian corn worth over £10,000, and in some years shipments were worth more than £20,000. We have less data for wheat, but in 1772 exports of this grain were valued at over £3,000.

Some planters, impressed by the success of South Carolina, experimented with rice and indigo. One landowner complained that while "we grapple with lightwood knots," South Carolinians had achieved "opulence" by "leaving the making of naval-stores to their more sharp-sighted neighbours, and pursuing the cultivation of rice, indigo and hemp; commodities which this province is equally capable of raising."[41] Planters in the Cape Fear region grew rice, but the quantities were small. Exports through North Carolina ports in 1771 were worth less than £2,000 sterling. Attempts to raise indigo came to little. As one planter noted: "Indico proves a very precarious crop." Exports in 1772 were valued at less than £500.[42]

OVERVIEW

Despite the mixed picture presented by this review of North Carolina products, there was evidence of overall growth. The driving force seems to be the spread of tobacco cultivation, the increased importance of Indian corn and wheat, and perhaps the rising prices of lumber and staves. Urban places remained small and contributed little to economic output. The impact of fluctuations in credit remains conjectural.

Several indications suggest increasing wealth. Perhaps the clearest sign was the expanding number of African Americans. The percentage of slaves in the total population climbed from 20 percent in 1755 to 26 percent in 1767 (fig 1.6). This increase was evident in all regions of North Carolina. The value of exports also rose faster than the population. The worth of goods shipped from North Carolina ports jumped from £8,000 sterling in 1736 to £76,000 in 1768–72. During the late colonial period the first signs of a colonial aristocracy were evident in the coastal counties, where the concentration of slaves and wealth was greatest.[43]

Still, North Carolina remained a poor cousin of the rice colonies. One observer remarked on the eve of Independence: "North Carolina is a striking Exception to the general Rule . . . that the Riches of a Country are in Proportion to the Number of Inhabitants." The tarheel economy contributed to the growth of the Lower South in the years after mid-century. But South Carolina and Georgia remained the engines of economic development for the region.[44]

PART II

Canada under the French Regime

—◡◡◡—

SEVEN

The French Connection

For Canada, as for the Thirteen Colonies, growth in the mother country was the all important determinant of the pace of colonial development. Hence a discussion of the economy of the St. Lawrence colony necessarily begins with an examination of fluctuations in France. On both sides of the Atlantic two broad cycles defined economic activity. The first swing, 1660 to 1713, was marked by slow growth. The second and far more vigorous wave of expansion lasted for the metropolitan power from 1713 to 1789, and for the colony from 1713 to the British Conquest in 1760.

A Long Cycle of Slow Growth, 1660–1713

During the quarter century after 1660 the French economy slowly, unevenly, but unmistakably gathered strength. Louis XIV's absolutist rule provided the stability necessary for recovery and expansion. It helped the country recover from the turmoil into which it had plunged during the Frondist wars of mid-century. Gains were evident in both the agricultural and commercial sectors.[1]

The output of France's farms, which accounted for perhaps 60 per cent of the domestic product, now kept pace with the demands of a growing population. Cereal prices declined from the early 1660s to the mid-1680s, and increased regional specialization was evident. The northwest abandoned wine production and raised more flax to serve the area's burgeoning linen industry.

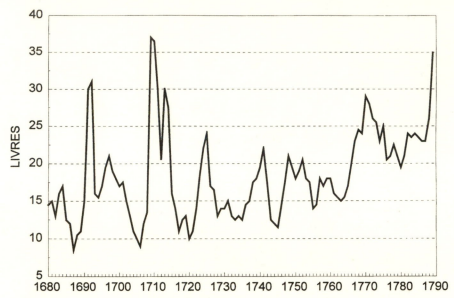

Figure 7.1. *Price of wheat in France, 1680–1789.* During the first long swing (1660–1713) recurrent agricultural crises led to high wheat prices. Conditions were more favorable during most of the next long swing (1713–89), although signs of scarcity appeared after 1770. [*Source:* Ernest Labrousse et al., *Histoire économique et sociale de la France*, vol. 2: *Des derniers temps de l'âge seigneurial aux préludes de l'âge industriel (1660–1789)* (Paris, 1970), 392. These prices are for Paris up to 1710, and for France after that date. Note that prices are for a setier of wheat, and 4 setiers = 1 minot.]

At the same time other regions, such as the Loire Valley and Burgundy, enlarged their vineyards.[2]

Although there was no broad commercial upturn, merchants in the western ports were buoyed by the rise of the Caribbean trade. During the 1670s, French investment in the West Indies climbed, fostering sugar culture and helping spur trade with the islands. While trade with the West Indies expanded, no such good fortune graced France's older, more valuable exchanges. Shipments of linens to Spain fared poorly, as did commerce with the Levant.[3]

Government policies also helped strengthen trade and manufacturing during this period. Louis XIV's controller general, Jean Baptiste Colbert, overhauled the tariff system in 1664 and 1667, raising duties to protect French industry from foreign competition while lowering internal barriers. Shipping was aided by subsidies as well as by a royal order prohibiting foreign vessels from taking part in the colonial trade. Colbert also bolstered French manufacturing through grants, regulations, and in some instances the establishment of state workshops. However, the pace of development must not be exaggerated. As early as 1672 the outbreak of the Dutch War forced Louis XIV to shift resources from domestic development to defense.[4]

As weak as the recovery of the 1660s and 1670s was, it soon ground to a halt. The European wars, which broke out in 1689 and continued with only

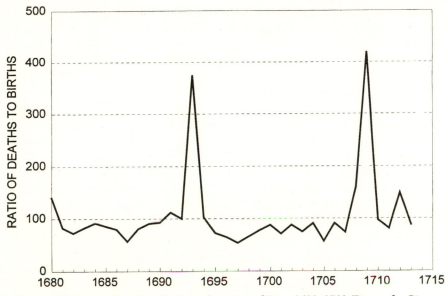

Figure 7.2. *Ratio of deaths to births in the region of Gien, 1680–1713.* Figures for Gien, which lies 130 kilometers south of Paris, make clear the devastation of the famines of 1693–94 and 1709–10. But even during "good" years births barely kept ahead of deaths. [*Source:* Jean Meuvret, "Les crises de subsistance et la démographie de la France d'ancien régime," *Population* 1 (1946): 646.]

brief interludes of peace, until 1713, were a grave blow to the French economy. Both farming and trade suffered during these years.

Agriculture went into a precipitous decline. Problems were evident in the south of France after 1680. By the mid-1680s the nation's farms — which had made few changes in technique or organization — were no longer able to sat-isfy the needs of a growing population. Perhaps most significant was the fail-ure of French agriculture to meet wartime demands. Bad weather produced disastrous conditions. Famine swept through the nation in 1692–94 and again in 1709–10, with grain prices soaring to extraordinary levels (fig. 7.1). Accord-ing to some estimates, between 10 and 20 percent of the population died dur-ing these two periods. The parish records of the region of Gien, which lay 130 kilometers south of Paris, illustrate the extraordinary jump in mortality with these two famines (fig. 7.2). A few areas, such as Brittany and the region near the Mediterranean Sea, fared better than the rest of the country. But transpor-tation remained poor, and surpluses in one province could not easily be shifted to feed other parts of the realm.[5]

Commerce also slumped. The Revocation of the Edict of Nantes in 1685 and the persecution of the Huguenots ended the fragile recovery of the pre-ceding decades. An estimated 200,000 Protestants, including some of the most prosperous and industrious citizens, fled from the provinces of the west and southwest.[6] During the war years the English navy dominated the shipping

lanes, closing several French ports. Such losses were hardly balanced by a flourishing, if short-lived, trade with Spanish America, and by the acquisition of Saint
Domingue in 1697.

A Long Cycle of Rapid Growth, 1713–1789

Beginning in 1713 the French economy gradually recovered, and by the 1730s
this improvement had become a broad wave of growth that encompassed farming, manufacturing, and commerce. This era of growth continued until 1770.

Agriculture, as the most important component of the national product, played
a pivotal role in this expansion. The output of French farms increased from the
1710s to the 1760s. Historians explain this rise by emphasizing favorable climatic
conditions, and note that abandoned land was brought into cultivation. Transportation also improved, so that by the 1730s the state was able to bring French
grain or supplies from abroad to areas where the crops had failed.

Favorable conditions in the countryside temporarily ended the threat of
famine, stimulated the growth of population, and enhanced the incomes of
landlords and peasants alike. With the exception of only a few years, such as
1739–41, supplies of food were ample. Grain prices fluctuated, but remained
well below the high levels recorded earlier in the century (fig. 7.1). The death
rate also declined. Figure 7.3 shows the drop in French mortality between 1740
(when this series begins) and 1770.[7]

Still, it is important to underscore the limits to progress in French agriculture. Unlike England, France experienced no widespread enclosure movement
or other structural changes. France remained a country of poor farmers. These
peasants cultivated small holdings and struggled to pay heavy taxes and meet
their obligations to the seigneur and Church.[8] The persistence of age-old patterns was evident even in the farms near Paris, probably the most commercial-
ized region in France. Philip Hoffman has studied the records of the estates
held by the Cathedral of Notre Dame. He found a rise in output, but no transformation of farm life.[9]

Manufacturing quickened after 1713, as domestic and foreign consumers
expanded their orders for goods. Recovery was evident in such districts as
Amiens and Dauphiné before 1720, and in most locales by the 1730s. Rising
peasant incomes underwrote the increased production of goods such as rough
cloth, shoes, cutlery, and soap, while the landlords' new wealth aided the industries that catered to the rich. In contrast to England, however, France lacked
a significant middle class that might have demanded the better but not luxuri-
ous fabrics. Nonetheless, France's woolen, linen, silk, and particularly cotton
industries all expanded briskly with foreign purchases reinforcing domestic
demand.[10]

French commerce also entered upon an era of growth, with colonial trade
the most dynamic component of this resurgence. During the 1720s, sugar
from Guadaloupe, Martinique, and Saint Domingue replaced the English
sweetener in northern European markets. In the 1730s coffee raised in the

Figure 7.3. *Crude death rate in France, 1740–1800.* The death rate dropped steadily from the 1740s to the 1770s and then temporarily rose as conditions worsened in the countryside. By the 1790s the trend to a healthier country was evident once more. [*Source:* Louis Henry and Yves Blayo, "La population de la France de 1740 à 1860," *Population* (November 1975) special issue: 109. Mortality rates are given for five-year periods. These have been graphed according to the midpoint of each period.]

French islands ended the dominance that Arabian producers had enjoyed. More generally, between 1725 and 1755 imports from the colonies rose from 20 million livres to nearly 100 million (fig. 7.4). French trade with other markets also increased. Reexports of tropical produce led this expansion, but shipments of French manufactures also climbed. France's cloth merchants achieved their greatest successes in the markets of Spain, Spanish America, Italy, and the Levant. Total exports soared from slightly more than 100 million livres to 300 million. Imperial wars, however, periodically if temporarily checked the triumphal ascent of French commerce. Trade fell sharply during the War of the Austrian Succession in the 1740s and the Seven Years' War (figs. 7.4 and 7.5).[11]

The era of expansion came to an abrupt end with the crisis of 1770, and the last two decades of the long swing were troubled ones for both farmers and city folk.

The crisis of 1770 marked a turning point in this long cycle of growth. This "panic" began in the countryside but quickly spread to the commercial centers. Like the crises of 1708–9 and 1740–41, hard times in 1769–71 were triggered by bad weather and disastrous crops. France remained a country of regions, and shortages in one area or another were common. But now harvests failed in one-third of France. The result was soaring grain prices, industrial

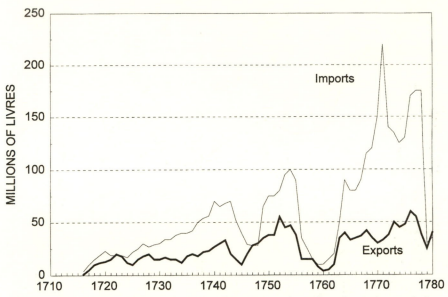

Figure 7.4. *French colonial trade, 1716–1780.* Imports from the colonies (particularly sugar from the Caribbean) increased strongly during this long swing. Exports to these possessions rose more slowly. Imperial wars delivered sharp if temporary setbacks to this commerce. [*Source:* Labrousse, *Histoire économique et sociale de la France,* 2: 502.]

stagnation, bankruptcies, and unemployment. Depending on the region, the worst year of this slump fell between 1769 and 1773.[12]

The crisis of 1770 and its aftermath revealed deeper problems in French agriculture. For the first time since the early years of the century, the production of foodstuffs failed to keep up with population growth. Shortfalls were evident even when "normal" harvests returned. The death rate, which had fallen for several decades, now soared (fig. 7.3). These shortages of grain and other foodstuffs culminated in the national crisis of 1788–89 with its famine level prices and angry protests (fig. 7.1).[13]

Manufacturing and commerce also slumped during the 1770s and 1780s. The woolen and linen industries stagnated after 1770, with declines evident in centers such as Amiens, Normandy, Rouen, Brittany, and Languedoc. In contrast to British producers, French textile manufacturers were slow to develop innovations that boosted productivity. When the Treaty of Vergennes lowered tariffs between the two countries in 1786, French goods had trouble competing with British products. Gains in coal, iron, and glass, and in the newer industries of chemicals and cotton textiles, did not balance the falling off in wool and linen.

Trade also expanded at a slower pace after 1770. Exports to the French colonies showed little growth. French shippers were hurt by the loss of the Canadian market with the Conquest in 1760 and by the slow increase of the European population in the French West Indies. Exchanges with Europe re-

Figure 7.5. *French noncolonial trade, 1716–1780.* Trade with Europe and the Mediterranean rose strongly from 1716 to the late 1760s. [*Source:* Labrousse, *Histoire économique et sociale de la France,* 2: 502.]

mained level. There were some advances in trade with the Baltic, and imports from the colonies climbed thanks to the spread of sugar cultivation on Saint Domingue. But French merchants lost ground in the important Mediterranean market. The War of the American Revolution, like imperial wars earlier in the century, sharply reduced French trade.[14]

These difficult years—and the long swing that began in 1713—came to a dramatic close with the economic and political crises of 1788–89. Only during the 1790s would France embark upon a new era of expansion.

—⌒∞⌒—

EIGHT

A Cycle of Slow Growth in Canada, 1665–1713

"The French [i.e., Canadian] inhabitant . . . ," observed the Jesuit priest and historian, François-Xavier de Charlevoix, "leaves his offspring involved in the same necessities he was in himself at his first setting out, and to extricate themselves as they can." Charlevoix, who visited Canada in the early eighteenth century, was struck by the lack of any noticeable rise in the standard of living.[1] His comments provide an apt introduction to the long swing of slow growth stretching from 1665 to 1713.

Viewed more closely, this cycle divides into three periods. The era began with generous French outlays and a brief surge of development from 1665 to 1672. However, these subventions declined, and between 1672 and 1689 the pace of growth slowed to a crawl. Finally, imperial war and difficult conditions in France dealt a hard blow to the colony and produced a downturn that lasted from 1689 to 1713.

Two sectors defined economic activity in Canada. One was staple production, which took place in rural areas and the colony's western reaches. Furs were the most valuable product, with grain a distant second. The other sector was the urban economy. Townsfolk managed trade, oversaw administrative and religious activities, and assisted the military. During this period, the prosperity of both sectors depended heavily on the fluctuating levels of financial support offered by the parent country.

A Brief Surge of Growth, 1665–1672

The years from 1665 to 1672 were a remarkable period of expansion for the infant colony. Government outlays underpinned this era of prosperity, boosting the fur trade, agriculture, and the development of the towns.

The burst of growth that began in the mid-1660s reflected the increasing vigor of the parent country and an important political decision: in 1663 Louis XIV took over Canada from the Company of One Hundred Associates, and made his new possession a royal colony. The king appointed a governor-general for military affairs and an intendant to handle civil matters. And he told Jean Talon, the first intendant to assume the duties of the office, that the King of France regarded the Canadians as his children. Louis XIV supported his new family with an unstinting hand. Between 1665 and 1672 annual expenditures on the colony were higher than these subventions would be between 1700 and 1730. Naturally, with a smaller population—Canada had a scant 3,250 souls in 1666—the impact of these outlays was proportionately greater.

French support strengthened earnings in the fur trade. In 1666 the newly arrived French regiment traveled deep into Iroquois territory, and imposed on the Indians a treaty favorable to New France. The troops also built a series of five forts stretching from Lake Champlain to the mouth of the Richelieu River. These aggressive moves assured Canada of a larger supply of beaver skins and helped establish a new pattern of trade. For many decades native peoples had brought their peltries to Montreal, and exchanged these skins for imported wares in a public marketplace. But the Indians gradually depleted local supplies and by the late 1660s brought few furs to town. Canadians were forced to venture farther into the interior for pelts, and thanks to the troops this commerce was set on a sound footing. While the supply of skins now expanded, profits were lessened by the downward spiral of peltry prices. The worth of coat beaver[2] fell from 210 sols a pound in the period 1659–64 to 135 sols in the years 1664–74 (fig 8.1).[3]

Louis XIV's policies also aided Canadian agriculture, expanding both the supply and demand for foodstuffs. French policies fostered immigration, sharply increasing the number of farmers. Some of the new arrivals went to the towns. But most settled in the countryside, and the proportion of the population dwelling in towns declined from 39 percent in 1667 to less than 25 percent a decade later (fig. 8.2). More than 2,000 individuals, about one-fifth of all persons who emigrated to the St. Lawrence colony in the French era, arrived in the colony between 1665 and 1672. This group included indentured servants and more than 400 soldiers who remained in Canada after their regiment returned to France in 1668. The soldiers received bonuses to help them begin farming.[4]

More land was now taken up, and requests for new seigneuries soared. Forty-six were created in 1672 alone. Compared with earlier decades, far more individuals settled the narrow rectangular farms that marked the countryside along the St. Lawrence. Talon encouraged the farmers by introducing pedigreed animals—horses, cows, and sheep—from France and by experimenting with different grains.[5]

The demand for foodstuffs also rose. The domestic market was strong, with 1,300 troops in the colony, as well as a comparatively large urban population. While Canadian supplies were not yet sufficient to satisfy local purchasers, some officials and traders dreamed of serving more distant markets. Talon had high

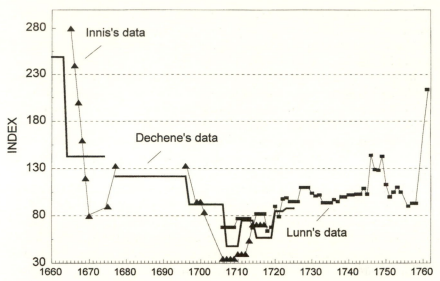

Figure 8.1. *Beaver price relatives, 1660–1760.* Beaver prices generally fell during the cycle of slow growth, 1660–1713, and rose during the cycle of stronger expansion, 1713–60. [*Sources:* Harold A. Innis, *The Fur Trade in Canada: An Introduction to Canadian Economic History* (rev. ed., Toronto, 1956), 63–73; A. J. E. Lunn, "Economic Development in New France, 1713–1760" (Ph.D. diss., McGill Univ., 1942), 459–61; Louise Dechêne, *Habitants et marchands de Montréal au XVIIe siècle* (Paris and Montreal, 1974), 141. This series combines (without weighting the existing data) the series for three kinds of beaver: gras ("coat" or "fatty"), sec ("dry" or "parchment") and demi-gras (or "half fatty"). In constructing each of the three component series the annual average for 1735–36 was taken as 100. So the following beaver prices, expressed in sols per pound, were made equal to 100: castor gras, 100; castor sec, 40; castor demi-gras, 70.]

hopes for trade with the French West Indies and the French settlements in Acadia. He declared: "There will be in fifteen years sufficient surplus in grain, vegetables, meat, and fish to supply the West Indies and even the mainland in this part of the world." However, despite Talon's optimism, dealings with the other French possessions remained limited to the occasional vessel. Exchanges with the Caribbean were sporadic in these years both because Canada had little grain to spare and because cane cultivation had not yet spread in the French West Indies.[6]

The towns also benefited from French subventions. The impact of these funds was evident in the growing military and religious establishments, as well as in the quickening of commerce and industry.[7] The number of troops stationed in the towns rose sharply in this era. The French noblemen who comprised the Company of One Hundred Associates rarely had kept more than 100 armed men in the colony. But in 1665 the military complement soared to more than 1,300 soldiers, who were headquartered in Quebec and Montreal. Marie de l'Incarnation, leader of the Ursuline nuns in Quebec, was struck by the change in the local economy. "Money, which was rare in this country is

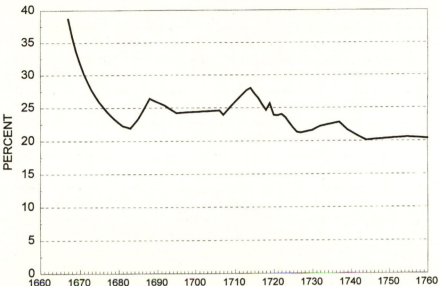

Figure 8.2. *Urban population as a percentage of total Canadian population, 1667–1760.* The proportion of the population living in the towns of Quebec, Montreal, and Trois Rivières was remarkably high but gradually declined. [*Sources:* Montreal and Trois Rivières figures from Richard C. Harris, *The Seigneurial System in Early Canada: A Geographical Study* (Madison, Wis., 1966), 90–133; Quebec statistics from John Hare et al., *Histoire de la ville de Québec, 1608–1871* (Montreal, 1987), 327. Canadian population from Louise Dechêne, *Habitants and Merchants in Seventeenth-Century Montreal* (Montreal and Kingston, 1992), 292–93. For Canadian population in 1760 see Guy Frégault, "The Colonization of Canada in the Eighteenth Century," in *Society and Conquest: The Debate on the Bourgeoisie and Social Change in French Canada, 1700–1850,* ed. Dale Miquelon (Toronto, 1977), 85, 95, 96. The graph was constructed by using straight-line interpolations in all the component series.]

now very common, these gentlemen having brought a great deal with them," she commented. "They pay for everything they buy with money, both their food and their other necessities, which suits our habitants very well." In the mid-1660s subsistence alone for these forces amounted to 150,000 livres a year.[8]

France supported a large religious establishment in Montreal and Quebec. These orders received generous grants of property as well as regular funds. Originally, the seigneury of Montreal Island was awarded to the Society of Notre-Dame of Montreal. But in 1663 the Society of Notre-Dame ceded its rights to the Seminary of Saint-Sulpice. The Sulpicians would remain the town's feudal lords for nearly 200 years, often exercising their customary rights to the annoyance of the commercial classes. Montreal was also home to the Recollets and Jesuits, while Quebec had orders of Recollets, Jesuits, Ursulines, and Hospitallers. In 1666 the capital had ninety-one clerics, or more than one for every eight inhabitants.[9]

The favorable conditions in the fur and dry goods trades also boosted the fortunes of townsfolk. Montrealers, who dominated the exchanges with the native people, profited from the expansion of the commerce in peltries. Importers in Quebec benefited from the quickened trade with France. However, within the Quebec merchant community French firms and their agents, rather than local merchants, controlled most of the exchanges. Foreign dominance of Canadian trade was strengthened in 1664 when Colbert awarded the West India Company a monopoly of colonial commerce. Talon and some of the Quebec merchants denounced this privilege, arguing that the monopoly slowed growth and dampened the spirit of enterprise. But for the moment Colbert resolutely defended his decision.[10]

French outlays made possible new industries, many of which were clustered in the capital. After ordering a survey of the colony's oak trees, Talon opened a shipyard in Quebec. Nearby he established a brick works, a brewery, a potash works, and a tannery. (Other enterprises, however, lay outside the two major cities. Talon helped create an ironworks at St. Maurice, near Trois Rivières, to take advantage of local ores. And at Baie St. Paul, Talon established a manufactory to produce tar, pitch, and resin.) None of Talon's ventures had been set on a firm footing. But they seemed a promising start for the new royal colony.[11]

While these forces for development drove the rapid expansion of Montreal and Quebec, they had less impact on the third Canadian city: Trois Rivières. This village, located midway between Montreal and Quebec, always remained a small regional administrative and trading center. One-half the size of Montreal in 1667 (210 people vs. Montreal's 400), it grew little. In 1739 it had only 375 inhabitants, in contrast to 4,200 in the western town.[12]

In sum, the years from 1655 to 1672 were ones marked by vigorous economic expansion. Like a summer breeze filling the sails of many skiffs, French funding propelled a variety of activities. The fur trade quickened, agriculture prospered, and the towns grew in size and wealth. Imports also rose, with tonnage from France sharply increasing from the low levels of the 1640s and 1650s. Virtually all vessels came from the port of La Rochelle, the chief destination for Canadian pelts; regular exchanges with Bordeaux would not begin until 1671 (fig. 8.3). However, the growth in imports was not yet evident in arrivals from the West Indies. The quantity of sugar used at the Quebec Hospital — one indication of the changing fortunes of Canada-Caribbean trade — remained relatively small (fig. 8.4).[13]

A Setback and Gradual Improvement, 1672–1689

The period from 1672 to 1689 was one of slow growth for the Canadian economy. The sharp decline in royal support was a setback for the colony, but continuing French outlays, as well as favorable conditions in the fur trade, agriculture, and towns kept the economy on an upward course.

This era opened with the shock of the French decision to end the generous expenditures that had characterized Talon's intendancy. With the start of the Dutch War in 1672 France was forced to cut back on its aid to Canada.[14] However, Versailles continued to support the colony, if at reduced levels. These

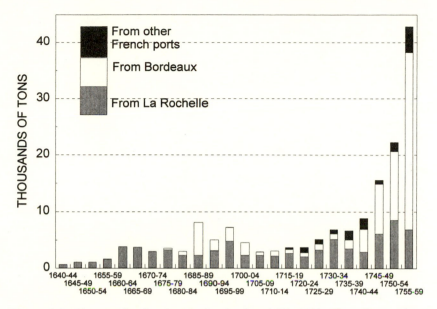

Figure 8.3. *Ships outfitted in France for Quebec, 1640–1759.* These figures show (1) the rise and fall of trade during the first long swing, which ended in 1713; (2) the upsurge during the second long swing, 1713–60, and (3) the shifting importance of the various French ports supplying this trade. [*Sources:* James S. Pritchard, "The Pattern of French Colonial Shipping to Canada before 1760," *Revue française d'histoire d'outre-mer* 63 (1976): 201–8; R. Cole Harris and Geoffrey J. Matthews, eds., *Historical Atlas of Canada,* vol. 1, *From the Beginning to 1800* (Toronto, 1987), plate 48. For several periods the tonnage arriving from the "other" ports has been estimated based on data in these sources. The "other" ports include Le Havre, Saint-Malo, Nantes, and Marseilles.]

subventions bolstered the economy during the 1670s as well as during the 1680s when the conflict with the Iroquois intensified once again. The most visible sign of French assistance was the decision of the ministry in 1685 to station a corps of *troupes de la Marine* permanently in Canada. This force of 1,300 to 1,600 men strengthened the defenses and in some years helped with the harvest. The soldiers were an appreciable increment of manpower in a colony whose population in 1685 was only about 11,000. The funds that paid for these forces lifted the local economy, and allowed Intendant Jacques Demeulles in 1685 to issue—and support—paper money. This was the famous "card money"—notes that were simply playing cards with the intendant's signature and a denomination added to the face. For the moment at least this currency remained stable.[15]

These years were buoyant ones for the fur trade: this commerce expanded, while new regulations set it on a firmer foundation. The governor, Louis de Buade, Comte de Frontenac, assisted by individuals such as Réné-Robert Cavelier, Sieur de la Salle, established a series of posts to tap the riches of the west. In 1673 these hardy imperialists erected Fort Frontenac at the eastern

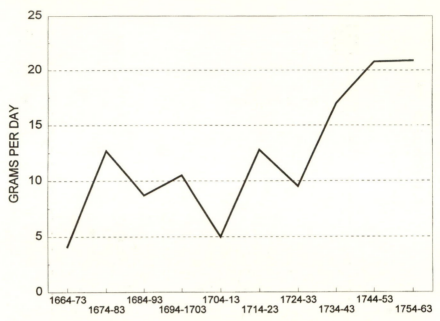

Figure 8.4. *Consumption of sugars at the Quebec Hospital, 1660–1763.* The consumption of sugar rose and fell during the first long swing (1660–1713) and then skyrocketed during the second long cycle (1713–60). [*Source:* François Rousseau, *L'oeuvre de chère en Nouvelle-France: le régime des malades à l'Hôtel-Dieu de Québec* (Quebec, 1983), 316. This series brings together the consumption of three items: white sugar, brown sugar, and molasses.]

end of Lake Ontario, and in 1676 built Fort Niagara near the western end of the lake. Beginning in 1679 the French constructed a chain of trading posts stretching from southern Lake Michigan to the Mississippi River. La Salle's voyage down the Mississippi in 1682 was only the continuation of this activity. To the north a group of Montreal traders established a base at Michilimackinac, at the juncture of Lakes Michigan and Huron.

The quantity of beaver—overwhelmingly the most important fur in the seventeenth century—received by the French companies doubled from about 70,000 pounds in the mid-1670s to 140,000 pounds in the late 1680s (fig. 8.5). French demand for furs strengthened, temporarily checking the decline in peltry prices (fig. 8.1).[16]

The government also reorganized the fur trade, providing greater stability and order for this commerce. Since the late 1660s many Canadians, some of whom were simply farmers hoping to supplement their income, had ventured west to barter imported wares for pelts. The intendant estimated that there were between 500 and 800 of these *coureurs de bois* seeking furs, but added: "I have been unable to ascertain the exact number because everyone associated with them covers up for them." The situation troubled importers because many of these casual traders provided little security for the goods advanced to them.

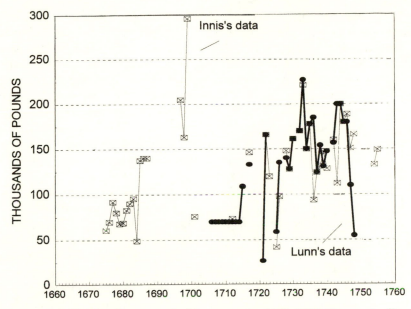

Figure 8.5. *Weight of beaver received by companies, 1675–1755.* These series illustrate the strengthening of the trade in the 1670s and 1680s, the glut and crash at the turn of the century, and the recovery of the trade after 1715. [*Sources:* Lunn, "Economic Development," 456–58; Innis, *Fur Trade,* 149–52. Not all furs, however, were received by the companies. Some were smuggled to the English in exchange for dry goods and other products. See Jean Lunn, "The Illegal Fur Trade Out of New France, 1713–1760," Canadian Historical Association, *Report of the Annual Meeting* (1939), 61–76. However, the relatively low value of the furs shipped from New York and from the other northern Thirteen Colonies (and the lack of change in these shipments after the Conquest) suggests that smuggling was less extensive than some have conjectured. U.S. Bureau of the Census, *Historical Statistics of the United States, Colonial Times to 1970,* 2 vols. (Washington, D.C., 1975), 2: 1188. Thomas Wien, "Castor, peaux, et pelleteries dans le commerce canadien des fourrures, 1720–1790," in *"Le Castor Fait Tout": Selected Papers of the Fifth North American Fur Trade Conference, 1985,* ed. Bruce G. Trigger et al. (Montreal, 1987), 89, presents still another set of figures for beaver shipments. But in most years these figures are similar to those of Innis and Lunn.]

Officials were disturbed by the willingness of the *coureurs de bois* to ignore French law and sell their pelts to Albany. In 1681 the authorities instituted a new system, which limited the western trade to the twenty-five firms receiving an official permit or *congé.* Smaller traders were forced out of this commerce, and the number of outfitters in Montreal fell from about thirty-five in 1681 to twenty at the end of the century.[17]

The new regulations, which would endure (with modifications) to the end of the French era, were no guarantee of prosperity for the fur traders. But they did provide a stable framework for this commerce, and would serve the colony well as these exchanges expanded in the eighteenth century.

Although agriculture was hurt by the sudden drop in spending with Talon's departure, it too gradually strengthened in the 1670s and 1680s. According to Cole Harris's data, fewer individuals took up farms in the 1670s, and the pace of settlement did not quicken again until the eighteenth century. Still, farmers had reason for optimism during these years. Until the late 1680s the fighting with the Iroquois was in areas well removed from the St. Lawrence and so did not directly threaten the colony's growers. A run of favorable harvests is suggested by wheat prices that fluctuated but remained well below the famine levels recorded after 1690. The broad downward trend in grain quotations during the 1670s and 1680s suggests that the colony was making headway in the task of feeding itself (fig. 8.6).[18]

For Quebec and Montreal these were years of both hardship and recovery. Talon's departure and the decline in French funding dealt a sharp blow to the capital, where much of the spending had been focused. The construction of large vessels ceased, and instead Governor Frontenac complained about the cost of hiring Canadian workmen. The workers, he stated, have "their heels on the necks of the habitants." The brewery and the other new enterprises in the capital closed. Several important merchants left Canada and returned to France. In addition to these problems a fire destroyed much of the Lower Town in 1682.[19]

But Quebec, which enjoyed continuing support for its religious and military establishments, gradually recovered from these blows. There were signs of vigor in the merchant community. In 1674 Colbert responded to the requests of Canadian importers and others, and ended the West India Company's monopoly of American trade. Quebec traders showed their initiative in 1682 by forming the Company of the North to tap the fur trade of Hudson's Bay by sea. They hoped to compete with the Hudson's Bay Company, which England had chartered in 1670. The 1682 fire proved a boon to builders, and stone houses now replaced wooden ones in the Lower Town. And in 1685 the capital welcomed new troops, who arrived from France. Several hundred soldiers were boarded temporarily in local hospitals to because of illnesses contracted on the voyage.[20]

Montreal also grew, though more slowly than the capital. Established traders benefited from the new regulations governing the commerce in peltries. Beginning in 1685 notaries recorded all loans advanced to the voyageurs, providing outfitters with added security. Montreal was also the point of embarkation for expeditions against the Iroquois and English. Nearly 800 men assembled in 1684, about 100 in 1686, and more than 1,700 in 1687 for these campaigns. But any rejoicing was tempered in 1687 by a smallpox epidemic. The population on the island of Montreal (which included the town and nearby farms) dropped by 20 percent between 1685 and 1688, from 2,727 to 2,192. More generally, before 1689 the population of Montreal increased more slowly than did the numbers in the capital (fig. 8.7).[21]

Whatever measure of success the urban upper classes enjoyed, these were difficult years for many of the common folk. In 1688 the Sovereign Council established *bureaux des pauvres*, or Offices of the Poor, in Quebec, Montreal, and Trois Rivières. These agencies were instructed to care for the indigent and

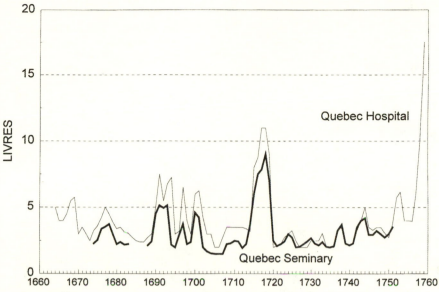

Figure 8.6. *Price of a minot of wheat in Quebec, 1664–1759.* Prices generally declined during the long swing of slow growth, 1660–1713, as Canada became more self-suffi-cient in its food supply. During the next long swing, 1713–60, strengthening demand in New France and abroad pushed up prices despite greater output. [*Sources:* Data for Quebec Hospital from Rousseau, *L'oeuvre de chère en Nouvelle France*, 72; data for Quebec Seminary from Jean Hamelin, *Economie et société en Nouvelle-France* (Quebec, 1960), 61. Note: 1 minot = 1.107 bushels.]

find jobs or apprenticeships for those capable of working. But the task would soon become too much for these boards.[22]

In sum, growth during the 1670s and 1680s was moderate at best. While there were hopeful signs, the overall record was a mixed one for the fur trade, agriculture, and the urban economies. Still, any effort to gauge the pace of expansion in these decades should also note one of the most favorable indica-tors: the boom in overseas trade.

Exchanges with both the mother country and the sugar islands expanded. Tonnage arriving from France reached a peak in 1689 when no fewer than eighteen French vessels, measuring collectively 2,500 tons, tied up at Quebec wharves. The needs of the soldiery drove this resurgence in trade. Shipments from La Rochelle, center of the fur trade and chief port in peacetime, declined in this era, while cargoes from the Bordeaux houses that outfitted the military transports soared. The tonnage arriving in Canada in the late 1680s would not be matched again until the 1740s (fig. 8.3).[23] Commerce with the French West Indies also increased. At the Quebec Hospital, sugar became a more impor-tant part of the patients' diet, and this sweetener held a prominent place on the menu until the first decade of the eighteenth century, when British war-ships closed the sea lanes (fig. 8.4).

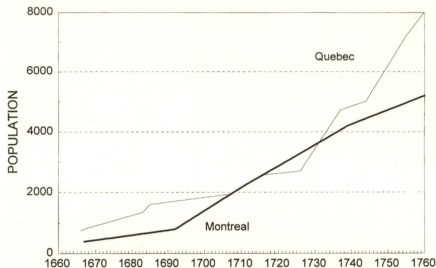

Figure 8.7. *Population of Montreal and Quebec, 1667–1760.* The changing population of the two towns reflected government spending more than commercial activities. [*Sources:* Montreal figures from Harris, *Seigneurial System*, 90–103. Louise Dechêne, "La croissance de Montréal au XVIIIe siècle," *RHAF* 27 (1973): 164, presents another set of statistics for Montreal, which suggests somewhat slower growth after 1720. Quebec data from Hare, *Histoire de la ville de Québec*, 324. Quebec population in 1760 from Harris.]

Growth in ocean-going trade suggests a solid recovery during this era. But those numbers can not stand alone. When those figures are brought together with data for the staple and urban sectors, the picture that emerges is one of a slow-paced expansion.

Wartime Depression, 1689–1713

In the late 1680s Canada's long cycle of slow growth reached its high point. During the next quarter century conditions worsened in the New World, much as they did in France. Hard times were evident through most sectors of Canada's economy. Only Montreal, which supplied the campaigns in the interior, flourished during this difficult period.

Uncertain, inconsistent French spending hurt the Canadian economy, and the shortfalls were particularly painful during these years of imperial conflict. Shipments from Bordeaux, the port that sent war materiel to Canada, serve as a proxy for government spending—and suggest reasonably high outlays before 1704. But these imports were below the level of the late 1680s—even though war in the New World had heightened the need for support (fig. 8.3).

Funding grew more precarious in the new century. In 1704 Versailles, strapped by a war-depleted treasury and fearing the dangers of the high seas, ended shipments of specie to New France. In response, the intendant discontinued the long-standing practice of annually redeeming the "card money." In 1705 France further undercut Canadian finances by refusing to honor bills of exchange drawn in the colony. Confessed the Minister of the Marine: "The unfortunate state of the kingdom in the past several years has prevented His Majesty from meeting both his expenses and those it was indispensable for him to make . . . to defend himself against the enemies of the state. . . . The King is not in a position to provide for the colony." At the same time that Versailles's commitment weakened, the demands of Canadian military campaigns increased—a situation that forced the intendants to issue ever larger quantities of card money to meet current expenses. Over one million livres of unsupported currency soon were in circulation, and inflation raged between 300 and 500 percent. "We can no longer live," keened one Quebecer with a fixed income. The problem was still unresolved in 1713.[24]

For the fur trade these were trying years. The difficulty was not a lack of pelts but rather overproduction and the collapse of the European market. While clashes with the Iroquois in the 1690s disrupted certain supply routes, they did not sever New France's links with Michilimackinac or the west. Traders now purchased record numbers of furs at these posts. The troops that Governor Frontenac dispatched often became trading parties, further enlarging the supply of skins. The Company of the Farm, which held the exclusive right of marketing the colony's beaver, was flooded with pelts. By 1695 it had furs worth 3,500,000 livres in its storehouses. Additional skins were turned over to the Company, climaxing in a record haul worth 296,000 livres in 1699 (fig. 8.5).

Paralleling this upsurge in production was a decline in European calls for beaver, and a precipitous fall in prices. These conditions reflected secular changes in taste as well as waning demand during this long swing. The beaver sent from Quebec to France and reexported to other countries was used to make hats, and by the end of the century popular tastes in headware were changing. The new styles had narrower brims and used less fur. More generally, hard times in France diminished the demand for elegant hats and other luxuries. Prices in Canada went into a tailspin beginning in 1699. Parchment beaver fell from roughly 50 sols a pound to 30 in 1706, and coat beaver was flatly refused at the company stores between 1706 and 1713 (fig. 8.1). The beaver trade would recover in the eighteenth century as the French economy gathered strength. But this commerce exhibited no long-term growth; furs other than beaver would become increasingly important in the eighteenth century (fig. 9.6). With the fur trade badly depressed, New France withdrew from the posts north and south of the Lakes. The founding of Detroit in 1701, however, indicated that the retreat was not to be a permanent one.[25]

Hard times in the fur trade led to a temporary change in the control of this commerce. Since 1675 Versailles had kept the beaver trade a monopoly. A single French corporation—in this era, the Company of the Farm—was responsible for purchasing the pelts, providing Indian goods, and financing its Canadian correspondents. When the trade slumped in 1700, the French licensees abandoned a difficult situation, and allowed a group of Canadian merchants, led by Aubert de la Chesnaye, to take over the monopoly. But the new enterprise, the Company of the Colony, had little French support and few resources of its own. The intendant, François de Beauharnois de la Chaussaye, observed: "The capital of this company is in reality a creation of the mind. No one has put a *sol* in it, and the private individuals only went into the partnership in the hope of sharing future profits." Unsurprisingly, the new firm soon collapsed, and in 1705 the monopoly was returned to France. But not until 1720 and the emergence of the French Indies Company did a truly solvent, dynamic French firm take over the beaver trade, and provide adequate financing for this important area of Canadian commerce.[26]

This era was also a difficult one for many farmers, who had to contend with Indians attacks as well as with bad weather. In August 1689 a force of 1,500 Iroquois burned Lachine, a small settlement near Montreal. Fighting with the Iroquois now intensified, with the settled areas very much the battleground. Intendant Jean Bochart de Champigny reported in 1691: "I found the people living above Trois Rivières in a state of great misery and the whole countryside ruined by the enemy, with the exception of the area around Boucherville and close by the forts, to which all the *habitants* have been forced to retire. This prevents them working on their distant fields or raising cattle except in very small numbers owing to the limited space within the fort walls." Bad weather compounded the farmers' problems. The result was a shortage of foodstuffs and soaring wheat prices. During most of the years between 1691 and 1701 the Quebec Hospital was forced to pay an unprecedented six livres or more for a minot (roughly a bushel) of grain, more than twice the price demanded in the 1680's. Quotations did not drop to more normal levels until 1703 (fig. 8.6). And because grain was in short supply, Canada was unable in many years to provision the garrisons at Placentia, Newfoundland, and Port Royal in Acadia.[27]

During these difficult years the two chief cities — Montreal and Quebec — fared better than did the countryside. Thanks to government spending, Montreal became a boom town. The population of the western metropolis caught up to, then surpassed, that of Quebec (fig. 8.7). Significantly, the growth of Montreal took place during years when the fur trade was depressed. Government outlays, not commerce, remained the primary engine of growth for the towns.

Montreal served as the staging ground for France's New World campaigns. In 1692 about 400 soldiers and their native allies came together in the city for an expedition to resupply Fort Chambly, on the Richelieu River. In 1695 Governor Frontenac assembled a force of more than 700 men in the city before setting out to reestablish the fort that bore his name. Frontenac's campaign the following year also began with extensive preparations at Montreal. The town continued to be the center of military activity in the new century. In 1709 Governor Claude de Ramezay brought more than 1,000 fighting men to the town to oppose the English and their native allies. Still other expeditions were launched from Montreal in 1710 and 1711. These campaigns provided work for artisans and laborers, and enriched the traders who provisioned the troops. The city also grew because it served as a refuge — particularly in the 1690s — for farmers who fled from the attacks of the Iroquois.[28]

To be sure, some Montrealers experienced hard times during these years. Crop failures in the early 1690s made it hard for many townsfolk to feed themselves. The devaluation of card money after 1700 hurt traders who depended on these government payments. The number of poor increased, and Montreal was forced to open a *hôpital-general,* or almshouse, to care for the indigent. A smallpox epidemic struck the town in 1703 (though losses were not as severe as in Quebec). But while some in Montreal suffered hardship, these years were also ones of bustle and construction.[29]

Quebec grew as well, although at a slower pace than Montreal. Like the western town, Quebec received money from the crown for lodging soldiers and for fortifications. But observers more often underscored the city's problems. Authorities remarked that it was difficult to find artisans and workers because so many had left for jobs in Montreal. Epidemics ravaged Quebec in 1699, 1700–01, 1702–03, and 1710–11. During the winter of 1702–3 smallpox claimed 302 victims or 16 percent of the population. Many Quebecers had to cope with poverty. The town opened an almshouse in 1692 to care for the beggars and to replace the Office of the Poor, recently created for that purpose. But the number of indigent people proved too much for the almshouse, and in 1698 the Office of the Poor was revived.[30]

In Canada, as in France, the years from 1689 to 1713 were marked by hard times. War, bad weather, uncertain French funds, and a decline in the demand for furs rocked the New World colony. This economic decline was reflected in imports from the mother country. Arrivals from France continued at relatively high levels during the 1690s, although tonnage fell below the peak five-year period, 1685–89. But the drop in trade was unmistakable after 1700, once England demonstrated its mastery of the high seas. Insurance rates doubled, and during several years no vessels arrived from France (fig. 8.3). Exchanges with the French Caribbean also were hurt. Sugar was nearly eliminated from the tables at the Quebec Hospital (fig. 8.4).[31]

In short, this cycle, which had started out so hopefully during Talon's intendancy, ended with depression in the new century. But the advent of peace, and the reopening of the sea lanes to the east and the land routes to the west, promised a new era of growth.

~ovo~

A Long Swing of Canadian Expansion, 1713–1760

Gilles Hocquart's arrival in Canada in 1729 was hardly auspicious. The *Eléphant*, the ship carrying him and his baggage, hit a rock in the St. Lawrence River and settled to the bottom. Hocquart had to proceed to the provincial capital in a small sloop. Landing in Quebec with little ceremony, the new intendant appeared unimpressive. He was overweight, with full jowls, and he made clear his love of fine food by bringing his personal chef. But Hocquart soon surprised his critics. During a term of service that lasted from 1729 to 1748, Hocquart proved singularly energetic and deeply concerned about the economic development of Canada. At least during the first dozen years of his administration he was successful in achieving his goal: the creation of a bustling economy based on a mix of private and public initiatives.[1]

But perhaps Hocquart was simply fortunate to serve as intendant when he did. The Canadian economy experienced a long wave of rapid development that began in 1713, accelerated after 1725, and did not slacken until the mid-1750s. This cycle, which closely paralleled the ascent of the French economy, was marked by the quickening of both the staple sector and the urban economy. The standard of living climbed about 0.5 percent a year, a pace comparable to that recorded in the Thirteen Colonies.[2] By 1755, however, growth yielded to hard times as war and ballooning government outlays increasingly distorted the patterns of business life.

The Beginnings of the Upturn, 1713–1725

Between 1713 and 1725 the Canadian economy recovered from the disruptions of imperial conflict and strengthened in ways that laid the foundation for future development. Both of the leading staples—furs and grain—exhibited growth, as did the towns. An increase in French funds reinforced favorable developments in commerce.

The fur trade entered upon a new era of expansion, with increases in both the supply and demand for skins. The quantities of pelts collected for shipment rose as New France strengthened its military presence in the interior. Governor Philippe de Rigaud de Vaudreuil visited Versailles shortly after the Treaty of Utrecht, and returned with ministerial support for an aggressive strategy. One of the first fruits of this policy was a victory in 1716 over the Fox Indians at their stronghold near Baie des Puants (now Green Bay, Wisconsin). With the establishment of new posts and the reopening of old ones, the quantity of beaver—still the mainstay of Canadian exports—readied for shipment rose sharply. Only about 70,000 pounds had been offered to the Company each year between 1706 and 1714. But in 1722 the amount soared to more than 150,000 pounds (fig. 8.5).

European demand quickened as growth resumed on the continent. French prices for both coat and parchment beaver jumped in the early 1720s, and quotations rose in Canada as well. Coat beaver, which earlier had been turned away by the company stores, by the mid-1720s commanded 100 sols a pound, and the value of parchment beaver also climbed, if less dramatically (figs. 8.1, 9.1, and 9.2). The emergence of the French Indies Company as the marketing agent boosted this commerce.[3]

Traders also benefited from improvements in the construction of canoes. This was a long-term development, although benefits were most apparent in periods such as this one when the boats were packed high with furs and supplies. Larger canoes raised productivity because they carried more cargo for each voyageur. In 1680 a typical canoe held three men, was perhaps 22 feet long, and carried 1,500 pounds of manufactures or furs. By 1715 these vessels had reached more than 30 feet in length, held five, and could be loaded with 3,000 pounds of skins. By the 1750s some of the canoes were 40 feet long, were paddled by eight voyageurs, and could transport 6,600 pounds of goods. Thus the number of pounds for each man had risen from about 500 in 1680 to more than 800 in 1760. The *congé* system, established in 1681, encouraged this steady improvement. These regulations allowed merchants to send only one cargo-load worth of trade goods to the west each year. So larger canoes meant more profits.[4]

Canadian farmers also increased their output during these years, but as yet produced little beyond local needs. External markets remained more important for their promise than their revenue. Following an ascending curve that dated back many decades, the per capita output of wheat rose. By the mid-1720s grain production consistently surpassed the level of twelve minots a person, roughly the point where the colony was able to feed its own citizenry and could begin gathering a surplus for shipment abroad (fig. 9.3). The wild gyrations that long had characterized wheat prices subsided. The latest, and most extreme fluctuations—the rise and fall of quotations from 1713 to 1720—reflected both a series of short crops and a period of inflation (fig. 8.6).[5]

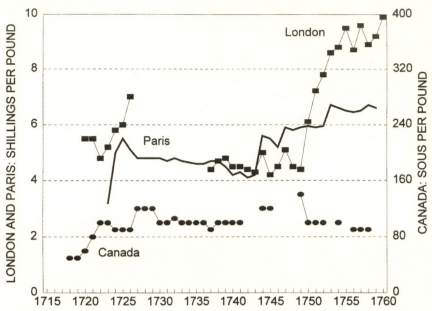

Figure 9.1. *Prices for coat beaver in London, Paris, and Canada, 1715–1760.* Canadian quotations for coat beaver (the skins worn and softened by the Indians) rebounded by the 1720s, but showed no further long-term growth. European prices climbed with the disruptions of war in the 1740s and 1750s. [*Sources:* A. J. E. Lunn, "Economic Development in New France, 1713–1760 (Ph.D. diss., McGill Univ., 1942), 459–61, presents the price the French Indies Company offered Canadians. Thomas Wien, "Selling Beaver Skins in North America and Europe, 1720–1760: The Uses of Fur-Trade Imperialism," *Journal of the Canadian Historical Association* 1 (1990): 308, provides Paris and London quotations.]

  The establishment of Louisbourg on Isle Royale shortly after the Peace of Utrecht created a new market for Canadian foodstuffs. By the mid-1720s Louisbourg was a town of more than 1,000 inhabitants and a garrison of 350 men. The new town boasted a splendid harbor, and was well located to oversee the New World fishery. It was soon handling exchanges with France, New England, the West Indies, and Canada. By the 1730s this fortress city would be the fourth busiest port in North America and an important destination for vessels leaving Quebec. However, before 1725 the lack of surplus grain kept Canada from sending regular shipments to the fortress town.[6]

  The French West Indies were another potentially rich market for Canadian food producers. But again success lay in the future. In the decade after 1715 no more than four vessels a year sailed in either direction between Canada and the French sugar islands (fig. 9.4).

  The towns expanded during this period, though not at the brisk pace of the war years. With over 20 percent of all the settlers, the urban places remained a crucial and dynamic component of the colonial economy. Continuing a trend that dated back to the 1690s, Montreal grew faster than Quebec (fig. 8.7). The

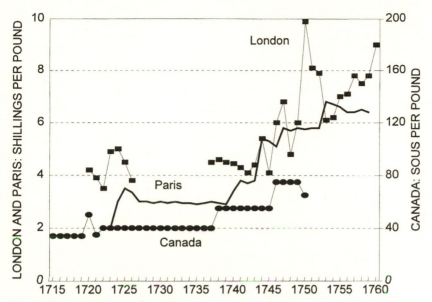

Figure 9.2. *Prices for parchment beaver in London, Paris, and Canada, 1715–1760.* Canadian quotations for parchment beaver (the skins dried in the sun) increased in value during the 1740s, the last decade for which we have data. Prices also climbed in Paris and London. [*Sources:* Lunn, "Economic Development," 459–61, presents the price the French Indies Company offered Canadians. Wien, "Selling Beaver Skins," 308, provides Paris and London quotations.]

western metropolis benefited from the revival of the fur trade and increased government spending. With peace the number of trips west soared, as did the earnings of the merchants. Equally important for Montreal were military outlays. In 1713 Intendant Michel Bégon called for the construction of stone ramparts to replace the wooden palisade that defended the city. The Crown supported this initiative, and sent a skilled architect and military engineer, Gaspard-Joseph Chaussegros de Léry, to supervise the project. Work began on the walls in 1717 and would continue until 1744. These fortifications provided steady employment for masons, carpenters, and other artisans. Although the king hoped local taxes would defray the cost of construction, in the end the royal treasury provided most of the funds.[7]

The development of Quebec, however, lagged. Agricultural exports, which would boost the town's fortunes in the 1730s and 1740s, did not surge until the late 1720s. And while Chaussegros de Léry designed ramparts for the capital, the Minister of the Marine offered little support for the project. Work on the walls stopped soon after it began in 1720. There was no further effort to complete the fortifications until after the fall of Louisbourg in 1745.[8]

The influx of money from France also strengthened the economy. These funds allowed Bégon to return the currency to a solid footing. In 1713 fully 1,600,000 livres of card money circulated, with a real worth that was only a

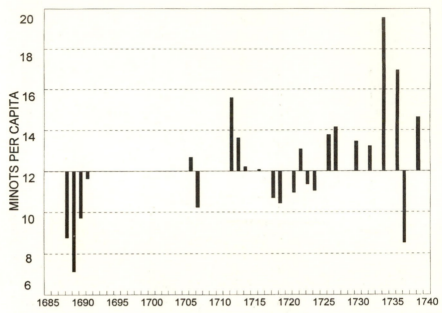

Figure 9.3. *Per capita wheat production in Canada, 1688–1739.* As the economy strengthened, Canada was able to feed itself and produce a surplus. The level of domestic consumption was roughly 12 minots per capita. [*Sources:* Lunn, "Economic Development," 443–44; F. W. Burton, "The Wheat Supply of New France," Royal Society of Canada, *Proceedings and Transactions*, 3d ser., 30 (1936): sect. 2, 140; on the subsistence level of 12 minots per capita, "Michel Bégon de la Picardière," *DCB* 3: 57.]

fraction of its nominal value. Now that the sea lanes were safe, France shipped supplies of coin to the New World. With these funds Bégon retired the card money, and in 1719 he made the money of France the money of Canada. But while this new specie currency was less troublesome than the inflated cards had been, it still was far from a satisfactory solution. The colony never received enough coin, and whatever amount arrived each year soon flowed back to France in payment for the imbalance of trade.[9]

In all, growth during these years was moderate. The limited nature of the gains recorded before 1725 was evident in the low level of imports. Arrivals from France remained at a low ebb, with rarely more than 1,200 tons' worth of shipping tying up at the Quebec docks in any one year (fig. 8.3).

The Heyday of Growth, 1725–1742

The period from 1725 to 1742 was the springtime of Canadian economic expansion. A wide variety of activities, including the fur trade and agriculture, commerce and manufacturing, displayed a new vitality. Both the countryside

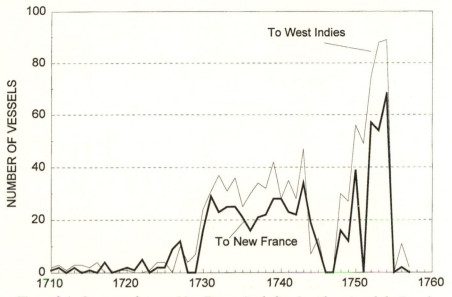

Figure 9.4. *Commerce between New France (including Louisbourg) and the French West Indies, 1710–1757.* Trade between New France and the French West Indies took off in the late 1720s. These exchanges were disrupted by the wars with Great Britain. [*Source:* Jacques Mathieu, *Le commerce entre la Nouvelle-France et les Antilles au XVIIIe siècle* (Montreal, 1981), 224–25.]

and towns benefited from this upturn. A dynamic mix of private and public capital characterized most enterprises, and the standard of living visibly improved. Underlying this quickening of business activity was the long swing of economic development that lifted the French economy.

FUR TRADE

The fur trade was one of the engines of growth in this period. Peltries accounted for almost three-fourths by value of the cargoes sent from Canada. Figure 9.5 shows the distribution of shipments in 1739. Mirroring the ascent of the metropolitan economy, the quantity of furs harvested in Canada and sent to France skyrocketed. The value of the skins received at La Rochelle maps this ascent, with 1727 the watershed year. Between 1718 and 1726 furs with an average worth of 280,000 livres were shipped to La Rochelle each year, but in 1727 the value of shipments jumped to more than a million livres. The annual average for the ensuing nine years, not including 1727, was 572,000 livres, fully 104 percent higher than the preceding period (fig. 9.5). Much of this rise came from the barrels of "other" furs, such as lynx and marten, directed to France (fig. 9.6).[10]

The resurgence of the fur trade should be kept in perspective. Although prices for parchment beaver rose in the late 1730s, those for coat beaver re-

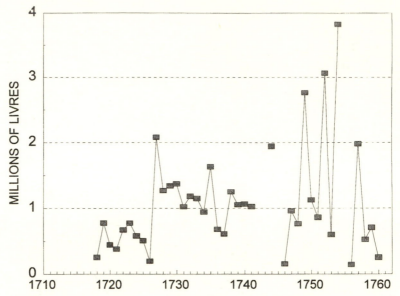

Figure 9.5. *Value of furs received at La Rochelle, 1718–1760.* The value of furs shipped from Canada to France jumped in the mid-1720s, and climbed again in the 1740s. [*Sources:* Lunn, "Economic Development," 464–65. This series is a good proxy for the Canadian fur trade, even though La Rochelle imports are not identical with Canadian exports. Some Canadian furs were smuggled to New York, and some were sent to other French ports. A small portion of the pelts received in La Rochelle came from Louisiana. See also U.S. Bureau of the Census, *Historical Statistics of the United States, Colonial Times to 1970,* 2 vols. (Washington, D.C., 1975), 2: 1188; Wien, "Selling Beaver Skins," 293–317.]

mained level between 1725 and 1742 (figs. 9.1 and 9.2).[11] And viewed in per capita terms, the shipments sent in the late 1720s marked a high point for the Canadian fur trade (fig. 9.7). While exports of peltries would rise again in the 1740s and 1750s, the relative importance of these shipments gradually declined. The Canadian economy was slowly shifting from its dependence on furs to an emphasis on grain. By the 1770s the value of grain exports, while fluctuating widely, would equal the worth of fur shipments.

Nonetheless, the fur trade clearly prospered in the 1720s and 1730s. Canadians now intensified their efforts in the area north and west of Lake Superior. The result was a second struggle with the Fox Indians, who had been defeated in 1716. This war, which disrupted the trade at Baie des Puants and on the western shore of Lake Superior, dragged on from 1727 to 1738, ending with a reaffirmation of Canadian power. Despite the steady march of New France toward Lake Winnipeg and, after 1742, toward the foothills of the Rockies, the area south of the Great Lakes always remained a far more important source of furs. Several times as many canoes headed each year for the southern region than set out for Lake Superior and the northwest.[12]

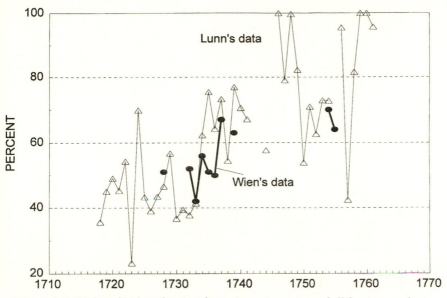

Figure 9.6. *Value of "other" furs (nonbeaver) as a percentage of all furs imported into La Rochelle, 1718–1761.* Gradually, furs other than beaver became the mainstay of the peltry trade. [*Sources:* Lunn, "Economic Development," 464–65; Thomas Wien, "Castor, peaux, et pelleteries dans le commerce canadien des fourrures, 1720–1790," in *"Le Castor Fait Tout": Selected Papers of the Fifth North American Fur Trade Conference, 1985,* ed. Bruce G. Trigger et al. (Montreal, 1987), 86, 89–92.]

AGRICULTURE

The production and sale of foodstuffs was another potent force for development. Because most grain was consumed in Canada, its importance was greater than its relative weight among Canadian exports (18 percent of the total in 1739) might suggest (fig. 9.8). Still, the fraction shipped from Canada was significant because it helped set prices and encouraged farmers to raise more grain. So at least in part the agricultural expansion of these years reflected the long cycle of growth in France and its possessions. This discussion surveys the prosperity of the countryside by looking at levels of production, markets, the terms of trade, and rural good fortune.

Soaring output now allowed Canadian farmers to supply external as well as domestic markets. The amount of improved land and the quantity of foodstuffs produced rose strongly in this era. This growth in production reflected the gradual shift in the colony from furs to farming as well as the impact of strengthening demand (and prices) in the French Atlantic empire. The number of *arpents* cultivated for each inhabitant—a figure that had changed little between 1705 and 1725—doubled between 1725 and 1739 (fig. 1.2). Land set aside for pasture also increased (fig. 9.9). Grain production climbed, continuing a trend that dated back many decades. Per capita output of wheat jumped from twelve minots in the mid-1720s to sixteen by the late 1730s, even though a crop failure in 1737 briefly checked this ascent (fig. 9.3).[13]

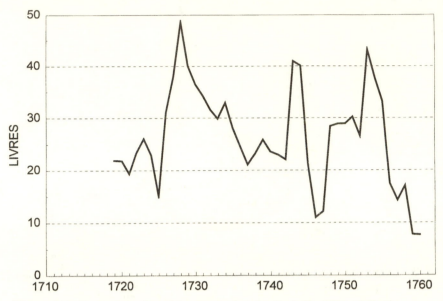

Figure 9.7. *Per capita value of furs received at La Rochelle, 1718–1760: three-year moving average.* Measured on a per person basis, the long-term trend for fur shipments after the 1720s was downward. [*Source:* Lunn, "Economic Development," 464–65. See the discussion of this series in the source note to figure 9.5.]

Vigorous demand from markets in Louisbourg and the French West Indies underwrote this era of rural prosperity. Louisbourg was the chief destination for the colony's agricultural products. Regular dealings between Quebec and the fortified town on Isle Royale began in 1728 when the Minister of the Marine initiated the practice of having Canada supply the garrison with its annual requirements of 2,165 quintals of flour and 340 quintals of peas. Departures for Louisbourg now rose to about thirty a year, and would remain at this high level for the next decade (fig. 9.10).

By the 1730s Louisbourg had come to play a major role in the economic life of New France. This outpost expanded in step with the growth of French imperial trade, taking off after 1725 as did its chief market, the French West Indies. The most valuable export from Louisbourg was fish, which came from the French vessels plying the waters near Newfoundland. Between 1732 and 1741 Louisbourg forwarded to the sugar islands cargoes of dried cod averaging more than 600,000 livres annually. The rise of Louisbourg helped French merchants in the Canada trade to secure return cargoes, or pursue triangular voyages. French houses sent dry goods to Louisbourg. Fish were then taken from Isle Royale to the West Indies, and finally sugar was brought back to France.

Isle Royale served as the chief market for Canadian biscuit, an export valued at 69,017 livres in 1739, and it absorbed foodstuffs totaling more than 180,000 livres in that year. But the entrepôt's very prosperity meant that Cana-

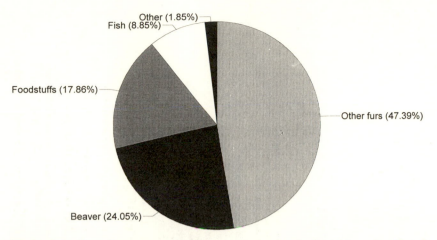

Figure 9.8. *Canadian exports, 1739.* Furs—beaver and other skins—dominated Canadian shipments in this era. Total exports were 1,504,742 livres. [*Source:* Denys Delâge, "Les structures économiques de la Nouvelle-France et de la Nouvelle-York," *l'Actualité économique* 46 (1970): 96.]

dians did not have the field to themselves. The administrators at Isle Royale usually opened the port to New Englanders. In 1739 fifty-nine ships came to Louisbourg from British Acadia and New England, frequently bearing provisions, and by 1743 the number had increased to seventy-eight. When crops were short, these ties with the English colonies proved a blessing for Canada, and more than once British American wheat helped feed New France. But in most years Canadians resented this competition.

Because Canadian stockpiles of grain always were limited, the West Indies remained a secondary market. Nonetheless, Quebec directed significant quantities of flour to the French sugar islands, whose economies also expanded strikingly during this long swing. France promoted these ties, much as it had encouraged Canadian commerce with Louisbourg. In 1726 the ministry requested that the government of New France prepare a "detailed memorandum" on ways of increasing trade with the Caribbean. The King instructed Governor Charles de Beauharnois de la Boische and Intendant Claude-Thomas Dupuy to discuss with their counterparts in Martinique and St. Domingue what products might be exchanged. In 1727 the French government lifted for ten years the duties on Caribbean products forwarded to Canada or Louisbourg, and commerce with the sugar isles gradually quickened.

By the 1730s Canadian trade with the sugar islands was flourishing, although the value of shipments remained well below the worth of cargoes sent to France or Isle Royale. In good years ten or more vessels might clear the St. Lawrence for the West Indies, carrying grain worth more than 100,000 livres.

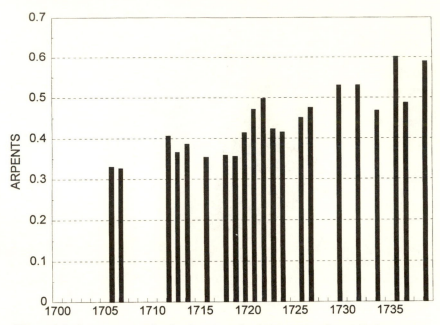

Figure 9.9. *Per capita meadowland in Canada, 1706–1739.* After 1713 the amount of meadowland rose more rapidly than did the population, reflecting the broad shift from furs to farming. [*Source:* Lunn, "Economic Development," 443–44.]

Canadian imports from the West Indies also increased, and at the Quebec Hospital sugar and molasses became ever more important parts of the regimen (fig. 8.4). Despite the expanded exports of cod and flour, supplies of foodstuffs from Canada invariably fell far short of the islands' needs. The French Antilles relied on cargoes from the mother country and the British provinces to feed their populations.[14]

Canadian farmers also benefited from a favorable movement in the terms of trade. Rising demand for grain helped reverse the secular fall of prices that dated back to the mid-seventeenth century. Despite remarkable increases in output, quotations for wheat remained around 2.5 livres from the mid-1720s to the mid-1730s, and began a steady climb after 1735 (fig. 8.6). At the same time quotations for the goods farmers bought stayed level or declined during the 1720s and 1730s. The account books of the Montreal merchant, Alexis Monière, illustrate the trends for the value of cloth, thread, shirts, blankets, and wine (fig. 9.11 and Appendix C). Bringing together the series for wheat and imported wares makes clear that a minot of grain purchased increasing quantities of dry goods between 1720 and the early 1740s. Some of these gains, however, were lost in the 1740s as wartime scarcities pushed up prices of imported wares (fig. 9.12). The records of the Quebec Hospital also depict the changing terms-of-trade between farm goods and imported wares. The hospital was forced to spend more and more on food in relation to its purchases of cloth (fig. 9.13).

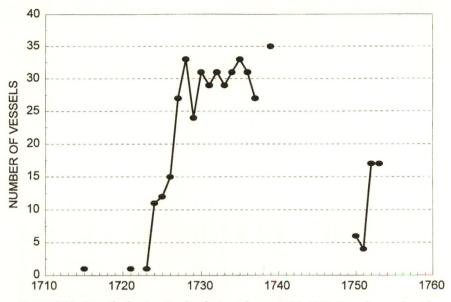

Figure 9.10. *Vessels clearing Quebec for Louisbourg, 1715–1753.* Canadian trade with Louisbourg boomed between 1725 and 1740, and then declined because of the disruptions of war. [*Source:* Mathieu, *Le commerce entre la Nouvelle-France et les Antilles,* 224–25. Mathieu presents a somewhat different set of figures for *arrivals* at Louisbourg from Quebec.]

Signs of rural prosperity became ever more apparent between 1725 and 1742. Pressure for the creation of new seigneuries increased. While only sixteen estates had been formed between 1700 and 1728, fully thirty-two were awarded from 1729 to 1743. Canadians improved their roads during this period, aiding settlement and communication. In 1737 laborers completed the King's Highway on the north shore of the St. Lawrence, making possible a four-day carriage ride from Quebec to Montreal. Furthermore, a new era of church building, the first since the 1670s, changed the skyline of many rural parishes. More than twenty-five churches, frequently with twin-towered baroque facades, were erected in a rush of work that began in the mid-1720s and continued through the 1730s. And a few of the wealthier *habitants* now built their houses of stone rather than wood.[15]

THE URBAN ECONOMY

The economies of Quebec and Montreal also recorded solid growth during this era. Quebec now was the more dynamic metropolis, reflecting the continuing influx of government money and the emergence of a more diversified export economy. And while Montreal did not keep pace with the capital, it too increased in both population and wealth (fig. 8.7).

Prosperity was a wind that filled the sails of many groups in Quebec. The noble families who resided in town enjoyed growing revenues from their

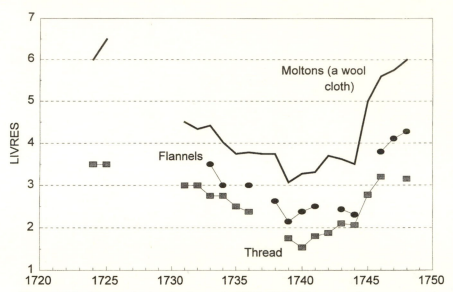

Figure 9.11. *Montreal prices for dry goods, 1724–1748.* The price of most imported dry goods remained level or declined between the early 1720s and 1745. During the mid-1740s the imperial conflict pushed up quotations. Moltons and flannels were sold in ells (a unit of length, roughly 45 inches), while thread was sold by spools. [*Sources:* These prices are drawn from the account book of Alexis Monière. See Appendix C for these data and more on their source. Monière was both an outfitter for the Indian trade and a merchant who sold to local customers. For more on his activities, consult Louise Dechêne, *Habitants and Merchants in Seventeenth-Century Montreal* (Montreal and Kingston, 1992), 97–98, 307–11.]

seigneuries and from their involvement in the fur trade. (Several seigneurs had a lucrative perquisite: the trading rights at a western post.) Importers also enjoyed favorable returns during these years. Although some of these individuals were independent Canadian merchants, the most important traders were still the representatives of Bordeaux, La Rochelle, and Rouen houses. Artisans and laborers found ample employment.[16]

Quebec also benefited from the quickening of industrial activity. The Quebec shipyards entered a period of unprecedented prosperity. These works, established by Talon in the 1660s, had never closed although production had been sporadic at best. Between 1700 and 1728, there was only one year (1724) when the colony launched more than three vessels. But increased wealth, trade, and government support dramatically changed the picture. Hocquart as usual played the promoter, assiduously lobbying for royal funds. In 1731 the crown agreed to pay bounties for all ships built in the provincial capital, and the first monies were dispersed the following year. Shipbuilding boomed, and in contrast to the dismal record of the preceding period, between 1729 and 1742 nine or more vessels rose on the stocks in most years. With the shipyards flourishing, Hocquart concurred with the decision to discontinue the bonuses in 1739, a step that had little immediate impact (fig. 9.14).

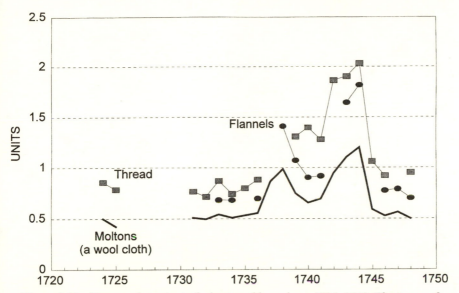

Figure 9.12. *How much a minot of wheat could purchase, 1724–1748.* The terms of trade became more favorable for Canadian farmers between 1720 and 1744. That is, a unit of wheat could be traded for more cloth or hardware in 1740 than in 1725. [*Sources:* Grain prices are drawn from Jean Hamelin, *Economie et société en Nouvelle-France* (Quebec, 1960), 61; for dry goods prices and units, see figure 9.11 and Appendix C.]

The bustling Quebec port and shipyard fostered an array of other industries. The 1739 census showed there were eleven sawmills in the Quebec region. There was also a rope factory and a manufactory for making tar. Coopers were kept busy with the demand for barrels. Butchers and bakers helped provision the vessels in the harbor.[17]

Montreal also expanded, if more slowly. Louise Dechêne's depiction of the town in 1731 suggests the components of the urban economy. About one-third of the working population drew their incomes directly from the fur trade. This group included about 30 merchant-outfitters, more than 60 merchant-voyageurs, 250 to 300 indentured servants, and 50 innkeepers, bakers, butchers, and other artisans. Perhaps 30 to 40 percent of those employed held positions supported by public funds. In this group were military, religious, and administrative personnel. The remaining 30 to 40 percent of the work force included servants, slaves, and domestics; artisans and builders; and other tradespeople.[18]

The growing wealth of Montreal was evident in the quickening pace of new construction. The hundreds of building contracts that have been preserved make clear the new structures were larger and more elegant. In 1721 Intendant Michel Bégon declared stone the proper building material for the towns of New France. But the impact of this decree was not evident until the late 1720s. After 1727 virtually all the contracts signed for new buildings in Montreal specified masonry. The size of houses grew. Before 1720 no con-

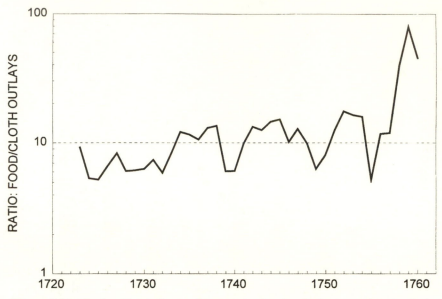

Figure 9.13. *Quebec Hospital expenditures: ratio of outlays for food to outlays for cloth, 1723–1760.* Food prices rose more rapidly than did the cost of imported manufactures. [*Source*: François Rousseau, *L'oeuvre de chère en Nouvelle-France: le régime des malades à l'Hôtel-Dieu de Québec* (Quebec, 1983), 48–51.]

tract signed in Montreal specified a home of more than 1,000 square *pieds* (roughly, 1,000 square feet). After 1730 one-half of all contracts called for structures of that size or greater. By the 1740s fully 80 percent of the new homes exceeded this benchmark. Many of the new buildings were in the graceful baroque style that now displaced the heavy lines of medieval architecture. This dramatic architecture appeared in Montreal as early as the mid-1720s with the construction of the Chateau Vaudreuil and the Parish Church of Notre-Dame.[19]

INDUSTRY OUTSIDE THE TOWNS

Several enterprises were established outside the environs of Quebec and Montreal. The number of sawmills rose from ten in 1716 to seventy in 1739. Work also began on a mine to exploit the copper deposits found near Lake Superior. Private funds — 25,411 livres from a Montreal fur trader — and royal backing financed the first stages of this project. However, the costs soon proved prohibitive, and the mine was abandoned.

The largest enterprise outside the cities was the ironworks at St. Maurice. Talon had established these forges, but after his departure they were closed, and the colony's rich ore deposits had lain untapped for over a half century. In 1729 Hocquart and Governor Beauharnois granted a Montreal merchant a twenty-year monopoly of iron production, and in turn this importer invested

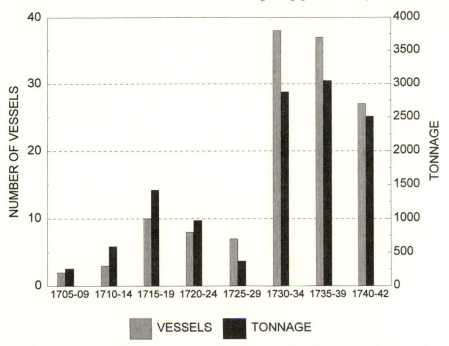

Figure 9.14. *Shipbuilding in Canada, 1705–1742.* Shipbuilding increased after 1713, but the great surge came in the 1730s. After 1743 the Crown took over the privately owned shipyards. [*Sources:* Lunn, "Economic Development," 473–76; Delâge, "Les structures économiques," 109.]

10,000 livres of his own funds. But difficulties mounted at the St. Maurice Forges, and government loans became ever more important. The resources of the Canadian merchant community were simply too limited to maintain an enterprise of this magnitude. Production gradually rose, and between 1737 and 1741, the forges turned out a million pounds of iron, most of which was exported to France. In 1741 the Canadian merchants managing the ironworks saw clearly that they would be unable to pay their debts to the King; they declared bankruptcy, preparing the way for a government takeover of the facilities.[20]

INFLUX OF FUNDS

The amount of capital offered to Canadians by private and government sources also increased during this era. A network of credit that began in France had characterized the colony since its earliest days.[21] French houses extended funds to Quebec and Montreal importers. They in turn provided credit to shopkeepers and outfitters in the fur trade, while the final links in this chain were the habitants and fur traders. A portion of this credit was retired annually, but much was not and became part of the working capital of the colony. In 1732 Intendant Gilles Hocquart observed: "A great proportion of the traders owe considerable sums in France, and I may state without risk that these amount to even more than 250 thousand livres." As French houses sought to increase their sales during this era, credit became one means of gaining new customers. Six years after Hocquart's remarks a single Rouen firm, Dugard & Co., had outstanding obligations in Canada of more than 100,000 livres. During the 1730s Dugard & Co. shipped no more than one-sixth of Quebec imports; therefore, these figures suggest a ballooning volume of credit that totaled well over 600,000 livres by the end of the decade.[22]

Government backing for economic growth also was important, and here too there seems to have been an expansion of funding. French support allowed Canadian authorities to reintroduce paper money—and keep it from depreciating. In 1729 the ministry acknowledged that the attempt to return Canada to a specie-based currency was a failure, and approved 400,000 livres of card money. But even this sum proved insufficient, and in 1733 an additional 200,000 livres were put into circulation, and in 1742 a further 120,000 livres. Despite these sharp increases in the quantity of currency, the cards retained their full value.

Direct government financing of Canadian development appears to have expanded during the 1730s, though the evidence is contradictory. Guy Frégault's figures for royal expenditures in New France show little increase until 1743, when military appropriations began their steep rise (fig. 9.15). But Frégault's statistics do not include the "loans" that Versailles extended for economic development— loans that typically were not repaid. For example, the production of tiles was aided in the early 1730s by a subvention of 6,000 livres, while by the end of the decade the French government had given more than 190,000 livres to the ironworks at St. Maurice near Trois Rivières. The Crown also contributed more than 300,000 livres to build the Montreal ramparts. Correspondence reinforces the picture of greater financial support. "As to the funds with which you believe the country must be assisted," the Minister of the Marine told Intendant Hocquart, "they have never been so considerable as during your administration."[23]

OVERVIEW

The years from 1725 to 1742 were ones of strong, diversified growth for the St. Lawrence colony. A mix of private and public funds underpinned this expansion, which mirrored the long cycle of development in France and its Atlantic empire. In Canada this expansion was evident in the fur trade, agriculture, and the urban economies.

The acceleration of the Canadian economy was also reflected in the rising imports from the mother country. Tonnage arriving from La Rochelle and Bordeaux increased. Moreover, now that the Canadian economy was wealthier and its needs more varied, merchants in other French ports, such as Rouen, Saint Malo, and Nantes, ventured cargoes to the New World. Indeed, in 1740 more tonnage arrived from these towns than from either La Rochelle or Bordeaux (fig. 8.3). Data for total Canadian trade also suggest the solid growth in the standard of living. Figures that cover the years from 1729 to 1743 show a steady rise in per capita imports and exports (fig. 9.16).[24] Growth would continue in the 1740s

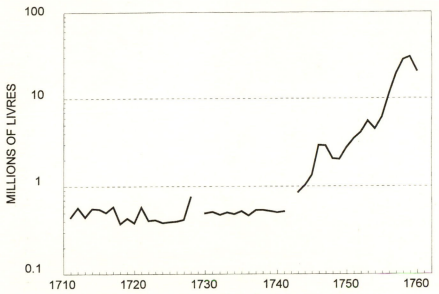

Figure 9.15. *Government expenditures in Canada, 1711–1760.* Government expenditures soared with the wars of mid-century. [*Sources:* Guy Frégault, *Le XVIIIe siècle canadien: études* (Montreal, 1968), 297, 302, 322, 336, 382; Lunn, "Economic Development," 478. Catherine M. Desbarats, "Colonial Government Finances in New France, 1700–1750" (Ph.D. diss., McGill University, 1993), 177–81, presents a slightly different set of figures for these outlays.]

and 1750s. But the vibrant, diversified economy, with its mix of private and public initiatives, would disappear as the colony shifted to a wartime footing.

French Spending Distorts the Economy, 1743–1760

Between 1743 and 1760 the steep rise in royal outlays and expanded military activity first fostered prosperity, and then—as the conflict widened and spending raced out of control—brought hardship and depression. Although the fur trade retained its vitality, the decisions of royal officials rather than private initiatives increasingly shaped business activity. During the years of prosperity (from 1743 to about 1753) French subventions aided both staple producers and town dwellers.

GOVERNMENT OUTLAYS

The new wartime economy began in 1743 as royal outlays, largely defense related, soared to an unprecedented 860,000 livres. The era of skyrocketing military expenditures continued until the British Conquest of 1760, despite a period of "peace" between 1748 and 1754. By 1745 subventions surpassed two million livres—a figure well above the value of the fur harvest. These grants

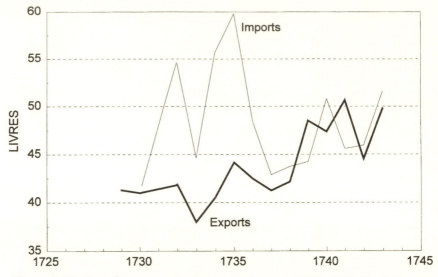

Figure 9.16. *Canadian per capita imports and exports, 1729–1743.* Trade figures suggest that the standard of living rose. However, these data must be used with care. A portion of the imports was directed to the fur trade, and so did not reflect the well-being of the European settlers. [*Source:* Lunn, "Economic Development," 443–44, 477, discusses the strengths and shortcomings of these figures. I have interpolated missing data for 1731.]

reached five million livres in 1753, and peaked at thirty million in 1759 (fig. 9.15). By the end of the 1750s, however, inflation had cut outlays in real money to less than half their nominal value.

Increased government spending was reflected in the record French exports to Canada and the changed nature of that commerce. As cargoes of war material and French foodstuffs (to feed the troops) grew more important, Bordeaux displaced La Rochelle as the chief port of origin for the Canada trade, and larger vessels became the norm (fig. 8.3). Before 1750 most ships leaving Bordeaux for Canada displaced fewer than 100 tons. During the Seven Years' War, however, the average size of vessels sailing from Bordeaux to Quebec was 273 tons.[25]

The financing of Canadian growth, which before 1743 had depended upon a mix of private and government funds, now rested almost exclusively with Versailles's escalating expenditures and its uncertain resolve. As generous as the increased outlays were, they did not keep pace with the enormous military costs that Canada incurred. Consequently, as early as 1747 Hocquart was forced to make bills on France payable in installments, and he had to juggle his books, transferring debts from one year to the next, to preserve a semblance of solvency. Grants matched spending in the early 1750s, but by 1753 delayed payment again became the norm, and bills of exchange circulated at substantial discounts. Observed a government official: "Those who in good faith make contracts with the king are cheated by the small degree of good faith and promptitude in both payments and receipts." In 1755 royal officials began to pay the regulars in specie instead of depreciated currency, and in 1759 the treasury suspended payments on the Canadian debt.[26]

FUR TRADE

Although disrupted by the fighting in the 1740s and 1750s, the fur trade continued to expand. Shipments were strong in the early 1740s until war dealt a harsh blow to this commerce. The British blockaded the St. Lawrence during 1744, 1745, and 1746, cutting off supplies for the Indian trade. Intendant Hocquart and Governor Beauharnois complained in 1745: "We are totally lacking in blankets, in dry goods, both for the needs of the inhabitants and for the Indians." Taking advantage of French weakness, the Miamis and Hurons attacked and burned several posts. Departures for the west from Montreal plummeted in 1745 and 1746. However, trade recovered in 1747 and surged once peace was concluded in 1748. Merchants forwarded record cargoes of peltries to La Rochelle in 1749, 1752, and 1754 (fig. 9.5). Canadians also benefited from rising fur prices in the Old World and New. Quotations for beaver climbed in France and England in the mid-1740s, and remained high during the 1750s. In Canada the value of parchment beaver rose in the 1740s. This series, however, ends in 1750. Canadian prices for coat beaver stayed level throughout this era (figs. 9.1 and 9.2).[27]

Fur traders also struggled to make the trade more efficient in the face of lengthening lines of supply. Merchants constructed ever larger canoes, and now used large freight-carrying *bateaux* to move goods on the St. Lawrence. The Crown also established a barque on Lake Ontario to facilitate shipments between Fort Frontenac and Fort Niagara. The growth of Detroit, which by 1751 had 600 inhabitants, further buttressed the expanding French empire. Detroit supplied foodstuffs to Michilimackinac and to traders heading for outlying posts. It also served as a headquarters for Quebec and Montreal agents. But all such efforts could not reverse the rising costs that came from the thinning of the animal populations and lengthening voyages.[28]

The resumption of war in the mid-1750s brought the brief boom in the fur trade to an abrupt end. In 1755 British warships and privateers prevented the French Indies Company from resupplying Canada with Indian wares, and during the next years, only a portion of the cargoes got through. The export of pelts suffered as well. Only in one war year, 1757, did large quantities of furs arrive in La Rochelle (fig. 9.5). The capture of Louisbourg in 1758 and Quebec in 1759 severed ties between France and its colony.[29]

AGRICULTURE

Although government spending boosted the fortunes of farmers in the 1740s, conditions worsened in the 1750s as the widening imperial conflict disrupted markets and production.

During 1740s farmers benefited from favorable crops, rising military demand, and higher prices for their produce. However, the era did not begin well.

Harvests in 1742 and 1743 were meager, and the colony had to import grain in 1743 and 1744 to cover the shortfall. But then Canada enjoyed six good harvests, beginning in 1744. At the same time, military purchases of foodstuffs expanded. Troop strength, to be sure, was well below the levels it would reach in the 1750s. Still, the governor commanded a force of 600 regulars, over 1,000 militia, as well as Indian allies. And all required Canadian grain and meat. Wheat prices now rose. Where a minot of wheat had cost about 2.5 livres in the 1720s and 1730s, the average climbed to 3 livres in the second half of the 1740s (fig. 8.6).[30]

Rising government outlays helped farmers weather difficulties during the War of the Austrian Succession. The fighting affected both exports and imports. The British blockade (and the capture of Louisbourg in 1745) cut Canadians off from valuable markets for foodstuffs. No supplies were sent to Louisbourg for several years, and shipments to the West Indies were ended. Wartime disruptions also raised the prices of imported wares (fig 9.11). The jump in the value of textiles and ironware reversed the favorable movement in the terms of trade. In the second half of the 1740s, a minot of wheat commanded fewer ells of cotton and woolen cloth than it had just a few years earlier (fig. 9.12). At the Quebec Hosptial the same reality was evident. Administrators had to spend proportionately more on clothing and less on food (fig. 9.13).

Despite such problems, the 1740s remained good years for Canadian farmers. Rising domestic consumption replaced the calls from external markets. Harvests were ample, grain prices were high, and military levies did not yet cut deeply into the rural work force. The unfavorable movement in the terms of trade after 1745 only reversed the striking gains of the early part of the decade. Visitors were impressed by the prosperity of the countryside in this period. Touring Canada in the late 1740s, Swedish naturalist Peter Kalm noted how well farmers lived: "The farmhouses are generally built of stone, but sometimes of timber, and have three or four rooms. . . . They have iron stoves in one of the rooms and fireplaces in the rest. . . ." He remarked further that "almost everybody finds it easy to be a farmer in this uncultivated country where he can live well, and at so small an expense that he does not care to work for others." And gazing upon the verdant banks of the St. Lawrence, Kalm concluded: "In a word this country was, in my opinion, one of the finest of North America that I had hitherto seen."[31]

During the 1750s, however, conditions in the countryside became increasingly difficult, and by 1755 rural prosperity had given way to hardship. Problems emerged because of the sheer size of the military demand, which quickly overwhelmed domestic sources of foodstuffs. Several hundred soldiers arrived in 1751. An additional 3,000 troops came in 1755, followed by 3,500 more in 1757. The militia also grew, as more and more Canadians were asked to bear arms. By 1754 there were about 4,000 militia serving in the West. The French also assumed responsibility for provisioning their Indian allies. In 1757 Bigot estimated that "between 14 and 15 thousand" individuals were receiving government supplies.[32]

The extraordinary demands of these years led to spiraling regulations — and corrupt practices by government officials. Poor harvests in 1750 and 1751 triggered the imposition of strict controls on the movement of grain. In 1751 Bigot halved the supplies directed to Louisbourg and prohibited private individuals from exporting flour. Farmers and traders also had to receive approval for shipments within the colony. The circle around Bigot used these regulations to manipulate markets and prices. The Châtelet Commission, which investigated the intendant and his associates after the Conquest, heard detailed testimony about corrupt practices. These included doctored records, inflated prices, and the high-handed dealings of the company (the Grande Société) that Bigot and his friends owned. So while the value of grain soared during the 1750s, much of the profit went into the hands of officials rather than landowners.[33]

Government requisitions made life increasingly difficult for the habitants. Military procurers demanded grain, horses for transport, and forage to feed these animals. At times, officials threatened to use the army to enforce their decrees. When supplies grew short in the winter of 1757, the commanders quartered their soldiers in the countryside and insisted that the peasants feed these troops. Landowners also resented the government decision to settle accounts with depreciating currency.

Farmers now had to contend with levies that took productive workers from the fields. Initially the French had tried to recruit soldiers without depleting the rural labor force. In mustering the habitants they sought to limit their service to the months between the spring sowing and fall harvest. But the need for troops became too great, and increasingly farmers were forced to serve in the militia. In 1756 an observer remarked that in the fields near Quebec only women, children, and the elderly were available for the harvest.[34]

Canada, which had been producing regular surpluses of foodstuffs since the 1720s, became ever more dependent on imported supplies — and these were never adequate. Substantial quantities of flour and other foodstuffs were brought in from France each year beginning in 1752. Shipments climbed in 1757, 1758, and 1759, reflecting the buildup of troops and a series of disastrous local harvests. Food shortages were common. While the troops ultimately received enough nourishment to take part in the campaigns of these years, rations fluctuated. Bread allotments were cut sharply, then restored when the supply ships arrived. Horsemeat was substituted for beef. By fall 1759 English troops controlled much of the area east of Quebec, and production had ended on many farms. The next year Canada was in English hands and farming was at a standstill.[35]

THE URBAN ECONOMY

The demands of imperial conflict bolstered the urban economies in the 1740s and early 1750s, but brought hardship to the towns after 1755. Quebec, which became the center of military preparations, expanded more rapidly than Montreal (fig. 8.7).

By the mid-1740s Quebec had become a key French stronghold, a busy entrepôt, and an important center for naval construction. The fall of Louisbourg in 1745 was a shock to Quebecers and reinvigorated plans to fortify the city. Chaussegros de Léry's designs, originally approved in 1718, now guided the building of the ramparts. Work proceeded briskly until 1752, and then fitfully until the fall of the city in 1759. France spent more than one million livres on these fortifications.

The expansion of commerce stimulated the Quebec economy. The number of vessels tying up at the docks soared, and recorded tonnage climbed from 8,900 tons in 1740–44 to 42,900 tons in 1755–59 (fig. 8.3). Higher levels of trade meant new wealth and more jobs for Quebecers, including merchants, artisans, and laborers. But these years were also marked by a shift in the control of these exchanges, as friends of Intendant Bigot replaced the established traders. Thus shipbuilding boomed in Quebec, but now under government rather than private management. A series of Crown commissions for warships kept workers busy during the 1740s. Bigot's crony, Jacques-Michel Bréard, took over direction of the yards and built a fleet that helped him gain a sizable share of the transport business.[36]

Reflecting this wartime activity, the population of Quebec rose from 5,010 in 1744 to 8,000 in 1760. Bigot remarked that farmers abandoned their lands and came to town, "to become carters, day laborers, or even innkeepers." The capital was also home to an increasing number of soldiers. The garrison grew from 169 individuals in 1748 to 1,000 in 1750, while during the 1750s thousands of troops were lodged temporarily in the town. The city was also a refuge for Acadians, who fled before the British onslaught. There were 1,300 Acadians present in 1757 and more than 1,500 in 1758. English prisoners were housed in Quebec before being sent to France. At least 1,700 were in the city in 1756 and 700 were counted a year later.

But the war also brought problems and, eventually, hardship to Quebec. By the mid-1750s grain was in short supply. Increasingly, the town depended on bread baked in the royal ovens. Louis-Antoine de Bougainville observed in 1756: "A police regulation has ruled here that bread will be distributed to the public only in the afternoon. I went to see this distribution. It presents the image of a famine. They fight to get near the wicket through which they pass the bread." Beef also became scarce. When authorities issued horsemeat to residents as part of the food rationing in 1757, a group of angry women piled the meat at the door to the governor's residence. Governor Pierre de Rigaud de Vaudreuil de Cavagnial admitted four of the protesters to his chambers. They told him "that religion forbade the killing of horses and that they would sooner die than eat them." Vaudreuil dismissed their arguments as "idle fancy." But despite all reassurances, conditions worsened. In 1758 a Quebecer remarked: "I am at a loss for terms to describe our misfortunes. The supply of animals is beginning to fail. . . . the mechanics, artisans and day-laborers exhausted by hunger, absolutely cannot work any longer; they are so feeble that 'tis with difficulty they can sustain themselves."[37] The capture of Quebec in 1759 and the arrival of English troops and provisions brought an end to this ordeal.

Montreal also grew during the war years and, like Quebec, experienced hardships in the late 1750s. The western town served as a base for a series of far-ranging expeditions during the War of the Austrian Succession, the interregnum of peace, and the Seven Years' War. Its population grew, though not as rapidly as that of Quebec, which benefited from the colony's swollen trade as well as the surge in military forces.[38] And like Quebecers, Montrealers suffered during the second half of the 1750s, even if conditions were never quite as grim as they were in the capital. The Montreal region was considered the "granary of Canada" and local supplies were more abundant than they were in Quebec. Still, the shortage of grain was felt in Montreal. After the cruel winter of 1757–58, the bread ration was reduced to two ounces a person. A new era for Montreal began only in 1760 with the English capture of the town.[39]

OVERVIEW

Although the era 1743–60 ended in turmoil and depression, most of the period was marked by prosperity and growth. The export of furs reached new heights. Farmers also fared well—at least until the mid-1750s. They benefited from higher prices and strong sales to government contractors. The towns grew, and industries such as shipbuilding provided employment for many artisans. Broadly viewed, Canadian prosperity paralleled the long swing of expansion in France. But the links between this long cycle of development and Canadian growth must be examined more closely.

French subventions were the chief force for growth, and the expansion of these outlays reflected not only wartime needs but also the greater wealth of the mother country. Never before had France directed such large outlays to its New World colony. And never before had France been able to afford such expenditures. Versailles could offer Canada far less assistance in the wars at the beginning of the century.

Commercial expansion in France and its empire was a secondary force for Canadian development—and again was a product of the long swing of growth. Economic development in France buoyed the market for furs. (This rising demand was reinforced by expansion in continental Europe.) European consumers now were able to purchase more peltries at higher prices. Exchanges in the France–West Indies–Louisbourg triangle also quickened—and helped the St. Lawrence colony. To be sure, Canada had little grain to spare for these booming markets. But Canadians benefited because Louisbourg traders now sent more tropical produce to Quebec. The Quebec Hospital recorded record levels of sugar consumption in the 1740s and 1750s (fig. 8.4).[40]

Unlike the cycle of growth in France, which continued its ascent until 1770, the long swing of Canadian expansion weakened well before 1760. Growth slowed by the mid-1750s as blockades, shortages, government regulations, inflation, and the incursion of enemy troops disrupted the economy of the St. Lawrence Colony. Only after 1763, with the return of peace and with Canada in English hands, would growth resume.

Concluding Note

The era of French rule in Canada ended with the British Conquest of 1760, a victory confirmed by the Treaty of Paris in 1763. British dominion over the Thirteen Colonies ceased with Independence in 1776. But these events did not mark the end of the dependency of the New World on the Old. Britain still remained an all-important source of manufactured goods and investment funds. Economic independence for Canada and the United States came only gradually as their economies matured in the nineteenth and twentieth centuries.

As the New World societies moved away from their heavy reliance on the export of a few staples, what happened to the ties between the economies in Europe and North America? Two long-term trends suggest the evolution from the world of the eighteenth century to the international economy of today.

First, for North America and Europe a growing interdependency replaced the one-sided relationships of the colonial era. The thesis of this work is that before 1760 (for Canada) and 1776 (for the Thirteen Colonies) the pace of development in the New World mirrored the fluctuations in the parent country. This relationship was the product of a set of conditions that defined these North American societies. These economies had weak internal markets, depended on the export of a few staples, were restricted by Acts of Trade, and desperately needed outside funds. Gradually these terms changed. Domestic markets grew stronger and production diversified. Imperial regulations disappeared; internal sources of funding emerged.

These developments transformed the links between the Old World and New. First, the imbalance between developing North American economies and powerful European states gradually was redressed. By the end of the nineteenth century, industrial production in the United States surpassed that in the United Kingdom. But the old relationships were not reversed. The United States did not shape the rhythms of commercial life for Europe (although the impact of the United States on Canada was far reaching). Rather, European dominance was replaced by a truly international economy, where the most powerful nations influence each other's worldly progress.[1]

Second, even closer ties developed among the advanced nations of Europe and North America. In the seventeenth and eighteenth centuries, long swings in Canada echoed those in France. Cycles in the Thirteen Colonies—thanks to the strong links the northern provinces had with the empire—tracked those in Britain. But fluctuations in England only coincidentally resembled those in France, and the northern colonies, Upper South, and Lower South were often out of phase with each other.

Gradually, the links between countries grew stronger. Trade, investment, and migration brought together states on the two sides of the Atlantic. Steady improvements in transportation and communication also helped coordinate patterns of development. In the nineteenth century, cycles of growth and price movements in Canada, the United States, and England moved in step with each other.[2] But short-term fluctuations were out of phase. In the twentieth century, not just long swings but parallel business cycles have gradually become the norm in developed nations. The prosperity of the 1920s and Great Depression of the 1930s were worldwide phenomena, as were subsequent recoveries and downturns. The recession of the early 1990s, for example, was experienced around the globe. As important as transatlantic ties were in the seventeenth and eighteenth century, recent years have been marked by closer coordination among the nations of Europe, North America, and (more recently) the Far East.[3]

Appendices

Appendix A: Philadelphia Textile Prices

These are the prices in Pennsylvania currency that merchants charged shopkeepers. They are drawn from John Reynell Day Books, 1747–64; John Reynell Cash and Sales Book C, 1764–75; Reynell & Coates Journal, 1771–72; Thomas Biddle Cash Book, 1771–74; Henry Drinker Day Book, 1773–75. All manuscripts are in the Historical Society of Pennsylvania, which is located in Philadelphia. The figures are quarterly. The length of checks was in ells, the width in yards.

Philadelphia Prices: Quarterly Data for Linen and Cotton Checks

	Linen Checks (Shillings/Ell)				Cotton Checks (Shillings/Ell)			
	Width in Yards					Width in Yards		
Year	3/4	7/8	1	6/4	3/4	7/8	1	6/4
1747	2.25	3.31	2.83	4.83	—	3.46	3.25	4.92
	2.23	3.50	3.33	4.83	—	3.50	—	4.99
	2.16	—	2.83	5.00	—	3.50	—	5.25
	2.15	—	—	4.77	—	3.60	—	—
1748	2.24	—	—	4.75	—	3.50	3.33	5.25
	2.15	—	3.08	5.13	—	3.50	3.33	5.01
	2.00	—	2.75	—	—	3.08	—	—
	2.00	—	2.50	—	—	3.08	—	4.58

(continued)

Year	Linen Checks (Shillings/Ell)				Cotton Checks (Shillings/Ell)			
	Width in Yards				Width in Yards			
	3/4	7/8	1	6/4	3/4	7/8	1	6/4
1749	1.85	2.72	2.50	—	—	2.92	—	4.05
	1.86	2.67	—	—	—	—	—	—
	1.83	—	2.50	4.00	—	2.83	—	4.00
	1.83	—	—	—	—	2.75	—	4.00
1750	1.83	—	—	4.00	—	—	—	—
	1.77	—	—	—	—	—	—	3.92
	1.75	2.12	—	—	—	2.82	—	4.17
	1.75	2.12	2.42	—	—	2.92	—	3.83
1751	1.75	—	2.33	3.83	—	2.89	—	3.89
	1.72	2.42	2.33	3.83	—	—	—	3.77
	1.75	2.50	—	3.29	2.25	—	—	3.90
	1.75	2.33	2.33	—	2.00	—	—	3.83
1752	1.72	—	—	—	2.25	—	—	3.75
	1.74	2.69	—	3.25	2.25	—	—	4.00
	1.73	2.50	—	—	—	2.42	—	3.65
	—	2.33	—	3.25	2.00	—	2.67	—
1753	1.72	2.75	—	—	2.00	2.33	2.67	3.83
	1.75	2.51	—	3.25	2.04	—	2.67	3.75
	—	2.67	—	—	2.08	2.42	—	3.75
	—	2.42	—	—	2.08	2.50	—	3.75
1754	1.75	2.96	—	—	2.08	—	—	3.75
	1.67	—	—	3.33	2.00	2.42	2.67	3.73
	—	—	—	—	—	—	2.67	3.58
	1.72	—	—	—	2.00	2.42	2.67	3.73
1755	1.71	—	—	—	—	2.42	—	3.67
	1.72	—	2.67	3.75	—	2.50	2.58	3.67
	1.69	3.17	—	—	2.00	2.42	2.58	3.67
	1.73	—	—	—	—	—	—	3.89
1756	1.75	—	—	3.25	—	—	—	—
	1.75	2.33	—	—	—	—	—	3.50
	1.75	2.04	—	—	—	2.52	2.79	—
	1.75	—	2.33	—	2.00	2.67	2.58	3.74
1757	1.67	—	2.33	—	2.00	2.83	2.47	3.72
	—	3.25	2.33	—	—	—	2.67	3.75
	—	—	—	—	—	—	—	—
	1.75	2.00	—	—	—	2.17	2.33	3.75
1758	1.75	—	—	—	—	2.75	3.00	3.75
	1.68	—	—	—	1.67	—	2.75	3.72
	1.67	—	—	3.33	—	—	—	3.75
	1.70	—	—	3.33	—	—	2.71	3.75

Year	Linen Checks (Shillings/Ell)				Cotton Checks (Shillings/Ell)			
	Width in Yards				Width in Yards			
	3/4	7/8	1	6/4	3/4	7/8	1	6/4
1759	1.67	2.17	2.25	—	—	2.67	2.83	3.67
	1.71	—	2.33	—	—	—	2.67	3.68
	1.63	—	2.33	—	—	2.46	2.92	3.67
	—	2.08	—	—	—	—	—	3.67
1760	1.58	—	—	—	—	2.33	2.54	3.58
	1.58	—	—	3.25	—	2.23	2.44	3.42
	—	2.08	—	—	—	—	—	—
	—	—	—	3.33	1.83	—	2.67	3.62
1761	1.75	—	—	3.33	1.83	—	2.67	3.67
	—	—	—	3.40	—	2.50	2.71	3.65
	1.87	—	—	3.50	—	2.46	2.67	3.70
	1.79	—	—	3.50	—	2.50	2.75	3.67
1762	1.84	—	—	3.50	—	2.48	—	3.72
	1.83	—	—	3.50	—	2.50	2.75	3.83
	—	—	—	—	—	2.67	3.06	4.00
	—	—	—	—	—	—	3.02	—
1763	—	—	—	—	—	—	—	—
	1.83	2.29	2.58	3.54	2.00	2.54	3.17	3.83
	1.83	2.29	2.58	—	—	2.52	2.75	3.75
	—	—	2.42	3.67	—	—	2.83	3.83
1764	—	—	—	—	—	2.58	2.67	3.75
	1.83	—	2.58	3.54	—	2.67	3.03	3.81
	—	—	—	—	—	2.50	2.96	3.75
	1.83	2.33	—	3.67	—	2.64	2.83	3.83
1765	1.85	2.25	—	3.56	—	2.57	2.90	3.74
	1.83	2.25	2.50	3.62	2.08	2.64	2.81	3.71
	—	—	2.50	3.50	—	2.54	2.75	3.75
	—	2.25	—	—	—	2.54	2.86	3.75
1766	1.83	2.21	—	3.50	2.17	2.62	2.83	3.70
	—	2.27	2.83	3.59	2.08	2.57	2.77	3.81
	—	2.25	—	—	—	2.56	3.25	3.83
	1.75	—	—	3.58	—	2.54	2.81	3.75
1767	—	—	2.33	3.50	—	2.58	2.92	3.73
	1.81	—	2.42	3.62	—	2.58	2.78	3.74
	1.75	—	2.42	3.50	—	2.50	2.75	3.69
	1.67	—	—	—	2.25	—	2.67	3.67
1768	1.67	2.25	—	—	—	2.58	2.67	3.67
	—	—	—	—	—	—	2.92	3.71
	—	2.21	—	—	—	2.50	—	3.67
	1.67	—	—	—	—	2.50	2.75	3.67

(*continued*)

Year	Linen Checks (Shillings/Ell) Width in Yards				Cotton Checks (Shillings/Ell) Width in Yards			
	3/4	7/8	1	6/4	3/4	7/8	1	6/4
1769	—	2.25	—	—	2.17	—	2.50	—
	1.58	—	2.17	—	—	2.50	2.58	3.50
	—	—	—	—	2.17	3.00	—	3.54
	—	—	—	—	—	2.50	—	3.53
1770	1.67	—	—	—	2.17	—	2.52	3.50
	1.62	2.17	—	—	2.21	2.46	2.72	—
	1.62	—	—	—	—	—	—	—
	—	—	—	—	—	—	—	—
1771	—	—	—	—	—	—	—	—
	1.50	2.00	—	—	—	—	2.37	3.33
	1.42	1.92	—	—	—	2.16	2.25	3.34
	1.42	2.00	—	—	—	2.25	2.42	3.35
1772	—	1.83	—	—	—	2.13	—	3.29
	—	1.83	2.17	—	—	2.13	2.33	3.29
	—	—	—	—	—	—	2.25	—
	—	1.67	—	—	—	—	2.33	—
1773	—	—	—	—	—	2.08	2.21	—
	—	—	2.08	—	1.83	2.08	2.34	—
	—	1.75	—	—	—	1.92	2.25	—
	—	—	2.08	—	—	1.95	2.24	—
1774	—	—	—	—	1.83	2.07	2.37	—
	—	1.88	—	—	—	2.06	2.28	3.25
	1.42	—	—	—	—	2.17	2.27	3.33
	1.50	2.00	—	—	—	2.17	2.42	3.33
1775	1.50	—	—	—	—	2.54	2.33	—
	1.50	—	—	—	—	2.67	2.69	—

Philadelphia Prices: Biannual Data for Other Textiles

Year	Princess Linen (Pence/Ell)	Oznabrigs (Pence/Ell)	Buckrams (Pence/Yard)	Red Flannels (Shillings/Yard)	Calamancos (Shillings/Yard)
1747	—	22.5	22.3	—	2.42
	—	23.2	22.0	3.33	2.50
1748	—	23.1	22.4	—	2.46
	—	21.5	20.3	2.79	2.24
1749	—	19.2	17.0	—	2.15
	18.0	18.8	17.8	—	2.08
1750	18.0	18.3	16.5	—	2.00
	18.0	18.4	16.3	2.25	2.00
1751	18.0	17.6	18.0	—	2.00
	17.9	19.5	16.5	2.33	—
1752	18.4	19.1	—	2.25	2.00
	18.9	18.4	16.0	2.38	—
1753	18.3	18.2	15.0	—	2.00
	17.5	19.0	15.0	2.50	2.00
1754	—	18.5	16.0	—	1.83
	—	18.0	16.0	—	—
1755	—	17.7	15.5	—	1.83
	—	17.9	16.0	—	1.86
1756	24.0	18.3	16.0	—	1.95
	—	20.3	17.0	2.75	1.83
1757	18.8	20.3	17.0	2.67	2.00
	18.2	19.8	17.0	—	2.00
1758	18.0	20.3	17.0	—	1.96
	18.5	19.1	17.0	2.63	1.98
1759	17.0	18.0	16.8	—	1.81
	19.0	—	16.0	2.58	1.92
1760	18.0	16.8	16.0	—	1.75
	17.0	17.0	16.0	2.50	1.79
1761	—	17.0	16.0	—	—
	—	—	16.0	—	2.00
1762	—	20.5	—	—	—
	—	24.0	16.0	2.50	1.96
1763	22.0	—	16.0	—	1.94
	—	21.5	—	—	1.92
1764	18.0	22.0	—	—	1.96
	—	—	—	—	1.92
1765	—	21.4	19.0	2.50	1.92
	—	24.0	19.0	2.50	1.90

(*continued*)

Year	Princess Linen (Pence/Ell)	Oznabrigs (Pence/Ell)	Buckrams (Pence/Yard)	Red Flannels (Shillings/Yard)	Calamancos (Shillings/Yard)
1766	17.5	21.3	20.0	—	—
	—	21.0	16.0	—	1.92
1767	—	20.0	—	—	1.83
	16.0	—	—	—	1.83
1768	—	20.0	21.0	2.50	1.83
	—	20.0	20.5	2.50	1.83
1769	—	20.0	—	—	1.92
	—	20.0	22.0	2.54	1.83
1770	—	20.5	20.1	—	—
	—	—	—	—	—
1771	—	20.7	20.0	2.50	—
	—	20.8	18.3	2.44	—
1772	—	18.8	20.0	2.31	—
	—	14.7	19.6	2.33	—
1773	—	12.7	18.3	—	—
	—	17.4	18.2	2.13	—
1774	—	16.6	17.0	—	—
	—	18.5	20.0	2.50	—
1775	—	21.8	18.0	2.67	—
	—	—	—	—	—

Appendix B: English Textile Prices

These are the prices in sterling that English exporters charged Philadelphia merchants. These prices have been taken from invoices in the Reynell Papers, 1747–61; Wharton Correspondence, 1754–61; Richard Waln Invoice Book, 1763–72; Clifford Papers, 1767. All manuscripts are in the Historical Society of Pennsylvania, which is located in Philadelphia. The length of checks was measured in ells, the width in yards.

English Prices: Biannual Data for Linen and Cotton Checks

| | Linen Checks (Pence/Ell) | | | Cotton Checks (Pence/Ell) | | | |
| | Width in Yards | | | | Width in Yards | | |
Year	3/4	7/8	1	3/4	7/8	1	6/4
1746	9	—	—	—	—	—	20
	9	—	12	—	15	13.5	20.5
1747	8.46	—	—	—	15	—	21.25
	—	—	—	—	—	—	—
1748	—	—	—	—	—	—	—
	—	—	—	—	—	—	—
1749	—	—	—	—	—	—	—
	9	—	12	—	14	—	—

(*continued*)

| Year | Linen Checks (Pence/Ell) Width in Yards | | | Cotton Checks (Pence/Ell) Width in Yards | | | |
	3/4	7/8	1	3/4	7/8	1	6/4
1750	9	—	—	—	—	—	20.5
	8.5	11	12	—	14.5	—	21
1751	9	13.25	—	11.25	13	—	22.5
	—	—	—	—	—	—	—
1752	—	—	—	—	—	—	—
	9.25	—	—	10.5	13	14	19.5
1753	—	—	—	—	—	—	—
	—	—	—	—	—	—	—
1754	9	—	—	10.5	13	13.5	19.5
	—	—	—	—	—	—	—
1755	—	—	—	—	—	—	—
	—	—	—	—	—	—	—
1756	8.25	10	11	9.5	12.75	13	18
	8.75	—	—	—	12.75	13.5	—
1757	—	—	—	—	—	12.5	—
	8.25	10	—	—	12	12.9	—
1758	8	—	—	—	—	—	—
	—	—	—	—	—	—	—
1759	—	—	—	—	—	13.75	—
	9.25	—	—	—	13.17	14.25	—
1760	—	—	—	—	—	—	—
	9.5	—	—	—	13	13.5	—
1761	10	—	—	—	13	14	—
	—	—	—	—	—	—	—
1762	—	—	—	—	—	—	—
	—	—	—	—	—	—	—
1763	9.5	12	13.5	—	14.25	15.5	—
	—	—	—	—	—	—	—
1764	—	13.25	14.75	—	15.5	18	—
	—	—	—	—	—	—	—
1765	—	—	—	—	—	—	—
	—	—	—	—	—	—	—
1766	—	—	—	—	—	—	—
	—	11.5	—	—	13	—	—
1767	—	—	—	—	—	—	—
	—	11.25	—	—	13	14	—

| | Linen Checks (Pence/Ell) | | | | Cotton Checks (Pence/Ell) | | | |
| | Width in Yards | | | | Width in Yards | | | |
Year	3/4	7/8	1		3/4	7/8	1	6/4
1768	—	—	—		—	12.5	—	—
	—	—	—		—	—	—	—
1769	—	—	—		—	—	—	—
	—	—	—		—	—	—	—
1770	—	—	—		—	—	—	—
	—	—	—		—	—	—	—
1771	—	—	13.5		—	12.5	13.5	—
	—	—	—		8.25	12.5	13.5	—
1772	—	—	—		—	—	—	—
	—	—	—		—	—	—	—
1773	8.75	11.5	15		—	—	—	—
	—	—	—		—	—	—	—
1774	—	—	—		—	—	—	—
	—	—	—		—	—	—	—

English Prices: Biannual Data for Other Textiles

Year	Buckrams (Pence/Ell)	Red Flannels (Pence/Yard)	Princess Linen (Pence/Ell)	Calamancos (Shillings/Piece)
1747	7.50	12.50	—	—
	—	—	—	—
1748	—	—	—	—
	—	—	—	—
1749	—	—	—	—
	—	11.50	7.50	—
1750	6.50	—	7.63	—
	—	—	—	—
1751	—	—	—	—
	6.88	—	8.50	—
1752	6.50	—	8.50	—
	—	—	—	—
1753	7.00	13.00	7.75	—
	—	—	—	—
1754	—	—	—	—
	7.50	13.00	—	—
1755	6.50	—	—	—
	—	—	—	—
1756	6.50	—	—	—
	7.15	—	6.75	—
1757	6.50	—	7.13	—
	—	—	—	32.0
1758	6.75	—	—	—
	—	12.00	—	—
1759	7.57	—	—	32.0
	6.75	—	—	—
1760	—	—	8.25	—
	—	15.00	7.75	—
1761	—	—	—	—
	7.50	—	—	—
1762	—	—	—	—
	—	—	—	—
1763	—	14.00	—	33.0
	—	14.00	—	—
1764	9.00	—	9.25	—
	—	—	—	—
1765	—	—	—	—
	—	—	9.25	—

Year	Buckrams (Pence/Ell)	Red Flannels (Pence/Yard)	Princess Linen (Pence/Ell)	Calamancos (Shillings/Piece)
1766	—	—	—	—
	8.88	—	—	31.5
1767	—	—	9.50	—
	—	12.70	—	—
1768	—	—	—	—
	—	—	—	31.0
1769	—	—	—	31.5
	—	—	—	—
1770	—	—	—	—
	9.50	—	—	—
1771	—	13.50	7.75	31.5
	9.50	—	—	31.5
1772	8.50	14.50	—	—
	—	—	—	—
1773	—	—	—	—
	—	—	—	—
1774	—	—	—	—
	—	—	—	—

Appendix C: Montreal Dry Goods Prices

These are the prices in French livres that Montreal merchant, Alexis Monière, charged *voyageurs* and other customers. The data are drawn from Monière's Journals 1 (1712–25), 3 (1731–37), and 4 (1737–48). These volumes are in the National Archives of Canada (located in Ottawa), and a microfilm version is available at the Michigan State Library (located in East Lansing), PAC roll nos. M847–M849. I am indebted to Matthew Laird for compiling the raw data on which these series are based, and for sharing his work with me.

Year	Flannels (Livres/Ells)	Moltons (Wool Cloth) (Livres/Ells)	Thread (Poitou Type) (Livres/Units)	Wine (Livres/Pots)	Women's Shirts (Livres/Units)	Hooded Blankets, Width 3.5 [Ells?] (Livres/Units)
1715	—	—	6.00	—	5.00	—
1721	—	—	—	1.20	6.00	—
1724	—	6.00	3.50	—	3.70	17.50
1725	—	6.50	3.50	—	3.83	18.00
1731	—	4.50	3.00	1.25	2.93	12.25
1732	—	4.33	3.00	—	3.00	12.50
1733	3.50	4.42	2.75	1.25	2.81	12.50
1734	3.00	4.02	2.75	1.25	2.75	12.25
1735	—	3.75	2.50	—	2.75	12.25
1736	3.00	3.78	2.38	1.25	3.00	12.25

Year	Flannels (Livres/Ells)	Moltons (Wool Cloth) (Livres/Ells)	Thread (Poitou Type) (Livres/Units)	Wine (Livres/Pots)	Women's Shirts (Livres/Units)	Hooded Blankets, Width 3.5 [Ells?] (Livres/Units)
1737	—	3.75	—	1.00	—	—
1738	2.63	3.75	—	1.25	—	—
1739	2.15	3.07	1.76	1.17	1.50	8.19
1740	2.38	3.28	1.54	—	1.43	—
1741	2.50	3.31	1.80	1.25	2.85	9.45
1742	—	3.70	1.88	1.50	—	9.98
1743	2.43	3.62	2.10	1.50	—	—
1744	2.31	3.50	2.07	—	—	—
1745	—	5.00	2.78	—	—	—
1746	3.80	5.60	3.20	—	—	—
1747	4.11	5.75	—	2.25	—	—
1748	4.28	6.00	3.15	1.13	—	—

Year	Kettles (Livres/Units)	Blankets, "Type 2" (Livres/Units)	Dourgne (Wool Cloth) (Livres/Ells)	Flat Shoes (Livres/Pairs)	Brandy (Livres/Pots)
1715	4.50	18.00	—	8.00	—
1721	—	—	—	2.50	—
1724	3.50	12.00	—	3.00	—
1725	3.83	14.00	—	3.90	—
1731	3.25	8.00	5.00	2.00	—
1732	3.17	8.00	3.00	5.00	2.00
1733	3.25	8.95	4.50	2.00	—
1734	3.17	8.00	5.00	2.50	—
1735	3.00	8.50	—	2.25	—
1736	3.50	8.83	2.85	5.00	1.96
1737	3.00	9.50	—	2.00	—
1738	—	6.63	—	2.00	—
1739	2.25	6.98	2.34	—	1.60
1740	3.00	7.28	2.48	4.50	2.20
1741	2.50	7.22	2.53	—	2.50
1742	—	7.88	2.85	4.50	2.50
1743	2.70	7.74	2.85	4.50	2.50
1744	2.52	—	2.66	4.50	3.00
1745	3.05	11.56	3.70	4.50	3.50
1746	—	—	4.00	4.50	4.50
1747	4.28	14.06	4.39	—	3.50
1748	4.22	—	4.50	5.00	4.00

Appendix D: Maritime Insurance, Philadelphia to or from London

This table presents premiums for maritime insurance for voyages between Philadelphia and London. Premiums are expressed as a percentage of the amount covered. The chief sources for these statistics are Wharton Correspondence; Reynell Papers; James & Drinker Letterbook; Willing Letterbook; Clifford Letterbook; and Richard Waln Invoice Book. All manuscripts are in the Historical Society of Pennsylvania, which is located in Philadelphia.

Year (Biannual Data)	Without Convoy	With Convoy	Year (Biannual Data)	Without Convoy	With Convoy
1744	—	9.0	1749	2.5	—
	12.8	—		2.5	—
1745	15.0	10.0	1750	2.5	—
	15.0	10.0		2.5	—
1746	15.0	10.0	1751	2.5	—
	15.0	10.0		2.5	—
1747	—	—	1752	2.5	—
	—	—		2.5	—
1748	5.0	—	1753	2.5	—
	—	—		2.5	—

Year (Biannual Data)	Without Convoy	With Convoy	Year (Biannual Data)	Without Convoy	With Convoy
1754	2.5	—	1763	2.5	—
	2.5	—		2.8	—
1755	2.5	—	1764	2.8	—
	—	—		—	—
1756	7.5	—	1765	2.0	—
	9.5	7.0		2.5	—
1757	13.3	8.0	1766	2.5	—
	22.5	—		2.1	—
1758	15.0	8.0	1767	2.1	—
	9.3	5.7		2.0	—
1759	8.7	4.5	1768	2.0	—
	6.7	4.0		2.0	—
1760	7.4	4.5	1769	2.0	—
	9.8	5.8		2.0	—
1761	12.0	6.0	1770	2.0	—
	11.0	5.5		2.0	—
1762	15.0	6.0	1771	3.0	—
	15.0	7.0		2.0	—

Appendix E: Antigua Prices

These figures are based on the "prices current" noted at the foot of letters in the Reynell Papers, Historical Society of Pennsylvania, which is located in Philadelphia. Many of these statistics are based on quotations drawn from several letters.

Year (Monthly Data)	Flour (Shillings/ Hundredweight)	Sugar (Shillings/ Hundredweight)	Rum (Shillings/ Gallon)	Exchange (Local Pounds for £100 Sterling)
1751 Apr	21.00	31.50	2.50	—
May	19.25	—	2.50	—
Jun	18.25	—	2.50	—
Jul	16.50	—	2.50	—
Aug	16.00	—	—	—
Sep	20.50	—	—	—
Oct	16.50	—	2.63	177.50
Nov	—	—	—	—
Dec	14.25	—	3.18	—
1752 Jan	15.03	33.75	3.10	175.00
Feb	14.25	—	2.75	173.75
Mar	15.50	—	—	—
Apr	19.00	—	2.50	175.00

Year (Monthly Data)	Flour (Shillings/ Hundredweight)	Sugar (Shillings/ Hundredweight)	Rum (Shillings/ Gallon)	Exchange (Local Pounds for £100 Sterling)
May	25.00	41.50	2.50	175.00
Jun	25.83	39.50	2.92	175.00
Jul	20.83	40.00	3.00	175.00
Aug	—	—	—	—
Sep	20.00	40.00	3.00	170.00
Oct	21.00	—	3.06	165.00
Nov	20.50	—	3.25	—
Dec	19.50	—	3.50	167.50
1753 Jan	16.19	40.00	3.25	165.00
Feb	16.47	40.00	3.25	167.50
Mar	15.75	40.00	3.13	170.00
Apr	15.92	34.00	2.28	165.00
May	14.50	33.30	2.25	161.88
Jun	14.25	33.80	2.25	161.25
Jul	16.00	—	—	—
Aug	15.63	34.00	2.00	162.50
Sep	15.50	—	—	—
Oct	20.25	31.50	2.25	165.00
Nov	22.00	—	2.25	165.00
Dec	—	—	—	—
1754 Jan	22.33	35.00	2.58	165.42
Feb	20.75	40.00	2.50	166.25
Mar	20.00	40.00	2.50	—
Apr	21.00	42.00	2.71	166.67
May	20.15	39.75	2.56	165.00
Jun	18.00	42.50	2.75	165.00
Jul	—	—	—	—
Aug	18.88	40.00	2.75	165.88
Sep	21.00	—	—	—
Oct	18.00	40.00	2.50	165.00
Nov	19.50	—	2.50	165.00
Dec	—	—	—	—
1755 Jan	21.00	—	—	165.00
Feb	21.00	—	—	—
Mar	—	—	—	—
Apr	18.67	30.00	1.96	—
May	19.00	30.00	1.92	—
Jun	19.00	—	—	—
Jul	—	—	—	—
Aug	19.50	30.00	2.00	—
Sep	22.17	31.50	1.92	—
Oct	28.00	—	—	—
Nov	27.00	—	—	—
Dec	—	—	—	—

(continued)

Year (Monthly Data)	Flour (Shillings/ Hundredweight)	Sugar (Shillings/ Hundredweight)	Rum (Shillings/ Gallon)	Exchange (Local Pounds for £100 Sterling)
1756 Jan	25.00	—	2.00	—
Feb	—	—	2.00	—
Mar	25.00	—	—	—
Apr	—	—	—	—
May	23.25	34.00	1.86	—
Jun	—	—	—	—
Jul	29.00	31.50	1.83	—
Aug	—	—	—	—
Sep	—	—	—	—
Oct	—	—	—	—
Nov	35.73	—	—	165.00
Dec	—	—	—	—

Notes

CHAPTER ONE

1. Cadwallader Colden to Board of Trade, Aug. 9, 1764, New York Historical Society *Collections* 9 (1876): 341–42.

2. In this book *economic growth* and *economic development* are synonyms, and both refer to the rise in the standard of living.

3. John J. McCusker and Russell R. Menard, *The Economy of British North America, 1607–1789* (Chapel Hill, N.C., 1985): 17–34, provides a valuable introduction to the staple thesis as well as to the literature on this topic. Also see Melville Watkins, "A Staple Theory of Economic Growth," *Canadian Journal of Economics and Political Science* 29 (1963): 141–58; Robert Baldwin, "Patterns of Development in Newly Settled Regions," *Manchester School of Economic and Social Studies* 24 (1956): 161–79; Richard E. Caves, "Export-Led Growth and the New Economic History," in *Trade, Balance of Payments, and Growth: Papers in International Economics in Honor of Charles P. Kindleberger*, ed. Jagdish N. Bhagwati et al. (Amsterdam, 1971), 403–42; Caves, "'Vent for Surplus' Models of Trade and Growth," in *Trade, Growth, and the Balance of Payments: Essays in Honor of Gottfried Haberler*, ed. Robert E. Baldwin et al. (Chicago, 1965), 95–115.

4. Albert O. Hirschman, *The Strategy of Economic Development* (New Haven, Conn., 1958), 98–103; Hirschman, "A Generalized Linkage Approach to Development, with Special Reference to Staples," *Economic Development and Cultural Change* 25 (Supplement, 1977): 72–89.

5. Watkins, "Staple Theory," quote on p. 141; Harold Innis, *The Fur Trade in Canada: An Introduction to Canadian Economic History*, rev. ed. (Toronto, 1956); Innis, *The Cod Fisheries: The History of an International Economy*, rev. ed. (Toronto, 1954); Innis, *Essays in Canadian Economic History* (Toronto, 1956). For other cri-

tiques of Innis, see Richard E. Caves and Richard H. Holton, *The Canadian Economy: Prospect and Retrospect* (Cambridge, Mass., 1959), 30, 141–44; and *Journal of Canadian Studies* 12 (Winter 1977), special issue, esp. R. F. Neil, "The Passing of Canadian Economic History," 73–95. James F. Shepherd and Gary M. Walton, in *Shipping, Maritime Trade, and the Economic Development of Colonial North America* (Cambridge, Eng., 1972), 6–26, also try to recast the staple thesis in more precise terms. But they conclude (p. 25n): "We wish to stress that this is a framework suggested to view and to aid in the explanation of the broad patterns of colonial economic development—it is not a theory to be tested in this book."

6. Douglass C. North, *The Economic Growth of the United States, 1790–1860* (Englewood Cliffs, N.J., 1961), quote on p. 68; Irving B. Kravis, "The Role of Exports in Nineteenth-Century United States Growth," *Economic Development and Cultural Change* 20 (1972): 387–405. Canadian scholars, including Watkins, have argued for the power of the staple thesis up to 1913. See Watkins, "Staple Theory," 142, 157; A. R. M. Lower, "The Trade in Square Timber," University of Toronto Studies, History and Economics, *Contributions to Canadian Economics* 6 (1933): 40–61; Gordon W. Bertram, "Economic Growth and Canadian Industry, 1870–1915: The Staple Model and the Take-off Hypothesis," *Canadian Journal of Economics and Political Science* 29 (1963): 163–84. Several of these essays are reprinted in *Approaches to Canadian Economic History*, ed. W. T. Easterbrook and M. H. Watkins (Ottawa, 1984).

7. W. W. Rostow, *The Stages of Economic Growth: A Non-Communist Manifesto* (Cambridge, Mass., 1960); for critiques of Rostow, see Robert W. Fogel, *Railroads and American Economic Growth: Essays in Econometric History* (Baltimore, 1964), 111–29; Douglass C. North, *Growth and Welfare in the American Past: A New Economic History* (Englewood Cliffs, N.J., 1966), 85–89; Diane Lindstrom, "American Economic Growth Before 1840: New Evidence and New Directions," *JEH* 39 (1979): 289–301; Paul A. David, "The Growth of Real Product in the United States Before 1840: New Evidence, Controlled Conjectures," *JEH* 27 (1967): 151–97. However, K. Berrill, "International Trade and the Rate of Economic Growth," *Economic History Review*, 2d Ser., 12 (1960): 351–59, develops an argument very similar to Rostow's.

8. What about the *quantity* of the staple produced? Why isn't this considered a key factor (along with changes in the terms of trade and the influx of funds) in fostering growth? Three related concerns explain why shifts in volume are not singled out as a leading influence on the pace of development. First, a rise in production that simply reflected the growth of population did not affect the standard of living. Because this study is concerned with changes in per capita income, the most common reason for rising output is not germane to our analysis. Second, some increases in the quantity of a staple reflected gains in productivity or in the capital stock, and so are treated under those headings. More rice was produced because farmers learned about the best soils for growing the crop (an advance in productivity). More tobacco was planted because farmers acquired plows (a rise in the capital stock). Those concerns are important, but are not best dealt with in a catch-all category of "quantity." Third, some sharp changes in the supply of staples *did* affect the standard of living, and are noted in the text. For example, the quantity of furs Canadians collected for shipment to France soared in 1699, driving down prices in an already depressed market—and hurting most producers. Similarly, the disruptions of war led to short crops in Canada in the late 1750s. Such circumstances were unusual but had a substantial impact on the standard of living, and are discussed in this work.

9. Before 1763 *Canada* refers to the French colony that lay along the banks of the St. Lawrence River, and *Quebec* to the capital (modern-day *Quebec City*).

10. The output of farms in Canada, the northern colonies, and Upper South is examined in Appendix B of Marc Egnal, *Divergent Paths: How Culture and Institutions Have Shaped North American Growth* (New York, 1996).

11. David W. Galenson and Russell R. Menard, "Approaches to the Analysis of Economic Growth in Colonial British America," *Historical Methods* 13 (1980): 10; Louise Dechêne, *Le partage de subsistances au Canada sous le régime français* (Quebec, 1994), 99–104.

12. Richard Colebrook Harris, *The Seigneurial System in Early Canada: A Geographical Study* (Madison, Wis., 1966), 90–103.

13. H. Roy Merrens, ed., *The Colonial South Carolina Scene: Contemporary Views, 1697–1774* (Columbia, S.C., 1977), 248–52, presents the 1768 tax account; James A. Henretta, "Economic Development and Social Structure in Colonial Boston," *WMQ*, 3d ser., 22 (1965): 75–92; Allan Kulikoff, "The Progress of Inequality in Revolutionary Boston," *WMQ*, 3d ser., 28 (1971): 375–412; Thomas M. Doerflinger, *A Vigorous Spirit of Enterprise: Merchants and Economic Development in Revolutionary Philadelphia* (Chapel Hill, N.C., 1986), 11–69; Louise Dechêne, "La Croissance de Montréal au XVIIIe siècle," *RHAF* 27 (1973): 173-79.

14. Output in 1800 provides a point of reference and suggests an upper bound for the contribution of the nonagricultural sector. Stanley Lebergott, "Labor Force and Employment, 1800–1960," in National Bureau of Economic Research, *Output, Employment and Productivity in the United States After 1800,* Studies in Income and Wealth, vol. 30 (New York, 1966), 118–19, suggests 74 percent of the labor force was in agriculture in 1800; David, "Growth of Real Product," 166, argues for 83 percent. David also (conservatively) estimates farm workers had a gross product 0.511 that of nonfarm workers (pp. 169–70). These figures mean that in 1800 nonagricultural production accounted for 30 to 40 percent of gross product. See also U.S. Bureau of the Census, *Historical Statistics of the United States, Colonial Times to 1970,* 2 vols. (Washington, D.C., 1975), 2:1168; Gary Nash, *The Urban Crucible: Social Change, Political Consciousness, and the Origins of the American Revolution* (Cambridge, Mass., 1979), 407–8; Lester J. Cappon et al., eds., *Atlas of Early American History: The Revolutionary Era, 1760–1790* (Princeton, N.J., 1976), 97–98; James T. Lemon, *The Best Poor Man's Country: A Geographical Study of Early Southeastern Pennsylvania* (Baltimore, 1972), chap. 5; Adrienne Hood, "The Gender Division of Labor in the Production of Textiles in Eighteenth-Century, Rural Pennsylvania (Rethinking the New England Model)," *Journal of Social History* 27 (1994): 537–61.

15. Harris, *Seigneurial System,* 90–103.

16. Lemon, *Best Poor Man's Country,* 122; John Flexer Walzer, "Transportation in the Philadelphia Trading Area, 1740–1775" (Ph.D. diss., Univ. of Wisconsin, 1968); Charles J. Farmer, *In the Absence of Towns: Settlement and Country Trade in Southside Virginia, 1730–1800* (Lanham, Md., 1993); Allan Kulikoff, *Tobacco and Slaves: The Development of Southern Cultures in the Chesapeake, 1680–1800* (Chapel Hill, N.C., 1986), 107, 119–25, 179.

17. Simon Kuznets, *Economic Change: Selected Essays on Business Cycles, National Income, and Economic Growth* (New York, 1953); Kuznets, *Cyclical Fluctuations: Retail and Wholesale Trade, United States, 1919–1925* (New York, 1926).

18. Moses Abramovitz, "The Nature and Significance of Kuznets Cycles," *Economic Development and Cultural Change* 9 (1961): 225–48; Stanley L . Engerman

and Robert E. Gallman, "U.S. Economic Growth, 1783–1860," *Research in Economic History* 7 (1983): 9.

19. N. D. Kondratieff, "The Long Waves in Economic Life," *Review of Economic Statistics* 17 (1935): 105–15; for a useful overview of long-wave theory, see Joshua S. Goldstein, *Long Cycles: Prosperity and War in the Modern Age* (New Haven, Conn., 1988). For criticisms of long-wave theory, see Nathan Rosenberg and Claudio R. Frischtak, "Long Waves and Economic Growth: A Critical Appraisal," *American Economic Review* 73 (1983): 146–51; Howard Brill, "Stepwise Polynomial Regression: Royal Road or Detour?" *Review: Fernand Braudel Center* 11 (1988): 393–411. Barry W. Poulson and J. Malcolm Dowling, "Background Conditions and the Spectral Analytic Test of the Long Swings Hypothesis," *Explorations in Economic History* 7 (1970–71): 343–51, argues the statistical evidence cannot resolve the question of whether long waves existed.

20. Along with the essays by Kondratieff cited in the previous note, consult the writings of several individuals who continue Kondratieff's emphasis on the role of long-term investments in explaining cycles. See Jay W. Forrester, "Business Structure, Economic Cycles, and National Policy," *Futures* 8 (1976): 195–214; A. Van der Zwan, "On the Assessment of the Kondratieff Cycle and Related Issues," in *Prospects of Economic Growth*, ed. S. K. Kuipers and G. J. Lanjouw (Amsterdam, 1980), 183–222; Nathaniel J. Mass, *Economic Cycles: An Analysis of Underlying Causes* (Cambridge, Mass, 1975), esp. 1–7, 15–19; Hans H. Glismann, Horst Rodemer, and Frank Wolter, "Long Waves in Economic Development: Causes and Empirical Evidence," in *Long Waves in the World Economy*, ed. Christopher Freeman (London, 1983), 135–63.

21. Joseph A. Schumpeter, *Business Cycles* (New York, 1939); Schumpeter, "Depressions: Can We Learn from Past Experiences?" in *Essays of J. A. Schumpeter*, ed. Joseph A. Schumpeter (Cambridge, Mass., 1951), 108–17. Gerhard Mensch, *Stalemate in Technology: Innovations to Overcome the Depression* (Cambridge, Mass., 1979), continues Schumpeter's emphasis on innovation, as does Joseph Delbeke, "Recent Long-Wave Theories: A Critical Survey," *Futures* 8 (1981): 246–57. See also Leon Trotsky, "The Curve of Capitalist Development" [1923] in Trotsky, *Problems of Everyday Life and Other Writings on Culture and Science* (New York, 1973), 273–80; Ernest Mandel, *Long Waves of Capitalist Development* (Cambridge, Eng., 1980); Mandel, "Explaining Long Waves of Capitalist Development," *Futures* 8 (1981): 332–38.

22. Albert Rose, "Wars, Innovations and Long Cycles," *American Economic Review* 31 (1941): 105–7; E. M. Bernstein, "War and the Pattern of Business Cycles," ibid., 30 (1940): 524–35; Norman J. Silberling, *The Dynamics of Business: An Analysis of Trends, Cycles, and Time Relationships in American Economic Activity Since 1700 and Their Bearing upon Governmental and Business Policy* (New York, 1943).

23. Fernand Braudel and Frank C. Spooner, "Prices in Europe from 1450 to 1750," in *The Cambridge Economic History of Europe*, ed. E. E. Rich and E. H. Wilson, 7 vols. (London, 1967), 4:374–486; Fernand Braudel, *The Mediterranean and the Mediterranean World in the Age of Philip II*, trans. by Sian Reynolds, 2 vols. (New York, 1972), 1:260-67; Phyllis Deane and W. A. Cole, *British Economic Growth, 1689–1959: Trends and Structure*, 2d ed. (Cambridge, Eng., 1967), chaps. 2, 3; Ernst Labrousse et al., *Histoire économique et sociale de la France*, vol. 2: *Des dernier temps de l'âge seigneurial aux préludes de l'âge industriel (1660–1789)* (Paris, 1970). Brinley Thomas, "The Rhythm of Growth in the Atlantic Economy of the Eighteenth Century," *Research in Economic History* 3 (1978): 1–46, attempts to carry his findings from the nineteenth century back to an earlier period and emphasizes the role of cycles in construction.

24. Diane Lindstrom, "Macroeconomic Growth: The United States in the Nineteenth Century," *Journal of Interdisciplinary History* 13 (1983): 704.

25. Carole Shammas, "The Decline of Textile Prices in England and British America Prior to Industrialization," *Economic History Review* 47 (1994): 483–507.

26. The concern here is with long-term price trends. Good and bad harvests did have an impact on annual fluctuations in prices. See Marc Egnal, "The Pennsylvania Economy, 1748–1762: A Study of Short-Run Changes in the Context of Long-Run Changes in the Atlantic Economy" (Ph.D. diss., University of Wisconsin, 1974). See also note 8 for a more general discussion of the impact of changes in demand.

27. "Trecothick's Observations on the Merchants' Petition," 1766, Add. MSS 33,030, fol. 215, BL.

28. Adam Smith, *The Wealth of Nations*, 2 vols. (1776; rpt., London, 1977), 1:301.

29. Ragnar Nurske, *Problems of Capital Formation in the Underdeveloped Countries* (Oxford, Eng., 1953), 1.

30. According to one estimate, capital goods accounted for less than 5 percent of national income in the late seventeenth and early eighteenth century. This percentage rose to 7 percent as industrialization accelerated at the end of the eighteenth century. See Deane and Cole, *British Economic Growth*, 260–63.

31. Russell R. Menard, "From Servants to Slaves: The Transformation of the Chesapeake Labor System," *Southern Studies* 16 (1977): 355–90; Allan Kulikoff, "A 'Prolifick' People: Black Population Growth in the Chesapeake Colonies, 1700–1790," *Southern Studies* 16 (1977), 392–428; Herbert S. Klein, "Slaves and Shipping in Eighteenth-Century Virginia," *Journal of Interdisciplinary History* 5 (1975): 383–412.

32. Literacy rose during the colonial era but had relatively little impact on productivity. Consult Kenneth A. Lockridge, *Literacy in Colonial New England: An Enquiry into the Social Context of Literacy in the Early Modern West* (New York, 1974); Alan Tully, "Literacy Levels and Educational Development in Rural Pennsylvania, 1729–1775," *Pennsylvania History* 39 (1972): 301–12; Allan Greer, "The Pattern of Literacy in Quebec, 1745–1899," *Histoire Sociale/Social History* 11 (1978): 295–335; Egnal, *Divergent Paths*, chap. 5.

33. Solomon Fabricant, *A Primer on Productivity* (New York, 1969), 3–11, 40–85; D. W. Jorgenson and Z. Griliches, "The Explanation of Productivity Change," *Review of Economic Studies* 24 (1956): 254–60; Winifred B. Rothenberg, "The Productivity Consequences of Market Integration: Agriculture in Massachusetts, 1771–1801," in *American Economic Growth and Standards of Living Before the Civil War*, ed. Robert E. Gallman and John J. Wallis (Chicago, 1992), 311–38.

34. For white immigration I have generally followed the figures in David W. Galenson, *White Servitude in Colonial America: An Economic Analysis* (Cambridge, Mass., 1981), 216–17; these have been supplemented by the data in Henry A. Gemery, "Emigration from the British Isles to the New World, 1630–1700: Inferences from Colonial Populations," *Research in Economic History* 5 (1980): 215. For black immigration, see Philip D. Curtin, *The Atlantic Slave Trade: A Census* (Madison, Wis., 1969), 119, 140; and the modifications made in Richard S. Dunn, "Servants and Slaves: The Recruitment and Employment of Labor," in *Colonial British America: Essays in the New History of the Early Modern Era*, ed. Jack P. Greene and J. R. Pole (Baltimore, 1984), 159, 165. Dunn estimates 300,000 servants and 50,000 convicts arrived between 1580 and 1775. See also Henry A. Gemery, "European Emigration to North America, 1700–1820: Numbers and Quasi-Numbers," *Perspectives in American History*, n. s., 1 (1984): 283–342. Abbot Emerson Smith, *Colonists in Bondage: White Servitude and Convict Labor in America, 1607–1776* (Chapel Hill, N.C., 1947), 336,

argues that between one-half and two-thirds of all white immigrants to the British colonies from 1630 to 1775 were servants. This contention has been repeated by other investigators. See Galenson, *White Servitude*, 17; and James Horn, "Servant Emigration to the Chesapeake in the Seventeenth Century," in *The Chesapeake in the Seventeenth Century*, ed. Thad W. Tate and David L. Ammerman (Chapel Hill, N.C., 1979), 51–95.

35. Peter N. Moogk, "Reluctant Exiles: Emigrants from France in Canada before 1760," *WMQ*, 3d ser., 46 (1989): 502–3; Mario Boleda, "Les migrations au Canada sous le régime français" (Ph.D. diss., University of Montreal, 1983), 41–55, 105–112, 339; Boleda, "Les migrations au Canada sous le régime français (1607–1760)," *Cahiers Québécois de demographie* 13 (1984): 23–28; J. N. Biraben, "Le peuplement du Canada français," *Annales de démographie historique* (Paris, 1967), 105–38. For a different set of emigration statistics, consult Leslie Choquette, "French Emigration to Canada, 1660–1760" (paper presented to American Historical Association, December 1989). For a fuller discussion of these issues, see Egnal, *Divergent Paths*, chap. 5.

36. Moogk, "Reluctant Exiles," quote on p. 473; Michael W. Flinn, *The European Demographic System, 1500–1820* (Baltimore, 1981), chap. 5; André Corvisier, *Armies and Societies in Europe, 1494–1789*, trans. by Abigail T. Siddall (Bloomington, Ind., 1979), 45, 131–33; J. F. Bosher, "French Colonial Society in Canada," *Transactions of the Royal Society of Canada*, 4th ser., 19 (1981): 152–53; J.-P. Poussou, "Les mouvements migratoires en France et à partir de la France . . . ," *Annales de démographie historique* (1970): 11–78, and esp. 72–73. There was also debate in France over the wisdom of allowing people to leave. While the general policy was to encourage such settlements, some officials disagreed. See Guy Frégault, "The Colonization of Canada in the Eighteenth Century," in *Society and Conquest: The Debate on the Bourgeoisie and Social Change in French Canada, 1700–1850*, ed. Dale Miquelon (Toronto, 1977), 94–95; John D. Brite, *The Attitude of European States Toward Emigration to the American Colonies . . . 1607–1820* (Chicago, 1939).

37. *Historical Statistics of the U.S.*, 2: 1168; Louise Dechêne, *Habitants and Merchants in Seventeenth-Century Montreal* (Montreal and Kingston, 1992), 292–93.

CHAPTER TWO

1. R. D. Lee and R. S. Schofield, "British Population in the Eighteenth Century," in *The Economic History of Britain Since 1700*, vol. 1: *1700–1860*, ed. Roderick Floud and Donald McCloskey (Cambridge, Eng., 1981), 17–22; J. D. Chambers, *Population, Economy, and Society in Pre-Industrial England* (London, 1972); see also the essays in D. V. Glass and D. E. C. Eversley, *Population in History* (London, 1965).

2. Lee and Schofield, "British Population," 25–32; Richard Brown, *Society and Economy in Modern Britain, 1700–1850* (London, 1991), 30–48; E. A. Wrigley and R. S. Schofield, *The Population History of England, 1541–1871: A Reconstruction* (Cambridge, Eng., 1981), 236–48, 265–69, 348–401.

3. Phyllis Deane and W. A. Cole, *British Economic Growth, 1689–1959: Trends and Structure*, 2d ed. (Cambridge, Eng., 1967), 62–97; B. R. Mitchell and Phyllis Deane, *Abstract of British Historical Statistics* (Cambridge, Eng., 1962), 94–95, 486–87. See also J. D. Gould, "Agricultural Fluctuations and the English Economy in the Eighteenth Century," *JEH* 22 (1962): 313–333; E. L. Jones, "Agriculture and Economic Growth in England, 1660–1750," ibid., 25 (1965): 1–18; A. H. John, "Agricultural Productivity and Economic Growth in England, 1700–1760," ibid., 25 (1965): 19–34. More recent studies have confirmed the existence of the agricultural depres-

sion of the 1730s and 1740s, while noting that not all farmers were affected. See J. V. Beckett, "Regional Variation and the Agricultural Depression, 1730–50," *Economic History Review*, 35 (1982): 35–51. More broadly on the role of agriculture in this era of growth, see three essays by Patrick K. O'Brien: "Agriculture and the Industrial Revolution," *Economic History Review* 30 (1977): 166–81; "Agriculture and the Home Market for English Industry, 1660–1820," *English Historical Review* 100 (1985): 773–99; and "Introduction: Modern Conceptions of the Industrial Revolution," in *The Industrial Revolution and British Society*, ed. Patrick K. O'Brien and Roland Quinalt (Cambridge, Eng., 1993), 19–24. Also see W. A. Cole, "Factors in Demand, 1700–80," in *Economic History of Britain*, 1:45–47; E. L. Jones, "Agriculture, 1700–80," ibid., 1:66–86; Brown, *Society and Economy*, 49–72.

4. Mitchell and Deane, *Abstract of British Historical Statistics*, 94; Deane and Cole, *British Economic Growth*, 82–95; J. H. Plumb, *England in the Eighteenth Century* (Baltimore, 1950), 82–83. Some economic historians, however, question this analysis, and the debate over agricultural growth is worth noting. N. F. R. Crafts contends that there was no acceleration in the pace of development in the 1740s. He argues that Deane and Cole underestimated the strength of the farm sector before 1745 and saw a turning point where there was none. R. V. Jackson (who builds on Crafts's work) goes one step further. He asserts that agriculture expanded more slowly after 1750 than before. Both writers argue there was no rise in the standard of living during the first eighty years of the century.

Crafts's analysis, although intriguing, is flawed. Crafts introduces no new information or series. Rather he reworks existing data and focuses on changes in supply. According to Crafts, falling agricultural prices before 1745 demonstrate the high productivity of the agricultural sector, while rising quotations after that date show that English farmers faltered in their efforts to increase production.

But Crafts and Jackson ignore the evidence documenting the agricultural depression of the 1730s and 1740s. And they largely ignore the impact of demand on prices. A decline in purchases helps explain the reduced value of wheat before mid-century, while increased calls for foodstuffs drove up prices in the 1750s. Nor do the conclusions of Crafts and Jackson fit with the data presented here for the growth of industry and commerce. N. F. R. Crafts's work includes "English Economic Growth in the Eighteenth Century: A Re-Examination of Deane and Cole's Estimates," *Economic History Review*, 2d ser., 29 (1976): 226–35; "British Economic Growth, 1700–1831: A Review of the Evidence," ibid., 2d ser., 36 (1983): 177–99; *British Economic Growth During the Industrial Revolution* (Oxford, 1985); and "The Eighteenth Century: A Survey," in *Economic History of Britain*, 1:1–16. Also consult R. V. Jackson, "Growth and Deceleration in English Agriculture, 1660–1790," *Economic History Review* 2d Ser., 38 (1985): 333–51. Cole, "Factors in Demand," 36–65, accepts many of Crafts's findings. On the agricultural depression, see G. E. Mingay, "The Agricultural Depression, 1730–1750," *Economic History Review*, 2d Ser., 7 (1955–56): 323–38; Richard A. Ippolito, "The Effect of the 'Agricultural Depression' on Industrial Demand in England, 1730–1750," *Economica*, n.s., 42 (1975): 298–312; Beckett, "Regional Variation," 35–51.

5. Deane and Cole, "British Economic Growth," 50–62. For N. F. R. Crafts's mild dissent, see Crafts, "British Economic Growth," 177–99. For critiques of Crafts, consult Julian Hoppit, "Counting the Industrial Revolution," *Economic History Review* 43 (1990): 173–93; and O'Brien, "Modern Conceptions," 7–14.

6. For a discussion of the long-term decline in textile prices, see Carole Shammas, *The Pre-industrial Consumer in England and America* (Oxford, Eng., 1990), 96–100;

Shammas, "The Decline of Textile Prices in England and British America Prior to Industrialization," *Economic History Review* 47 (1994): 483–507. Shammas argues that "fierce competition" from European and Asian producers kept English prices low (504).

7. David Richardson, "The Slave Trade, Sugar, and British Economic Growth, 1748–1776," *Journal of Interdisciplinary History* 17 (1987): 739–69, provides a thoughtful discussion of the links between domestic growth and trade. See also Deane and Cole, *British Economic Growth*, 41–62; Cole, "Factors in Demand," 38–45; Donald McCloskey and Robert P. Thomas, "Overseas Trade and Empire, 1700–1860," in *Economic History of Britain*, 1:88–90, 100–1.

8. David W. Galenson, *Traders, Planters, and Slavers: Market Behavior in Early English America* (New York, 1986), analyzes slave sales in the West Indies between 1673 and 1725; for overall figures, see Philip Curtin, *The Atlantic Slave Trade: A Census* (Madison, Wis., 1969); David Richardson, "The Eighteenth-Century British Slave Trade: Estimates of Its Volume and Coastal Distribution in Africa," *Research in Economic History* 12 (1989): 151–95; Richardson, "The British Slave Trade to Colonial South Carolina," *Slavery and Abolition* 12 (1991): 125–72; Paul E. Lovejoy, "The Volume of the Atlantic Slave Trade: A Synthesis," *Journal of African History* 23 (1982): 473–501.

9. U.S. Bureau of the Census, *Historical Statistics of the United States, Colonial Times to 1970*, 2 vols. (Washington, D.C., 1975), 2: 1168, 1176–78; Deane and Cole, *British Economic Growth*, 85–86.

10. Ralph Davis, "English Foreign Trade, 1700–1774, *Economic History Review*, 2d ser., 15 (1962): 285–303; T. S. Ashton, *An Economic History of England: The 18th Century* (London, 1955), 150–63.

11. Deane and Cole, *British Economic Growth*, 28–30, 40–96; Crafts, "The Eighteenth Century," 1–3; Cole, "Factors in Demand," 39.

CHAPTER THREE

1. J. Hector St. John de Crèvecoeur, *Letters from an American Farmer* (1782; rpt. New York, 1957), 39–40.

2. Marc Egnal, *A Mighty Empire: The Origins of the American Revolution* (Ithaca, N.Y., 1988), passim.

3. James F. Shepherd and Gary M. Walton, *Shipping, Maritime Trade, and the Economic Development of Colonial North America* (Cambridge, Eng., 1972), 135, places shipping earnings second in the period, 1768–1772, among the goods and services sold by the English colonies in North America. They provide this list:

Tobacco	£766,000
Shipping earnings	610,000
Bread and flour	412,000
Rice	312,000
Fish	287,000
Indigo	117,000

But Shepherd and Walton's estimate appears high, and does not account for voyages where traders failed to cover costs. See ibid., 114–36; Marc Egnal, "The Changing Structure of Philadelphia's Trade With the British West Indies, 1750–1775," *Pennsylvania Magazine of History and Biography* 99 (1975): 156–79.

4. U.S. Bureau of the Census, *Historical Statistics of the United States, Colonial Times to 1970*, 2 vols. (Washington, D.C., 1975), 2:1179–83; William S. Sachs,

"The Business Outlook in the Northern Colonies, 1750–1775" (Ph.D. diss., Columbia Univ., 1957), 175–88, 273–76; James G. Lydon, "Philadelphia's Commercial Expansion, 1720–1739," *Pennsylvania Magazine of History and Biography* 91 (1967): 415; James F. Shepherd and Samuel H. Williamson, "The Coastal Trade of the British North American Colonies, 1768–1772," *JEH* 32 (1972): 783–810; David C. Klingaman, "Food Surpluses and Deficits in the American Colonies, 1768–1772," *JEH* 31 (1971): 553–69. During the period 1720–1775 the increase in the percentage of tonnage involved in the coasting trade was most marked for Philadelphia and Boston.

5. Egnal, *A Mighty Empire*, discusses conflicting visions of American growth. Also see Merrill Jensen, *The Founding of a Nation: A History of the American Revolution, 1763–1776* (New York, 1968), 386–88; Jack M. Sosin, *Whitehall and the Wilderness: The Middle West in British Colonial Policy, 1760–1775* (Lincoln, Neb., 1961).

6. Simon Kuznets, "Notes on the Pattern of U.S. Economic Growth," in *The Reinterpretation of American Economic History*, ed. Robert W. Fogel and Stanley L. Engerman (New York, 1971), 18.

7. See the "amenities index" constructed by Lois Green Carr and Lorena S. Walsh, and used by Gloria L. Main; Carr and Walsh, "The Standard of Living in the Colonial Chesapeake," *WMQ*, 3d ser., 45 (1988): 135–59; Main, "The Standard of Living in Southern New England, 1640–1773," ibid., 124–34.

8. Alice Hanson Jones, *Wealth of a Nation to Be: The American Colonies on the Eve of the Revolution* (New York, 1980), 61–64, quote on p. 63.

9. Thomas Weiss, "U.S. Labor Force Estimates and Economic Growth, 1800–1860," in *American Economic Growth and Standards of Living Before the Civil War*, ed. Robert E. Gallman and John Joseph Wallis (Chicago, 1992), 26–35.

10. See John J. McCusker, *Money and Exchange in Europe and America, 1660–1775: A Handbook*, 2d ed. (Chapel Hill, N.C., 1992), 8, 116–31; for price levels in 1774 and 1840, see John J. McCusker, *How Much Is That in Real Money? A Historical Price Index for Use as a Deflator of Money Values in the Economy of the United States* (Worcester, Mass., 1992), 325, 327.

11. This estimate of average income must be used with care. We can question the utility of an average that encompasses such a diverse population—one with a large slave population as well as wealthy planters and merchants. Still, the largest group in society was the middling farmers, and their relative prosperity did much to shape the average. Jones's figures show that the average income in the North, where there were few slaves, differed little from the average income in the South.

CHAPTER FOUR

1. Benjamin Franklin, *The Autobiography and Other Writings*, ed. L. Jesse Lemisch (New York, 1961), 71–72.

2. Council and assembly of Jamaica to Board of Trade, May 2, 1735, CO 137/21/217–218, PRO. See also president, council, and assembly of Jamaica to King, Nov. 23, 1736, CO 137/22/101–102, PRO.

3. Governor William Mathew to [Board of Trade?], 1734, quoted in David B. Gaspar, "The Antigua Slave Conspiracy of 1736: A Case Study of the Origins of Collective Resistance," *WMQ*, 3d Ser., 35 (1978): 316.

4. Fairchild & Caddell to John Yeats, Sept. 28, 1744, John Bayley to John Yeats, Jan. 16, 1738, Yeats Papers, HSP. See the in-letters in the Yeats Papers for a depiction of West Indian conditions during these years.

5. George Metcalf, *Royal Government and Political Conflict in Jamaica, 1729–1783* (London, 1965), 38–48; Peter H. Wood, *Black Majority: Negroes in South Carolina from 1670 through the Stono Rebellion* (New York, 1974), 225.

6. Richard B. Sheridan, *Sugar and Slavery: An Economic History of the British West Indies, 1623–1775* (Baltimore, 1973), 496–97, presents sugar prices.

7. For the magnitude of trade with the English and French islands see "Calculations of Sugars Made in the Different Isles . . . ," 1747, Add. MSS 38,331, fol. 97, BL; "An Inquiry into the Causes of the Present Scarcity of Money . . . ," Jamaica, 1750, Add. MSS 30,163, fols. 13–14, BL; "Memorial Respecting the Trade Carried on by His Majesty's Subjects to the French Settlements in Hispaniola . . . ," Dec. 1760, C.O. 137/60, 321–30, PRO; "An Estimate of the Tea, Sugar, and Molasses Illegally Imported . . . ," ca. 1764, Add. MSS 38,335, fol. 243, BL; "Calculations Concerning the Molasses Duty," ca. 1766, T. 1/434, 52, PRO. New France included Canada, Acadia, Isle Royale, and the settlements in the west such as Detroit. The other large French colony in North America was Louisiana. See R. Cole Harris and Geoffrey J. Matthews, eds., *Historical Atlas of Canada*, vol. 1: *From the Beginnings to 1800* (Toronto, 1987), plate 40.

8. U.S. Bureau of the Census, *Historical Statistics of the United States, Colonial Times to 1970*, 2 vols. (Washington, D.C., 1975), 2:1180–81, presents tonnage figures for Boston and New York.

9. Helen L. Klopfer, "Statistics of Foreign Trade of Philadelphia, 1700–1860" (Ph.D. diss., University of Pennsylvania, 1936), 176; Anne Bezanson et al., *Prices in Colonial Pennsylvania* (Philadelphia, 1935), appendix.

10. Robert to Alida Livingston, June 27, July 1, 1724, quoted in Lawrence H. Leder, *Robert Livingston, 1654–1728, and the Politics of Colonial New York* (Chapel Hill, N.C., 1961), 273–74.

11. Duane E. Ball and Gary M. Walton, "Agricultural Productivity Change in Eighteenth-Century Pennsylvania," *JEH* 36 (1976): 106; Bruce C. Daniels, "Economic Development in Colonial and Revolutionary Connecticut: An Overview," *WMQ*, 3d ser., 37 (1980): 430–34; Edward Byers, *The Nation of Nantucket: Society and Politics in an Early American Commercial Center, 1660–1820* (Boston, 1987), 77.

12. Gloria L. Main, "The Standard of Living in Colonial Massachusetts," *JEH* 43 (1983): 101–8.

13. Terry L. Anderson, "Economic Growth in Colonial New England: 'Statistical Renaissance'," *JEH* 29 (1979): 243–57. Anderson's work overlaps with Main's, because Hampshire County is one of the three counties that Main samples.

14. Douglas C. North, "Sources of Productivity Change in Ocean Shipping, 1600–1850," in *The Reinterpretation of American Economic History*, ed. Robert W. Fogel and Stanley L. Engerman (New York, 1971), 163–74; James F. Shepherd and Gary M. Walton, *Shipping, Maritime Trade, and the Economic Development of Colonial North America* (Cambridge, Eng., 1972), chaps. 4 and 5; Christopher J. French, "Productivity in the Atlantic Shipping Industry: A Quantitative Study," *Journal of Interdisciplinary History*, 17 (1987): 613–38; William S. Sachs, "The Business Outlook in the Northern Colonies, 1750–1775" (Ph.D. diss., Columbia Univ., 1957), 270; Byers, *The Nation of Nantucket*, 5, 82, shows the difficulties the whaling industry faced before 1745.

15. J. Bridger to Board of Trade, 1719, quoted in Rolla M. Tryon, *Household Manufactures in the United States, 1640–1860* (Chicago, 1917), 77–78.

16. Board of Trade to House of Commons, February 1731/32, quoted in Tryon, *Household Manufactures*, 80; Adrienne Hood, "The Gender Division of Labor in the

Production of Textiles in Eighteenth-Century, Rural Pennsylvania (Rethinking the New England Model)," *Journal of Social History* 27 (1994): 537–61.

17. Credit flows and the terms offered are discussed in more detail later in this chapter.

18. Jackson Turner Main, *Society and Economy in Colonial Connecticut* (Princeton, N.J., 1985), 127–29.

19. Frank W. Pitman, *The Development of the British West Indies, 1700–1763* (New Haven, 1917), 21, 307; Metcalf, *Royal Government*, 197; Frances Armytage, *The Free Port System in the British West Indies: A Study in Commercial Policy, 1766–1822* (London, 1953), 1–51; J. R. Ward, *British West Indian Slavery, 1750–1834: The Process of Amelioration* (Oxford, 1988), 80–98; for maps showing the spread of cane culture in Jamaica, see David Watts, *The West Indies: Patterns of Development, Culture, and Environmental Change Since 1492* (Cambridge, Eng., 1987), 227, 293, 295. Sheridan, *Sugar and Slavery*, 487–89, presents quantity figures; see also B. R. Mitchell and Phyllis Deane, *Abstract of British Historical Statistics* (Cambridge, Eng., 1962), 285–91, 309–11.

20. Arthur M. Schlesinger, *The Colonial Merchants and the American Revolution, 1763–1776* (New York, 1918), 570–75, discusses the large exportations to Britain at the end of the colonial era; Byers, *The Nation of Nantucket*, 140–41, examines the rising demand for whale oil; so does James B. Hedges, *The Browns of Providence Plantations: The Colonial Years* (Providence, 1968), 89–93. There were two other, minor markets for northern goods. Ireland was important chiefly as a consumer of flaxseed, and Africa took New England rum as part of the slave trade.

21. Bezanson, *Prices in Colonial Pennsylvania*, 118.

22. Klopfer, "Statistics of Foreign Trade," 176.

23. The sharp rise in Iberian demand reflected the disappearance of British grain surpluses, as the burgeoning population of the mother country pressed upon agricultural output in the 1760s. Britain had long been an important supplier of foodstuffs to southern Europe. Mitchell and Deane, *Abstract of British Historical Statistics*, 94–95, provides data on Britain's grain trade; see also Phyllis Deane and W. A. Cole, *British Economic Growth, 1688–1959: Trends and Structure* (Cambridge, Eng., 1967), 2d ed., 65, 93–94.

24. William Pollard to Sericold & Jackson, Dec. 18, 1772, Pollard Letterbook, HSP.

25. The grain growers of the North were one of the most prosperous groups in the Thirteen Colonies. Strong demand meant they fared better than staple producers in the other regions. Between 1740 and Independence the number of barrels of flour exported from Philadelphia increased at approximately 70 percent a decade, compared to 20 percent for growth in the quantity of tobacco sent from the Chesapeake, and 34 percent for shipments of rice from the Lower South. See David Klingaman, "Food Surpluses and Deficits in the American Colonies, 1768–1772," *JEH* 31 (1971): 553–69; Sachs, "Business Outlook," 273–75.

26. For flour exports, Klopfer, "Statistics of Foreign Trade," 173; for tobacco and rice, *Historical Statistics of the U.S.*, 2:1190, 1192–93. The rice economy of South Carolina and Georgia remained more prosperous in the late colonial period than the grain economy of Pennsylvania and New York.

27. Morse quoted in John J. McCusker and Russell R. Menard, *The Economy of British America, 1607–1789* (Chapel Hill, N.C., 1985), 305; Howard S. Russell, *A Long, Deep Furrow: Three Centuries of Farming in New England* (Hanover, N.H., 1976); David O. Percy, "An Embarrassment of Richness: Colonial Soil Cultivation

Practices," *Associates N[ational] A[gricultural] L[ibrary] Today*, n.s., 2 (1977): 4–11.
Ball and Walton, "Agricultural Productivity Change," 106–10; John Flexner Walzer,
"Transportation in the Philadelphia Trading Area, 1740–1775" (Ph.D. diss., Univer-
sity of Wisconsin, 1968); Richard L. Bushman, "Opening the American Countryside,"
in *The Transformation of Early American History: Society, Authority, and Ideology*, ed.
James A. Henretta et al. (New York, 1991), 239–56; Lucy Simler, "Tenancy in Colo-
nial Pennsylvania: The Case of Chester County," *WMQ*, 3d ser., 43 (1986): 550–51;
Paul G. E. Clemens and Lucy Simler, "Rural Labor and the Farm Household in
Chester County, Pennsylvania, 1750–1820," in *Work and Labor in Early America*,
ed. Stephen Innes (Chapel Hill, N.C., 1988), 142; Peter O. Wacker, *Land and People:
A Cultural Geography of Preindustrial New Jersey: Origins and Settlement Patterns*
(New Brunswick, N.J., 1975), 361.

28. For a further discussion of these figures, and a graph for gross profits showing the computations for individual fabrics, see Marc Egnal, *A Mighty Empire: The
Origins of the American Revolution* (Ithaca, N.Y., 1988), 133–36.

29. W. T. Baxter, *The House of Hancock: Business in Boston, 1724–1775* (New
York, 1965), 78–91, 93, 125–28, 272; Kenneth Morgan, *Bristol and the Atlantic Trade
in the Eighteenth Century* (Cambridge, Eng., 1993), 189–99.

30. Michael Atkins to John Reynell, July 5, 1751, Reynell Papers, HSP; Thomas Riche to Parr & Bulkley, May 26, 1770, Riche Letterbook, HSP; William Pollard
to Sericold & Jackson, Dec. 18, 1772, to Brian Bentley, Mar. 9, 1773, Pollard
Letterbook, HSP; Thomas Clifford to Roach & Niles, Apr. 5, 1765, Clifford Letterbook,
HSP; more generally on this topic, see Marc Egnal, "The Changing Structure of
Philadelphia's Trade With the British West Indies, 1750–1775," *Pennsylvania Magazine of History and Biography* 99 (1975): 156–79.

31. Richard Waln, Jr., to Harford & Powell, Apr. 18, 1769, Richard Waln letterbook, HSP. More generally, see Egnal, *A Mighty Empire*, 138–39, 161–66, 187–89,
206–12.

32. Franklin quoted in Merrill Jensen, *The Founding of a Nation: A History of
the American Revolution, 1763–1776* (New York, 1968), 173.

33. William Pollard to Benjamin & John Bower, Apr. 6, 1773, Pollard Letterbook,
HSP; Schlesinger, *Colonial Merchants*, 64–67, 77, 109–11, 122–24, 130–31. Ball and
Walton, "Agricultural Productivity Change," 113, shows that in Chester County
nonagricultural activity rose rapidly. By 1768 12 percent of farm labor was engaged in
nonagricultural pursuits. See also Victor S. Clark, *History of Manufactures in the United
States*, 3 vols. (1929; rpt. New York, 1949), 1:215–19; Subscribers for Manufactory,
Mar. 15, 1768, Ezekiel Price Papers, Massachusetts Historical Society. These enterprises met with mixed success, but failure often was followed by the establishment of
another, larger manufactory. See Tryon, *Household Manufactures*, 86–88, 245–46;
T. Wharton to Benjamin Franklin, Apr. 26, 1766, in *The Papers of Benjamin Franklin*,
ed. Leonard W. Labaree et al. (New Haven, Conn., 1959–), 12:252. See also ibid.,
11:314–16; Gary Nash, *The Urban Crucible: Social Change, Political Consciousness,
and the Origins of the American Revolution* (Cambridge, Mass., 1979), 332–37; Douglas
Lamar Jones, "The Strolling Poor: Transiency in Eighteenth-Century Massachusetts,"
Journal of Social History 8 (1975): 28–54.

34. Tryon, *Household Manufactures*, 200; Clark, *History of Manufactures*, 1:116,
207–8; Gov. William Stuart to Secretary of State Dartmouth, Dec. 24, 1773, CO 71/
4, 71, PRO; James & Drinker to Thomas Evans, Dec. 3, 1761, James & Drinker
Letterbook, HSP. The fabrication of alkalis and whale products also expanded between
1760 and 1775. See also *Historical Statistics of the U.S.*, 2:1183–88; Sachs, "Business

Outlook," 188–92; Paul G. Faler, *Mechanics and Manufacturers in the Early Industrial Revolution: Lynn, Massachusetts, 1780–1860* (Albany, 1981), 8–14; D. W. Meinig, *The Shaping of America: A Geographical Perspective of 500 Years of History*, vol. 1, *Atlantic America, 1492–1800* (New Haven, 1986), 294–95; Daniels, "Economic Development," 438–39.

35. Tryon, *Household Manufactures*, 171–77; Clark, *History of Manufactures*, 1:438–63; Clemens and Simler, "Rural Labor and the Farm Household," 111. The success of local manufactures in the North helps explain why that region had somewhat lower levels of per capita imports from Britain than did the Upper or Lower South but was no less prosperous. See Paul F. Paskoff, "Labor Productivity and Managerial Efficiency against a Static Technology: The Pennsylvania Iron Industry, 1750–1800," *JEH* 40 (1980): 129–35; Clark, *History of Manufactures*, 1:165–81; William B. Weeden, *Economic and Social History of New England, 1620–1789*, 2 vols. (Boston, 1891), 2:501–3; Robert Plumstead to John Scott, Sept. 3, 1757, Robert Plumstead Letterbook, Cambridge University Library. For a different view of progress in flour milling before 1776, consult Greville and Dorothy Bathe, *Oliver Evans: A Chronicle of Early American Engineering* (Philadelphia 1935), 1–18. The Bathes minimize the technical advances occurring before Evans's inventions in the early 1780s.

36. Thomas M. Doerflinger, *A Vigorous Spirit of Enterprise: Merchants and Economic Development in Revolutionary Philadelphia* (Chapel Hill, N.C., 1986), 70–164; Virginia D. Harrington, *The New York Merchant on the Eve of the Revolution* (New York, 1935), 47–163; Hedges, *The Browns of Providence Plantations*, 123–54.

37. Information on credit practices is provided by English letters preserved in North American archives, Parliamentary hearings, and scattered references in colonial letterbooks. Lacking for the most part are the letterbooks of the great houses dealing with the northern colonies. One of the few exceptions is the letterbook of Robert Plumstead, Cambridge University Library, Cambridge, England. The record is much fuller for the British firms shipping to the Chesapeake.

38. Thomas Crowley to Thomas Wharton, Aug. 6, 1754, Wharton MSS, HSP.

39. Committee on the American Papers, Feb. 11, 1766, Add. MSS, 33,030, fol. 91, BL; James Beekman to Thomas Harris, Oct. 17, 1767, in *The Beekman Mercantile Papers, 1746–1799*, ed. Philip L. White, 3 vols. (New York, 1956), 3:789; John Hancock to Harrison & Barnards, Dec. 3, 1766, in Abram E. Brown, *John Hancock: His Book* (Boston, 1898), 136; James & Drinker to John Lindoe, Aug. 26, 1760, James & Drinker Letterbook, HSP.

40. David & John Barclay to James Pemberton, Jan. 14, 1771, Pemberton Papers, HSP. The discussion in the text focuses on London. The credit period in the outports generally was shorter, but followed the same pattern. On outport credit, see Joseph Broadbent to John Pemberton, Nov. 26, 1753, Pemberton Papers, HSP; John and Henry Gurney to John Pemberton, Jan. 12, 1754, Pemberton Papers, HSP; Christopher Rawson to Thomas Wharton, July 19, 1773, Wharton MSS, HSP; Gerard G. Beekman to William Beekman, *Beekman Papers*, 2:357. See also testimony of Robert Dawson, Feb. 11, 1766, and William Reeve, Feb. 13, 1766, Add. MSS, 33,030, fols. 142, 152–53, BL.

41. James Pemberton to John Pemberton, July 27, 1750, Pemberton Papers, HSP.

42. John Kidd to Neate & Neave, May 31, 1750, Mar. 27, 1751, Kidd Letterbook, HSP; Michael Bland to James Pemberton, Mar. 30, 1750, John Hunt to Israel Pemberton, Jr., Nov. 21, 1751, Pemberton Papers, HSP.

43. James & Drinker to William Neate, June 1, 1761, to Neate & Pigou, May 11, 1763, James & Drinker Letterbook, HSP; more generally, see Marc Egnal, "The

Pennsylvania Economy, 1748–1762: An Analysis of Short-Run Fluctuations in the Context of Long-Run Changes in the Atlantic Trading Community" (Ph.D. diss., Univ. of Wisconsin, 1974), chaps. 4, 5, 6.

44. James & Drinker to John Clitherall, May 9, 1760, James & Drinker Letterbook, HSP. The French and Indian War paralleled but was not coterminous with the Seven Years' War. The fighting in North America began in 1754; with the fall of Canada in 1760 the large-scale confrontations between the French and English ended.

45. Gov. Henry Moore to earl of Hillsborough, May 14, 1768, quoted in Joseph A. Ernst, *Money and Politics in America, 1755–1775: A Study in the Currency Act of 1764 and the Political Economy of Revolution* (Chapel Hill, N.C., 1973), 254.

46. Christian Wirtz to John Steinmetz, Oct. 10, 1769, Aubrey Roberts to John Steinmetz, Feb. 4, 1769, William and Young Keene to John Steinmetz, Feb. 13, 1769, John Steinmetz Mercantile Correspondence, HSP; Richard Waln, Jr., to Harford & Powell, Nov. 1769, Richard Waln Letterbook, HSP.

47. Gerrit Lansing, Jr., to James Beekman, Apr. 24, 1769, *Beekman Papers*, 3:973; Cadwallader Colden to earl of Hillsborough, July 11, 1769, quoted in Carl Becker, *The History of Political Parties in the Province of New York, 1760–1776* (Madison, Wis., 1909), 79n; Sachs, "Business Outlook," 240.

48. Carol Shammas, *The Pre-industrial Consumer in England and America* (Oxford, Eng., 1990), 270–83.

49. John Watts to William Brymer, May 15, 1764, *Letter Book of John Watts, Merchant and Councillor of New York*, New York Historical Society, *Collections*, 61 (New York, 1928), 254; John Hancock to Devonshire & Reeve, Dec. 7, 1764, *John Hancock: His Book*, 57.

50. Thomas Clifford to Nathaniel Green & Co., Sept. 17, 1765, Clifford Letterbook; Israel Pemberton to John Pleasants, Nov. 11, 1765, Pemberton Papers, HSP; Daniel Roberdeau to Meyer & Hall, Oct. 21, Nov. 9, 1765, Roberdeau Letterbook, HSP; John Dickinson, *The Late Regulations*, 1765, in *The Writings of John Dickinson*, ed. Paul L. Ford, Memoirs of the Historical Society of Pennsylvania, vol. 14 (Philadelphia, 1895), 227–28.

51. John Hancock to Harrison & Barnard, July 29, 1767, Hancock to Harrison, Barnard & Sprag, Oct. 16, 1767, Hancock to George Haley, Oct. 16, Dec. 15, 1767, *John Hancock: His Book*, 146, 150–51; Thomas Riche to Smyth & Sudler, Nov. 5, 1767, Riche Letterbook, HSP.

52. Egnal, *A Mighty Empire*, 129–39, 140–42; economic conditions during the first half of the 1770s are abundantly documented in several letterbooks, including those of Henry Drinker, Thomas Clifford, Reynell & Coates, William Pollard, and Richard Waln, Jr. All of these are located in HSP.

53. Eliot quoted in Richard L. Bushman, *From Puritan to Yankee: Character and the Social Order in Connecticut, 1690–1765* (Cambridge, Mass., 1967), 135.

54. Roger Wolcott is quoted in Oscar Zeichner, *Connecticut's Years of Controversy, 1750–1776* (Chapel Hill, N.C., 1949), 246.

CHAPTER FIVE

1. Roy Harvey Pearce, ed., *Colonial American Writing*, 2d ed. (New York, 1969), 588–608, quote on p. 589. The evidence about Cooke's life is sketchy, but the likelihood is that he was born in England and inherited property in Maryland, where he went on to be a lawyer and poet. See "Ebenezer Cooke," *Dictionary of American Bi-*

ography, ed. Allen Johnson and Dumas Malone, 20 vols. (New York, 1928–1937), 9: 189–90.

2. Robert "King" Carter to son, Feb. 14, 1721, quoted in John M. Hemphill II, *Virginia and the English Commercial System, 1689–1733: Studies in the Development and Fluctuations of a Colonial Economy under Imperial Control* (New York, 1985), 52; Russell R. Menard, "The Tobacco Industry in the Chesapeake Colonies, 1617–1730: An Interpretation," *Research in Economic History* 5 (1980): 110–16.

3. Robert "King" Carter to Haswell & Brooks, May 13, 1727, quoted in Hemphill, *Virginia*, 82.

4. Jacob M. Price, *France and the Chesapeake: A History of the French Tobacco Monopoly, 1674–1791, and of Its Relationship to the British and American Tobacco Trades*, 2 vols. (Ann Arbor, Mich., 1973), 2:852, presents Virginia tobacco prices at Amsterdam. Also consult Price, "The Economic Growth of the Chesapeake and the European Market, 1697–1775," *JEH* 24 (1964): 496–511; Paul B. E. Clemens, *The Atlantic Economy and Colonial Maryland's Eastern Shore: From Tobacco to Grain* (Ithaca, N.Y., 1980), 111–14.

5. Gov. William Gooch to Board of Trade, May 27, 1732, quoted in Allan Kulikoff, *Tobacco and Slaves: The Development of Southern Cultures in the Chesapeake, 1680–1800* (Chapel Hill, N.C., 1986), 85.

6. John Randolph to Board of Trade, Jan. 17, 1729, quoted in Hemphill, *Virginia*, 96; Lois Green Carr, "Diversification in the Colonial Chesapeake: Somerset County, Maryland, in Comparative Perspective," in *Colonial Chesapeake Society*, ed. Lois Green Carr, Philip D. Morgan, and Jean B. Russo (Chapel Hill, N.C., 1988), 342–88; Jean B. Russo, "Self-sufficiency and Local Exchange: Free Craftsmen in the Rural Chesapeake Economy," ibid., 389–432; Carole Shammas, *The Pre-industrial Consumer in England and America* (Oxford, Eng., 1990), 53–60.

7. The number of pounds of tobacco that the average worker produced fell off in the 1720s and 1730s and would not rise again until the 1740s. The drop was most marked along the York and lower Rappahannock Rivers — areas that grew sweetscented (as opposed to oronoco) tobacco. See Lorena S. Walsh, "Plantation Management in the Chesapeake, 1620–1820," *JEH* 49 (1989): 395–97; Paul G. E. Clemens, "The Operation of an Eighteenth-Century Chesapeake Tobacco Plantation," *Agricultural History* 49 (1975): 517–22.

8. For data on slave population, see U.S. Bureau of the Census, *Historical Statistics of the United States, Colonial Times to 1970*, 2 vols. (Washington, D.C., 1975), 2:1168.

9. Price, "Economic Growth," 496–511; Clemens, *Atlantic Economy*, 111–17; Kulikoff, *Tobacco and Slaves*, 109–10; Hemphill, *Virginia*, 151–57; Price, *France and the Chesapeake*, 1:266; Gloria L. Main, *Tobacco Colony: Life in Early Maryland, 1650–1720* (Princeton, N.J., 1982), 23.

10. Price, "Economic Growth," 501.

11. Bladen quoted in Kulikoff, *Tobacco and Slaves*, 114; Vertrees J. Wyckoff, *Tobacco Regulation in Colonial Maryland*, Johns Hopkins University Studies in Historical and Political Science, n.s., 22 (Baltimore, 1936), chap. 8.

12. George Washington to Robert Cary & Co., June 20, 1768, *Writings of George Washington*, ed. John C. Fitzpatrick, 39 vols. (Washington, D.C., 1931–1944), 2: 491; *Historical Statistics of the U.S.*, 2:1190; Jacob M. Price, "The Rise of Glasgow in the Chesapeake Tobacco Trade, 1707–1775," *WMQ*, 3d ser., 11 (1954): 177–99; Kulikoff, *Tobacco and Slaves*, 123; Gregory Nobles, "Breaking into the Backcountry: New Approaches to the Early American Frontier," *WMQ*, 3d ser., 46 (1989): 657. The

activities of the Scots and the planters involved in the consignment trade could well be considered the "commercial" sector of the Upper South, a region that lacked the large towns found in the other sections. On the commercial activities of an area without cities, see several excellent studies of the Southside: Michael L. Nicholls, "Origins of the Virginia Southside, 1703–1754: A Social and Economic Study" (Ph.D. diss., College of William and Mary, 1972); Richard R. Beeman, *The Evolution of the Southern Backcountry: A Case Study of Lunenburg County, Virginia, 1746–1832* (Philadelphia, 1984); Charles J. Farmer, *In the Absence of Towns: Settlement and Country Trade in Southside Virginia, 1730–1800* (Lanham, Md., 1993).

13. *Historical Statistics of the U.S.*, 2:1190; Price, "Rise of Glasgow," 177–99.

14. French, "Productivity in the Atlantic Shipping Industry," *Journal of Interdisciplinary History* 17 (1987): 623–32; Gary M. Walton, "Sources of Productivity Change in American Colonial Shipping, 1675–1775," *Economic History Review* 20 (1967): 74–76; James F. Shepherd and Gary M. Walton, *Shipping, Maritime Trade, and the Economic Development of Colonial North America* (Cambridge, Eng., 1972), 77–90.

15. Shepherd and Walton, *Shipping, Maritime Trade*, 56–66; Menard, "Tobacco Industry," 146–47; French, "Atlantic Shipping Industry," 635.

16. Walsh, "Plantation Management," 393–406; Lois Green Carr and Russell R. Menard, "Land, Labor, and Economies of Scale in Early Maryland: Some Limits to Growth in the Chesapeake System of Husbandry," *JEH* 49 (1989): 407–418; Russell R. Menard, "Economic and Social Development of the South," in *The Cambridge Economic History of the United States*, vol. 1, *The Colonial Era*, ed. Stanley L. Engerman and Robert E. Gallman (New York, 1996), 261–70.

17. Washington to Capel and Osgood Hanbury, May 5, 1768, *Writings of George Washington*, 2:485; also see Washington to Stewart & Campbell, Sept. 4, 1766, to Robert Cary & Co., May 17, 1767, July 25, 1769, ibid., 2:442, 454, 513.

18. Shepherd and Walton, *Shipping, Maritime Trade*, 214–25; David Klingaman, "The Significance of Grain in the Development of the Tobacco Colonies," *JEH* 29 (1969): 272. Klingaman provides figures for coastal shipments from Virginia, and I have assumed that a similar portion (29 percent) of Maryland corn exports was sent to other American colonies.

19. See Chapters 2 and 4.

20. Kulikoff's study of grain exports for four Virginia naval districts (South Potomac, Rappahannock, York, and Upper James) shows that gains in per capita output came after 1745, with the greatest strides recorded between 1760 and 1770; Kulikoff, *Tobacco and Slaves*, 120–21. Paul Clemens's analysis of the Eastern Shore counties of Maryland also makes clear both the growth of the wheat trade during the 1760s, and its reorientation toward Southern Europe; Clemens, *Atlantic Economy*, 168–79.

21. Klingaman, "Significance of Grain," 273–74; Kulikoff, *Tobacco and Slaves*, 123–27; Beeman, *Evolution of the Southern Backcountry*, 34.

22. Andrew Burnaby, *Travels through the Middle Settlements in North America* . . . (1798; rpt. New York, 1970), 59–60; Lois Green Carr and Russell R. Menard, "Land, Labor, and Economies of Scale," 414–15.

23. Gov. Francis Fauquier to Board of Trade, Jan. 30, 1763, quoted in T. H. Breen, *Tobacco Culture: The Mentality of the Great Tidewater Planters on the Eve of Revolution* (Princeton, N.J., 1985), 179–80.

24. In 1770 Williamsburg had only 2,000 inhabitants, and Annapolis 3,700. See James J. O'Mara, "Urbanization in Tidewater Virginia during the Eighteenth Century: A Study in Historical Geography (Ph.D. diss., York University, 1979); Carville

V. Earle and Ronald Hoffman, "Staple Crops and Urban Development in the Eighteenth-Century South," *Perspectives in American History* 10 (1976): 5–78; Edward C. Papenfuse, *In Pursuit of Profit: The Annapolis Merchants in the Era of the American Revolution, 1763–1805* (Baltimore, 1975); Paul Kent Walker, "Business and Commerce in Baltimore on the Eve of Independence," *Maryland Historical Magazine* 71 (1976): 296–309; G. Terry Sharrer, "Flour Milling in the Growth of Baltimore," 1750–1830," ibid., 322–33; *Pennsylvania Chronicle*, Jan. 26, Feb. 16, Mar. 16, 1767, discusses the growing rivalry between Philadelphia and Baltimore for the grain trade.

25. Burnaby, *Travels through the Middle Settlements*, 46.

26. In Talbot County, Maryland, artisans made up 10 percent of those inventoried, compared to 25 percent of those whose estates were recorded in Connecticut. Russo, "Self-sufficiency and Local Exchange," 389–482; Carr, "Diversification in the Colonial Chesapeake," 342–88; Lois G. Carr and Lorena S. Walsh, "Changing Life Styles in Colonial St. Mary's County," Regional Economic History Research Center, *Working Papers*, 1, no. 3 (1978): 107–9; Kulikoff, *Tobacco and Slaves*, 102–3.

27. Jerman Baker to Duncan Rose, Feb. 15, 1764, WMQ, 1st ser., 12 (1904): 242; Jacob M. Price, "Credit in the Slave Trade and the Plantation Economies," in *Slavery and the Rise of the Atlantic System*, ed. B. L. Solow (Cambridge, Eng., 1991), 293–339.

28. John Wayles to Farrell & Jones, Aug. 30, 1766, *Virginia Magazine of History and Biography* 66 (1958): 305.

29. Richard B. Sheridan, "The British Credit Crisis of 1772 and the American Colonies," JEH 20 (1960): 180–81; Shammas, *Pre-industrial Consumer*, 267–71.

30. Samuel Galloway to unknown, Oct. 28, 1764, quoted in Ronald Hoffman, "Economics, Politics, and Revolution in Maryland" (Ph.D. diss., Univ. of Wisconsin, 1969), 61–62.

31. John Baylor to John Norton, Sept. 18, 1764, in *John Norton & Sons, Merchants of London and Virginia, Being the Papers from their Counting House for the Years 1750 to 1795*, ed. Frances N. Mason (Richmond, 1937), 11–12; Marc Egnal, *A Mighty Empire: The Origins of the American Revolution* (Ithaca, N.Y., 1988), 144–47.

32. Col. Thomas Moore to George Washington, Oct. 21, 1766, *Letters to Washington and Accompanying Papers*, ed. Stanislaus M. Hamilton, 5 vols. (Boston, 1898–1902), 3:288.

33. John Hook to [William?] Donald & Co., May 29, 1768, John Hook Papers, microfilm at Colonial Williamsburg Foundation; David Jameson to John Norton, Dec. 8, 1769, *John Norton & Sons*, 113; Robert Beverley to Samuel Athawes, Sept. 6, 1769, Robert Beverley Letterbook, microfilm at Colonial Williamsburg Foundation.

34. Kulikoff, *Tobacco and Slaves*, 129; Joseph A. Ernst, *Money and Politics in America, 1755–1775: A Study in the Currency Act of 1764 and the Political Economy of Revolution* (Chapel Hill, N.C., 1973), 67, 231; Calvin B. Coulter, Jr., "The Virginia Merchant" (Ph.D. diss., Princeton Univ., 1944), 225. These store debts are in Virginia currency.

35. Testimony of John Glasford, Feb. 13, 1766, Add. MSS 33,030, fols. 160–63, BL; Jacob M. Price, "Capital and Credit in the British–Chesapeake Trade, 1750–1775," in *Of Mother Country and Plantations: Proceedings of the Twenty-Seventh Conference in Early American History*, ed. Virginia B. Platt and David C. Skaggs (Bowling Green, Ohio, 1971), 8–9, quotation on p. 8; Price, *Capital and Credit in British Overseas Trade: The View from the Chesapeake, 1700–1776* (Cambridge, Mass., 1980), 8–12; John Pleasants to [Israel Pemberton], Oct. 14, 1765, Pemberton Papers, HSP.

36. Samuel M. Rosenblatt, "The Significance of Credit in the Tobacco Consignment Trade: A Study of John Norton and Sons, 1768–1775," WMQ, 3d ser., 19 (1962): 383–87.

37. William Wiatt to Francis Wiatt, June 26, 1773, WMQ, 1st ser., 12 (1903–4): 113–14; Sheridan, "British Credit Crisis," 170–78.

38. Kulikoff, *Tobacco and Slaves*, 129–31; Ernst, *Money and Politics*, 329–34; Sheridan, "British Credit Crisis," 161–86.

39. Price, "Capital and Credit," 8.

40. William Lux to Russell and Molleson, October 1764, to William Alexander and Sons, Jan. 29, 1767, quoted in Ernst, *Money and Politics*, 144, 166; Hoffman, "Economics, Politics, and Revolution," 107–24.

41. Kulikoff, *Tobacco and Slaves*, 118–122; Allan Kulikoff, "The Economic Growth of the Eighteenth-Century Chesapeake Colonies," JEH 39 (1979): 277–86; Alice Hanson Jones, *Wealth of a Nation To Be: The American Colonies on the Eve of the Revolution* (New York, 1980), esp. 109, 127–29; Alice Hanson Jones, *American Colonial Wealth: Documents and Methods*, 3 vols. (New York, 1977), table 3.10.

42. Kulikoff, *Tobacco and Slaves*, 133–34; James A. Henretta, "Wealth and Social Structure," in *Colonial British America: Essays in the New History of the Early Modern Era*, ed. Jack P. Greene and J. R. Pole (Baltimore, 1984), 275.

43. Lois Green Carr and Lorena S. Walsh, "The Standard of Living in the Colonial Chesapeake," WMQ, 3d ser., 45 (1988): 135–59.

44. A more general criticism of statistics based on probate records is that these data ignore the conditions of a large group of individuals with little property. Billy G. Smith, "Comment," WMQ, 3d ser., 45 (1988): 163–66, discusses the bias in various surveys of colonial wealth.

45. Maryland law, 1768, quoted in Kulikoff, *Tobacco and Slaves*, 299. Kulikoff observes that "as many as a third of the white families of tidewater were poor on the eve of the Revolution" (298–99).

46. Ibid., 128–34. In Prince George's County, for example, the proportion of tenants increased from a third at the beginning of the century to more than half in the 1770s.

CHAPTER SIX

1. The geographical inequality of wealth was also striking *within* the rice colonies. The lowcountry was far richer than the backcountry. See Peter A. Coclanis, *The Shadow of a Dream: Economic Life and Death in the South Carolina Low Country, 1670–1920* (New York, 1989), 65–91.

2. Russell R. Menard, "Slavery, Economic Growth, and Revolutionary Ideology in the South Carolina Lowcountry," in *The Economy of Early America: The Revolutionary Period, 1763–1790*, ed. Ronald Hoffman et al. (Charlottesville, Va., 1988), 250, offers a similar periodization of South Carolina growth.

3. Francis Yonge, *A View of the Trade of South-Carolina . . .* , reprinted in *The Colonial South Carolina Scene: Contemporary Views, 1697–1774*, ed. H. Roy Merrens (Columbia, S.C., 1977), 70–71; R. C. Nash, "South Carolina and the Atlantic Economy in the Late Seventeenth and Eighteenth Centuries," *Economic History Review* 45 (1992): 684–85, 690, discusses rice growing in northern Italy and gives figures for the size of the harvest; Robert M. Weir, *Colonial South Carolina: A History* (New York, 1983), 165–66; Converse D. Clowse, *Economic Beginnings in Colonial South Carolina, 1670–1730* (Columbia, S.C., 1971), 219, 244; Henry C. Dethloff, "The Colonial Rice Trade," *Agricultural History* 56 (1982): 235–37.

4. Governor, council, and assembly to king, May 11, 1745, George Dunbar to duke of Newcastle, Aug. 24, 1743, South Carolina Public Records, XXII, 92, XXI, 166, South Carolina Archives; Charles Boschi to secretary of Society for Propagation of Gospel, Oct. 30, 1745, *South Carolina Historical Magazine* 50 (1949): 183; Eliza Lucas [Pinckney] to George Lucas, July 25, 1740, Sept. 8, 1742, *The Letterbook of Eliza Lucas Pinckney, 1739–1762,* ed. Elise Pinckney (Chapel Hill, N.C., 1972), 9, 55; M. Eugene Sirmans, *Colonial South Carolina: A Political History, 1663–1763* (Chapel Hill, N.C., 1966), 210–16; Alexander Hewatt, *An Historical Account of the Rise and Progress of the Colonies of South Carolina and Georgia,* 2 vols. (1779, rpt. Spartanburg, S.C., 1971), 2:111–222.

5. Governor James Glen to Board of Trade, Oct. 10, 1748, South Carolina Public Records, XXIII, 211–230, South Carolina Archives.

6. C. R. Boxer, "The Dutch Economic Decline," in *Economic Decline of Empires,* ed. C. Cipolla (London, 1970), 235–63; A. C. Carter, *The Dutch Republic in Europe in the Seven Years War* (London, 1971), 129–35; Carter, *Neutrality or Commitment: The Evolution of Dutch Foreign Policy (1667–1795)* (London, 1975), 85–87.

7. Nash, "South Carolina," 682, 690–92; Weir, *Colonial South Carolina,* 166; U.S. Bureau of the Census, *Historical Statistics of the United States, Colonial Times to 1970,* 2 vols. (Washington, D.C., 1975), 2:1193.

8. *Historical Statistics of the U.S.,* 2:1192–93; David Chesnutt, "South Carolina's Penetration of Georgia in the 1760's: Henry Laurens as a Case Study," *South Carolina Historical Magazine* 73 (1972): 194–208; Douglas C. Wilms, "The Development of Rice Culture in Eighteenth-Century Georgia," *Southeastern Geographer* 12 (1972): 45–57. More generally, on the slow development of Georgia before 1750 and the accelerated growth in the late colonial period, Kenneth Coleman, *Colonial Georgia: A History* (New York, 1976), 111–16, 203–220; Betty Wood, *Slavery in Colonial Georgia, 1730–1775* (Athens, Ga., 1984), 91–98; Julia Floyd Smith, *Slavery and Rice Culture in Low Country Georgia, 1750–1860* (Knoxville, Tenn., 1985), 15–28.

9. Ramsay quoted in Menard, "Slavery, Economic Growth, and Revolutionary Ideology," 250.

10. James M. Clifton, "The Rice Industry in Colonial America," *Agricultural History* 55 (1981): 266–75; Peter Wood, *Black Majority: Negroes in Colonial South Carolina from 1670 through the Stono Rebellion* (New York, 1974), 35–62, discusses the possible contribution of slaves to rice cultivation; David L. Coon, *The Development of Market Agriculture in South Carolina, 1670–1785* (New York, 1989), 168–75; Joyce E. Chaplin, *An Anxious Pursuit: Agricultural Innovation and Modernity in the Lower South, 1730–1815* (Chapel Hill, N.C., 1993), 228–32.

11. Chaplin, *Anxious Pursuit,* quote on p. 230; Joyce E. Chaplin, "Tidal Rice Cultivation and the Problem of Slavery in South Carolina and Georgia, 1760–1815," *WMQ,* 3d ser., 49 (1992): 28–48.

12. Chaplin, *Anxious Pursuit,* 232–51; David Doar, *Rice and Rice Planting in the South Carolina Low Country* (Charleston, S.C., 1936), 7–42; Clifton, "Rice Industry," 275–77; Philip D. Morgan, "The Development of Slave Culture in Eighteenth-Century Plantation America" (D. Phil. diss., University College, London, 1977), 67–83; Coon, *Development of Market Agriculture,* 181–86.

13. Figures drawn from various sources all point to the same conclusion: increased productivity. See Clowse, *Economic Beginnings,* 170; Philip D. Morgan, "Work and Culture: The Task System and the World of Lowcountry Blacks, 1700 to 1880," *WMQ,* 3d ser., 39 (1982): 565–77; Coclanis, *Shadow of a Dream,* 96–97; Chaplin, *Anxious Pursuit,* 262–76; Weir, *Colonial South Carolina,* 150.

14. Nash, "South Carolina," 696; Chaplin, *Anxious Pursuit*, 251–62; Coclanis, *Shadow of a Dream*, 99–101; Clifton, "Rice Industry," 278; Morgan, "Development of Slave Culture," 72–75; Morgan, *Development of Market Agriculture*, 186–90.

15. Eliza Lucas to Mrs. Boddicott, May 2, [1740], *Letterbook of Eliza Lucas Pinckney*, xv–xvi, 7; Harriott Horry Ravenel, *Eliza Pinckney* (1896; rpt. Spartanburg, S.C., 1967), 1–9.

16. Quoted in *Letterbook of Eliza Lucas Pinckney*, 8; Ravenel, *Eliza Pinckney*, 7.

17. Eliza Lucas Pinckney to Charles Cotesworth Pinckney, Sept. 10, 1785, *Colonial South Carolina Scene*, 145–46; *Letterbook of Eliza Lucas Pinckney*, xvii–xx.

18. *Colonial South Carolina Scene*, 144–46; David L. Coon, "Eliza Lucas Pinckney and the Reintroduction of Indigo Culture in South Carolina," *Journal of Southern History* 42 (1976): 61–76; Lewis Cecil Gray, *History of Agriculture in the Southern United States to 1860*, 2 vols. (Washington, D.C., 1933), 2:290–97.

19. Menard, "Slavery, Economic Growth, and Revolutionary Ideology," 253–55; Chaplin, *Anxious Pursuit*, 190–208. The bounty fluctuated, but there was no close link between these changes and variations in the worth of exports. On this issue, see John J. McCusker and Russell R. Menard, *The Economy of British America, 1607–1789* (Chapel Hill, N.C., 1985), 186–87.

20. Nash, "South Carolina," 695; Weir, *Colonial South Carolina*, 150; [Charles Woodmason], "Expense of Purchasing a Plantation in South Carolina . . . ," in *Colonial South Carolina Scene*, 160–63, quote on p. 163; Ravenel, *Eliza Pinckney*, 4–14.

21. Ramsay quoted in McCusker and Menard, *Economy of British America*, 188; Alice Hanson Jones, *Wealth of a Nation To Be: The American Colonies on the Eve of the Revolution* (New York, 1980), 375–82.

22. Clowse, *Economic Beginnings*, 40–41, 63–66, 116–22, 162–66, 198–99, 207–8, 237–38; Coclanis, *Shadow of a Dream*, 80–81; James F. Shepherd and Gary M. Walton, *Shipping, Maritime Trade, and the Economic Development of Colonial North America* (Cambridge, Eng., 1972), 211–27; Verner W. Crane, *The Southern Frontier, 1670–1732* (Durham, N.C., 1928), 109–12, 177, 328–31.

23. Clowse, *Economic Beginnings*, 132–40, 170–76, 208–12, 232–42, 256–58; Coclanis, *Shadow of a Dream*, 80–81; Weir, *Colonial South Carolina*, 143–50.

24. Joseph A. Ernst and H. Roy Merrens, "Camden's Turrets Pierce the Skies!": The Urban Process in the Southern Colonies during the Eighteenth Century," *WMQ*, 3d ser., 30 (1973): 549–74; Coclanis, *Shadow of a Dream*, 67–77; Weir, *Colonial South Carolina*, 147; *Colonial South Carolina Scene*, 232–47, with quote from *Boston Chronicle* on p. 247. Efforts were also made to encourage the production of silk, but exports of this thread were rarely worth more than £1,000 sterling. See Lester J. Cappon et al., *Atlas of Early American History: The Revolutionary Era, 1760–1790* (Princeton, N.J., 1976), 26–31; Clowse, *Economic Beginnings*, 223–24; Coleman, *Colonial Georgia*, 113–16, 209.

25. Richard Splatt to William Cripps, Jan. 17, 1726, in *Colonial South Carolina Scene*, 77, 80.

26. Governor Robert Johnson to the Board of Trade, Jan. 12, 1720, in *Colonial South Carolina Scene*, 66.

27. Weir, *Colonial South Carolina*, 155–56; *Colonial South Carolina Scene*, 248–52, presents the 1768 tax account; on the changing status of merchants, also see the information presented in *Biographical Directory of the South Carolina House of Representatives*, vol. 2: *The Commons House of Assembly, 1692–1775*, ed. Walter B. Edgar and N. Louise Bailey (Columbia, S.C., 1977), passim.

28. Moses Lopez to Aaron Lopez, May 3, 1764, quoted in "Charlestown in 1764," ed. Thomas J. Tobias, *South Carolina Historical Magazine* 67 (1966): 67–68.

29. Peter Timothy to Benjamin Franklin, Sept. 3, 1768, *The Papers of Benjamin Franklin*, ed. Leonard W. Labaree et al. (New Haven, Conn., 1959–), 15:201–2; Henry Laurens to James Grant, Mar. 23, 1767, *The Papers of Henry Laurens*, ed. Philip M. Hamer et al. (Columbia, S.C., 1968–), 5:238–39.

30. Richard Walsh, *Charleston's Sons of Liberty: A Study of the Artisans, 1763–1789* (Columbia, S.C., 1959), 29–42; Marc Egnal, *A Mighty Empire: The Origins of the American Revolution* (Ithaca, N.Y., 1988), 139–42, 147–49.

31. Walsh, *Charleston's Sons of Liberty*, 56–68; *Atlas of Early American History*, 26–31.

32. Weir, *Colonial South Carolina*, 155–56.

33. Henry Laurens to Grubb & Watson, July 14, 1763, Laurens to Joseph Bower, Jan. 13, 1763, Laurens to Alexander & James Baillie, Apr. 28, 1763, *Papers of Laurens*, 3:489, 216, 429.

34. Lieutenant Governor William Bull noted in 1769: "Our back settlers . . . persist in their resolution not to be drawn down to Charleston by lawsuits, where by high fees and unprofitable sale of their lands and chattels so far from their homes they are often ruined without being able thereby to pay their creditors." See Lt. Gov. William Bull to earl of Hillsborough, Sept. 7, 1769, South Carolina Public Records, XXXII, 101; Henry Laurens to Capt. Robert Dodson, Sept. 13, 1768, *Papers of Laurens*, 6:110–11.

35. Lt. Gov. William Bull to Board of Trade, Dec. 17, 1765, South Carolina Public Records, XXX, 300; Laurens to Isaac King, Sept. 30, 1767, *Papers of Laurens*, 5:320; *Commons House of Assembly*, 460–61; E. Donnan, "The Slave Trade into South Carolina before the American Revolution," *American Historical Review* 33 (1928): 804–28; D. C. Littlefield, *Rice and Slaves: Ethnicity and the Slave Trade in Colonial South Carolina* (Baton Rouge, La., 1981), 20–21, 63–66, 135.

36. A. Roger Ekirch, *"Poor Carolina": Politics and Society in Colonial North Carolina, 1729–1776* (Chapel Hill, N.C., 1981), 18, quote on p. 4.

37. Ibid., quotes on p. 15; Harry Roy Merrens, *Colonial North Carolina in the Eighteenth Century: A Study in Historical Geography* (Chapel Hill, N.C., 1964), 142–55.

38. Anne Bezanson et al., *Prices in Colonial Pennsylvania* (Philadelphia, 1935), 151, appendix. The statistical evidence bearing on North Carolina must be treated with caution. Philadelphia prices are an uncertain proxy for southern staples. To be sure, Philadelphia quotations are reasonably representative of movements in the value of South Carolina rice, but they correlate less clearly with the changing worth of Chesapeake tobacco. See Ekirch, *"Poor Carolina"*, 12. Also note that data on the value of North Carolina naval stores is contradictory. Merrens, in *Colonial North Carolina*, 90–91, 94–96, presents quantity figures that suggest exports of over £40,000 sterling. That high figure is based on Merrens's quantities and price data extracted from Shepherd and Walton, *Shipping, Maritime Trade*, 213–27. However, Shepherd and Walton's own figures based on Customs 16:1 and those presented in *Historical Statistics of the U.S.*, 2:1184, indicate a value closer to £30,000 sterling.

39. Merrens, *Colonial North Carolina*, 90–96; Ekirch, "*Poor Carolina*," 12.

40. Ekirch, "*Poor Carolina*," 4, 12; Merrens, *Colonial North Carolina*, 120–23; Shepherd and Walton, *Shipping, Maritime Trade*, 213–27.

41. Merrens, *Colonial North Carolina*, 109–15, quote on p. 131; Ekirch, "*Poor Carolina*," 4, 12–15.

42. Ekirch, "*Poor Carolina,*"13–14, quote on p. 14; Merrens, *Colonial North Carolina*, 125–31; James M. Clifton, "Golden Grains of White: Rice Planting on the Lower Cape Fear," *North Carolina Historical Review* 50 (1973): 365–69.

43. Ekirch, "*Poor Carolina,*"11–26; Merrens, *Colonial North Carolina*, 73–79; Charles C. Crittenden, *The Commerce of North Carolina, 1763–1789*, Yale Historical Publications, *Miscellany*, vol. 30 (New Haven, 1936), 1–13, 53–58, 75–76.

44. Quote from Ekirch, "*Poor Carolina*," 3.

CHAPTER SEVEN

1. Most historians see evidence of both slow growth during this long swing and (in the years before 1689) signs of renewal. F. Crouzet, "England and France in the Eighteenth Century: A Comparative Analysis of Two Economic Growths," in *The Causes of the Industrial Revolution in England*, ed. R. M. Hartwell (London, 1967), 139–74, has a dour view of the years from 1660 to 1715, and comes close to the idea of the "tragic seventeenth century," a concept that dominated an earlier generation of economic historians. But even Crouzet sees stirrings of growth in these decades. By contrast, Ralph Davis, *The Rise of the Atlantic Economies* (London, 1973), 90–96, 227–30, is thoroughly revisionist, though never arguing that the pace of development in the seventeenth century approached that evident in the eighteenth. Like Davis, Ernest Labrousse et al., *Histoire économique et sociale de la France*, vol. 2, *Des derniers temps de l'âge seigneurial aux préludes de l'âge industriel (1660–1789)* (Paris, 1970), 331–34, takes a balanced but positive view of this era. See also Emmanuel Le Roy Ladurie, *The Territory of the Historian* (Sussex, England, 1979), 200–1.

2. Davis, *Rise of the Atlantic Economies*, 98–104, 218–23; Labrousse, *Histoire économique*, 104–18; Micheline Baulant, "Le prix des grain à Paris de 1431 à 1788," *Annales* 23 (1968): 520–37; Pierre Goubert, "Recent Theories and Research in French Population between 1500 and 1700," in *Population in History*, ed. D. V. Glass and D. E. C. Eversley (Chicago, 1965), 466–69; Roger Dion, *Histoire de la vigne et du vin en France, des origines au XIX siècle* (Paris, 1959).

3. Davis, *Rise of the Atlantic Economies*, 168–69, 226–27, 235–36; Pierre Dardel, *Navires et marchandises dans les ports de Rouen et du Havre au XVIIIe siècle* (Paris, 1963), 96–100, 122–25; Labrousse, *Histoire économique*, 195–98; Jean-Michel Deveau, *La traite rochelaise* (Paris, 1990), 15–17; Robert Louis Stein, "The Nantes Slave Traders, 1783–1815" (Ph.D. diss., York University, 1975), 2–14.

4. Labrousse, *Histoire économique*, 267–68, 351; Davis, *Rise of the Atlantic Economies*, 223–24, 294–95; Louis-Philippe May, *Histoire économique de la Martinique (1635–1763)* (Paris, 1930), 54–85.

5. Taxes, which fell largely on the rural poor, climbed during the war years. See Labrousse, *Histoire économique*, 269–72, 360–63; Crouzet, "England and France," 146–47; Davis, *Rise of the Atlantic Economies*, 119–20, 168–70, 229–30; Jean Meyer, *L'armement nantais dans la deuxième moitié du XVIIIe siècle* (Paris, 1969), 81–88; Pierre Goubert, *Familles marchandes sous l'Ancien Régime: Les Danse et les Motte, de Beauvais* (Paris, 1959), 94–108. Marcel Lachiver, *Les anneés de misère: La famine au temps du Grand Roi, 1680–1720* (Paris, 1991), 96–123, 349–84, shows how bad weather led to ruined harvests and starvation. Consult also David R. Weir, "Markets and Mortality in France, 1600–1789," in *Famine, Disease, and Social Order in Early Modern Society*, ed. John Walter and Roger Schofield (Cambridge, Eng., 1989), 201–34; François Lebrun, "Les crises démographiques en France aux XVIIe et XVIIIe

siècles," *Annales* 35 (1980): 205–34; Pierre Léon, "La Crise de l'économie française à la fin du règne de Louis XIV (1685–1715)," *L'Information historique*, 4 (1956): 127–37. Andrew Appleby, "Grain Prices and Subsistence Crises in England and France, 1590–1740," *JEH* 39 (1979): 865–87, argues that the lack of diversification in French agriculture exacerbated these crises. Unlike England, the French did not have other, cheaper grains to turn to when wheat failed. Jacques Dupâquier, "Demographic Crises and Subsistence Crises in France, 1650–1725," in *Famine, Disease, and Social Order*, 189–99, modifies Appleby's argument.

6. Labrousse, *Histoire économique*, 12–13, 269–70, 359–65; Crouzet, "England and France," 141–45; Davis, *Rise of the Atlantic Economies*, 122–24, 228–29.

7. David R. Weir, "Life Under Pressure: France and England, 1670–1870," *JEH* 44 (1984): 21–41; Weir, "Les crises économiques et les origines de la Révolution Française," *Annales* 46 (1991): 917–36; Labrousse, *Histoire économique*, 367–78; Goubert, "Recent Theories," 471–73; Jean Meuvret, "Les crises de subsistances et la démographie de la France d'ancien régime," *Population* 1 (1946): 643–50; David S. Landes, "The Statistical Study of French Crises," *JEH* 10 (1950): 195–211, argues that the relationship between harvest fluctuations and prosperity was a complex one.

8. Davis, *Rise of the Atlantic Economies*, 289–95; Labrousse, *Histoire économique*, 383–91; Pierre Dardel, *Commerce, industrie, et navigation à Rouen et au Havre au XVIIe siècle: Rivalté croissante entre ces deux ports*, La conjoncture (Rouen, 1966), 21–36, 73–77; Appleby, "Grain Prices," 885–87; Weir, "Markets and Mortality," 218–32; Jacques Dupâquier, "Demographic Crises and Subsistence Crises in France, 1650–1725," in *Famine, Disease, and Social Order*, 189–99.

9. Philip T. Hoffman, "Land Rents and Agricultural Productivity: The Paris Basin, 1450–1789," *JEH* 51 (1991), 771–805.

10. Crouzet, "England and France," 152–53; Davis, *Rise of the Atlantic Economies*, 220–23.

11. Davis, *Rise of the Atlantic Economies*, 250–63; Paul Butel, *Les négociants bordelais l'Europe et les Iles au XVIIIe siècle* (Paris, 1974) 24–35, 107–110; Crouzet, "England and France," 148–49.

12. J. F. Bosher, "The French Crisis of 1770," *History* 57 (1972): 17–30; Ernest Labrousse, *Esquisse du mouvement des prix et des revenus en France au XVIIIe siècle*, 2 vols. (Paris, 1933), 1:106–14.

13. Davis, *Rise of the Atlantic Economies*, 113–14, 118–19; Crouzet, "England and France," 152–54; L. M. Cullen, "History, Economic Crises, and Revolution: Understanding Eighteenth-century France," *Economic History Review* 46 (1993): 635–57; Weir, "Les crises économiques," 917–47; Ernst Labrousse, *La crise de l'économie française à la fin de l'Ancien Régime et au début de la Révolution* (Paris, 1944), 278–83, 321–61. Labrousse, *Histoire économique*, 23–49, 130–47, argues for a long-term ascent that stretched from 1715 to 1789, and suggests that the problems evident after 1770 were really short-term fluctuations.

14. Labrousse, *Histoire économique*, 380–99, 418–432, 453–61, 473–95, 545–62; Crouzet, "England and France," 150–57; Robert Stein, "The State of French Colonial Commerce on the Eve of the Revolution," *Journal of European Economic History* 12 (1983): 105–17, provides valuable statistics on French trade. See also Charles P. Kindleberger, "Financial Institutions and Economic Development: A Comparison of Great Britain and France in the Eighteenth and Nineteenth Centuries," *Explorations in Economic History* 21 (1984): 103–5; Ladurie, *Territory of the Historian*, 201–2; Davis, *Rise of the Atlantic Economies*, 292–93.

CHAPTER EIGHT

1. François-Xavier de Charlevoix, *Journal of a Voyage to North America*, 2 vols. (1761; facsimile rpt., Ann Arbor University Microfilms, 1966), 1:113–114: "Pierre-François-Xavier de Charlevoix," *DCB*, 3:103–110. Charlevoix visited Canada in 1705–8 and again in 1720–21. While the 1720-21 visit came during the beginnings of the second long swing, more rapid growth was not yet evident.

2. Coat beaver (*castor gras*) was the fur that had been worn by the native people. These pelts were prized because contact with the skin softened them. Parchment beaver (*castor sec*) was sun dried, and had not been softened by wear.

3. A. J. E. Lunn, "Economic Development in New France, 1713–1760" (Ph.D. diss., McGill Univ., 1942), 235; Denys Delâge, "Les structures économiques de la Nouvelle France et de la Nouvelle York," *L'Actualité économique* 46 (1970): 113; Louise Dechêne, *Habitants et marchands de Montréal au XVIIe siècle* (Paris and Montreal, 1974), 143; Harris, *The Seigneurial System in Early Canada: A Geographical Study* (Madison, Wis., 1966), 90–91, 113; Marcel Trudel, *Introduction to New France* (Toronto, 1968), 67–71, 95; W. J. Eccles, *The Canadian Frontier, 1534–1760* (New York, 1960), 56–57, 64, 71, 85, 104–106; Eccles, *Canada under Louis XIV, 1663–1701* (Toronto, 1964), 23–76; James Pritchard, "Commerce in New France," in *Canadian Business History: Selected Studies, 1497–1971*, ed. David S. Macmillan (Toronto, 1972), 30; R. Cole Harris and Geoffrey J. Matthews, eds., *Historical Atlas of Canada*, vol. 1, *From the Beginnings to 1800* (Toronto, 1987), 86–87, plates 35–38.

4. Only a third of those settling along the St. Lawrence were female. Harris, *Seigneurial System*, 109; Guy Frégault, "The Colonization of Canada in the Eighteenth Century," [orig. pub. in *Cahiers de L'Académie canadienne-française* 2 (1957): 53–81], trans. and rpt. in *Society and Conquest: The Debate on the Bourgeoisie and Social Change in French Canada, 1700–1850*, ed. Dale Miquelon (Toronto, 1977), 95; Trudel, *Introduction to New France*, 1–67; Leslie P. Choquette, "French Emigration to Canada in the 17th and 18th centuries," 2 vols. (Ph.D. diss., Harvard University, 1988), 2: 523–27; Jan Noel, "New France: Les Femmes Favorisées," in *Rethinking Canada: the Promise of Women's History*, ed. Veronica Strong-Boag and Anita Clair Tellman, 2d ed. (Toronto, 1991), 36–41; Louise Dechêne, *Habitants and Merchants in Seventeenth-Century Montreal*, trans. Liana Vardi (Montreal and Kingston, 1992), 16–17, 292–93; Eccles, *Canada under Louis XIV*, 47.

5. Harris, *Seigneurial System*, 90–91, 179; Trudel, *Introduction to New France*, 67–68.

6. Talon to Colbert, Oct. 4, 1665, quoted in F. W. Burton, "The Wheat Supply of New France," Royal Society of Canada *Proceedings and Transactions*, 3d Ser., 30 (1936), section 2:138.

7. In 1667 Quebec, Montreal, and Trois Rivières had about 1,420 residents, a remarkable 39 percent of the settlers in Canada. While this proportion soon dropped, it stood well above 25 percent in 1672 (fig. 8.2). See Hubert Charbonneau and Jacques Légaré, "La population du Canada aux recensements de 1666 et 1667," *Population* 22 (1967): 1031–54; Charbonneau and Légaré, "Recensements et registres paroissiaux du Canada durant la période 1665–1668," ibid., 97–124. The two articles discuss the strengths and shortcomings of the population data.

8. Marie de l'Incarnation, 1665, quoted in W. J. Eccles, "The Social, Economic, and Political Significance of the Military Establishment in New France," *Canadian Historical Review* 52 (1971): 1–22, quote on p. 3; Pritchard, "Commerce in New

France," 30; Jack Verney, *The Good Regiment: The Carignan–Salières Regiment in Canada, 1665–1668* (Montreal, 1991), 110, and passim.

9. John Hare, Marc Lafrance, and David-Thierry Ruddel, *Histoire de la ville de Québec, 1608–1871* (Montreal, 1987), 23, 39; Dechêne, *Habitants and Merchants*, 55–57, 260–78; Dechêne, "La croissance de Montréal au XVIIIe siècle," *RHAF* 27 (1973): 175; Phyllis Lambert and Alan Stewart, eds., *Opening the Gates of Eighteenth-Century Montréal* (Montreal, 1992), 55-57; Pierre-Georges Roy, *La ville de Québec sous le régime français*, 2 vols. (Quebec, 1930), 1:317–22; *Historical Atlas of Canada*, 1:114, plate 49.

10. Eccles, *Canada under Louis XIV*, 20–27, 54–76, 101; Eccles, *Canadian Frontier*, 62, 105; Dechêne, *Habitants and Merchants*, 5–8, 91–92; Lambert and Stewart, *Opening the Gates*, 52.

11. Eccles, *Canadian Frontier*, 71, 106; Lunn, "Economic Development," 235; Trudel, *Introduction to New France*, 67; Delâge, "Les structures économiques," 113; Pritchard, "Commerce in New France," 30; Roy, *La ville de Québec*, 1:329–32.

12. Harris, *Seigneurial System*, 89.

13. Delâge, "Les structures économiques," 97; Trudel, *Introduction to New France*, 67; Pritchard, "Commerce in New France," 29; J. F. Bosher, "The Political and Religious Origins of La Rochelle's Primacy in Trade with New France, 1627–1685," *French History* 7 (1993): 286–312; Bosher, *The Canada Merchants, 1713–1763* (Oxford, Eng., 1987), 12–15, 22–43.

14. Joseph-Noël Fauteux, *Essai sur l'industrie au Canada sous le régime français*, 2 vols. (Quebec, 1927), 1:40–41, 174–76.

15. James S. Pritchard, "The Pattern of French Colonial Shipping to Canada before 1760," *Revue Française d'Histoire d'Outre-mer* 63 (1976): 193, 201; Eccles, *Canada under Louis XIV*, 100; Pritchard, "Commerce in New France," 32–33; Eccles, "Social, Economic, and Political Significance," 5–6; Eccles, *Canadian Frontier*, 101; Adam Shortt, ed. *Documents Relating to Canadian Currency, Exchange and Finance During the French Period*, 2 vols. (Ottawa, 1925),1:65–81; Jay Cassell, "The Troupes de la Marine in Canada, 1683–1760: Men and Materiel" (Ph.D. diss., University of Toronto, 1987), 45–50, 142–43, 218–34, 437–49; Demeulles would have been unable to pay the troops without issuing card money.

16. Harris, *Seigneurial System*, 144; Eccles, *Canada under Louis XIV*, 104, 119–147; Eccles, *Canadian Frontier*, 107–109; W. J. Eccles, "The Fur Trade and Eighteenth-Century Imperialism," *WMQ*, 3rd ser., 40 (1983), 342; *Historical Atlas of Canada*, 1: 87, plate 38.

17. Quote from Eccles, *Canadian Frontier*, 110; Dechêne, *Habitants and Merchants*, 85–94.

18. Harris, *Seigneurial System*, 144; Eccles, *Canada under Louis XIV*, 119–47; Robert A. Goldstein, *French–Iroquois Diplomatic and Military Relations, 1609–1701* (The Hague, 1969), 166–69; Louise Dechêne, *Le Partage des subsistances au Canada sous le régime français* (Quebec, 1994), 16.

19. Roy, *La ville de Québec*, 1:443–44; Pritchard, "Commerce in New France," 30; Eccles, *Canada under Louis XIV*, 100, quotes Frontenac. See also ibid., 125–27. In 1673 the tar furnaces at Baie St. Paul also closed because of the decline in French funding. Quebec, as modern visitors are aware, is divided into a Lower Town and an Upper Town with a steep set of steps connecting the two. During the French regime the merchants lived in the Lower Town near the river, while most Church buildings were in the Upper Town.

20. Hare, *Histoire de la ville de Québec*, 62–64; Eccles, *Canada under Louis XIV*, 138–40; J. F. Bosher, "Les origines cosmopolite du commerce canadien à Bordeaux," *Etudes Canadiennes* (Bordeaux), 17 (1994): 29–36; Harold Innis, *The Fur Trade in Canada: An Introduction to Canadian Economic History*, rev. ed. (Toronto, 1956), 58; Dechêne, *Habitants and Merchants*, 72–78; "Aubert de la Chesnaye," *DCB*, 2: 28–29. The end of the West Indies Company did not mean free trade. In 1675 the Company of the Farm, based in France, was given the right to market all beaver pelts.

21. See Dechêne, *Habitants and Merchants*, 59–60, 101, 297; Eccles, *Canada under Louis XIV*, 133–51.

22. Hare, *Histoire de la ville de Québec*, 52–53, 94; Dechêne, *Habitants and Merchants*, 59; Eccles, *Canadian Frontier*, 69; Trudel, *Introduction to New France*, 228–30; Roy, *La ville de Québec*, 1:485–86; Tony Gelfand, "Medicine in New France," in *Medicine in the New World: New Spain, New France, and New England*, ed. Ronald L. Numbers (Knoxville, Tenn., 1989), 85–90.

23. J. F. Bosher, "Political and Religious Origins," 286–312; Jacques Mathieu, *Le commerce entre la Nouvelle-France et les Antilles au XVIIIe siècle* (Montreal, 1981), 1–20.

24. Minister of the Marine to intendant and governor of New France, 1712, quoted in Frégault, "Colonization of Canada," 91–92; Pritchard, "Commerce in New France," 33, 39; Pritchard, "Pattern of French Colonial Shipping," 193–194, 201; "Michel Bégon de la Picardière," *DCB*, 3:58, quotes Charles de Monseignat; Lunn, "Economic Development," 386; Dechêne, *Habitants et marchands*, 136–40. Most individuals, to be sure, were not on fixed incomes. But some members of the military, religious, and civil establishments were in that category.

25. Innis, *Fur Trade in Canada*, 68–81; Eccles, *Canadian Frontier*, 120–125; Dale Miquelon, *New France, 1701–1744: "A Supplement to Europe"* (Toronto, 1987), 56–58; "Antoine Laumet, dit de Lamothe Cadillac," *DCB*, 2:353–54.

26. "François de Beauharnois de la Chaussaye, Baron de Beauville," *DCB*, 3: 52, quotes the intendant; Guy Frégault, "La compagnie de la colonie," in *Le XVIIIe siècle Canadien: études* (Montreal, 1968), 242–288; Jean Hamelin, *Economie et société en Nouvelle-France* (Quebec, 1960), 48–65; Dechêne, *Habitants et marchands*, 144, 228; Eccles, *Canadian Frontier*, 126–137; Pritchard, "Commerce in New France," 39; "Beauharnois de la Chaussaye," *DCB*, 3:52; Eccles, *Canada under Louis XIV*, 202, 245; Lunn, "Economic Development," 136–156; "Aubert de La Chesnaye," *DCB*, 2: 32–33; Gratien Allaire, "Les engagements pour la traite des fourrures," *RHAF* 34 (1980): 3–15; Allaire, "Officiers et marchands: les sociétés de commerce des fourrures, 1715–1760," ibid., 40 (1987): 424–25; Allaire, "Le commerce des fourrures à Montréal: documentation et méthode d'analyse," in *"Le Castor Fait Tout": Selected Papers of the Fifth North American Fur Trade Conference, 1985*, ed. Bruce C. Trigger et al. (Montreal, 1987), 93–121; Thomas Wien, "Selling Beaver Skins in North America and Europe, 1720–1760: The Uses of Fur-Trade Imperialism," *Journal of the Canadian Historical Association* 1 (1990): 293–317; Philippe Haudrère, *La Compagnie française des Indes au XVIIIe siècle (1719–1795)*, 4 vols. (Paris, 1989).

27. "Philippe de Rigaud de Vaudreuil," *DCB*, 2:566; Eccles, *Canada under Louis XIV*, 185–209, with Champigny quote on p. 185.

28. Lambert and Stewart, *Opening the Gates*, 19–20, 34–36; Dechêne, "Croissance de Montréal," 167; Dechêne, *Habitants and Merchants*, 17.

29. Dechêne, *Habitants and Merchants*, 59; Hare, *Histoire de la ville de Québec*, 29.

30. Eccles, *Canadian Frontier*, 69; Trudel, *Introduction to New France*, 228–230; "Antoine-Denis Raudot," *DCB*, 2:551–552; "François de Beauharnois de la Chaussaye,

Baron de Beauville," *DCB*, 2:52; "Bégon," *DCB*, 3:59; "Vaudreuil," *DCB*, 2:570; W. J. Eccles, "Social Welfare Measures and Policies in New France," in *Essays on New France*, ed. W. J. Eccles (Toronto, 1987), 38–49; Antoine Silvy, *Letters from North America*, trans. I. A. Dickson (Belleville, Ont., 1980), 96–97; Hare, *Histoire de la ville de Québec*, 36–40, 52; Roy, *La ville de Québec*, 1:485–86, 527–28; 2:17–18.

31. Pritchard, "Pattern of Commerce in New France," 31–39; Pritchard, "French Colonial Shipping," 198–200.

CHAPTER NINE

1. Donald James Horton, "Gilles Hocquart, Intendant of New France, 1729–1748" (Ph.D. diss., McGill Univ., 1974), 28–40; "Gilles Hocquart," *DCB*, 4:354–65; Jean-Claude Dubé, *Les intendants de la Nouvelle-France* (Montreal, 1984), 78–79. When Hocquart arrived in Canada in 1729 he was, technically, financial commissary and *acting* intendant. Only in the 1730s did he receive a full appointment as intendant.

2. Morris Altman, "Economic Growth in Canada, 1695–1739: Estimates and Analysis," *WMQ*, 3d ser., 45 (1988): 684–711.

3. A. J. E. Lunn, "Economic Development in New France, 1713–1760" (Ph.D. diss., McGill Univ., 1942), 115, 142–48, 351, 450; "Vaudreuil," *DCB*, 2:570–71; Louise Dechêne, *Habitants et marchands de Montréal au XVIIe siècle* (Paris and Montreal, 1974), 510, 512, presents graphs detailing the number of individuals heading west and the volume of credit extended. See also Harold A. Innis, *Fur Trade in Canada: An Introduction to Canadian Economic History*, rev. ed. (Toronto, 1930, 1956), 72–73; R. Cole Harris and Geoffrey J. Matthews, eds., *Historical Atlas of Canada*, vol. 1, *From the Beginnings to 1800* (Toronto, 1987), plates 39–41. John Law's Compagnie d'Occident was granted a monopoly of the beaver trade. In 1720 the Compagnie des Indes gained this privilege and kept it until 1760.

4. Louise Dechêne, *Habitants and Merchants in Seventeenth-Century Montreal*, trans. Liana Vardi (Montreal and Kingston, 1992), 67, 95; *Historical Atlas of Canada*, 1:87.

5. F. W. Burton, "The Wheat Supply of New France," Royal Society of Canada, *Proceedings and Transactions*, 3d ser., 30 (1936): section 2, 137–50; Lunn, "Economic Development," 443–44; Dechêne, *Habitants et marchands*, 338–47; Louise Dechêne, *Le partage des subsistances au Canada sous le régime français* (Quebec, 1994), 23–27, discusses the group of peasants who supplied grain for export.

6. Christopher Moore, "The Other Louisbourg: Trade and Merchant Enterprise in Ile Royale, 1713–58," *Histoire Sociale/Social History* 12 (1979): 79–96; Julian Gwyn, *The Enterprising Admiral: The Personal Fortune of Admiral Sir Peter Warren* (Montreal, 1974), 15, 19–20; Charles de la Morandière, *Histoire de la pêche française de la Morue dans l'Amérique Septentrionale*, 3 vols. (Paris, 1962–66), 2:662–64, 687; "Antoine-Denis Raudot," *DCB*, 2: 551; Dale Miquelon, *Dugard of Rouen: French Trade to Canada and the West Indies, 1729–1770* (Montreal, 1978), 11; Guy Frégault, "The Colonization of Canada in the Eighteenth Century," in *Society and Conquest: The Debate on the Bourgeoisie and Social Change in French Canada, 1700–1850*, ed. Dale Miquelon (Toronto, 1977), 98; James Pritchard, "The Voyage of the *Fier*: An Analysis of a Shipping and Trading Venture to New France, 1724–1728," *Histoire Sociale/ Social History* 6 (1973): 77, 85–86; *Historical Atlas of Canada*, 1: plate 24; Christopher Moore, *Louisbourg Portraits: Life in an Eighteenth-Century Garrison Town* (Toronto, 1982), 209, 296–97; J. S. McLennan, *Louisbourg: From Its Foundation to Its Fall, 1713–1758* (Sydney, Nova Scotia, 1975), 71–76.

7. Phyllis Lambert and Alan Stewart, eds., *Opening the Gates of Eighteenth-Century Montréal* (Montreal, 1992), 15–26; Robert Rumilly, *Histoire de Montréal*, 5 vols. (Ottawa, 1970), 1: 321–23; Dechêne, *Habitants and Merchants*, 310, 312, presents graphs showing the revival of the fur trade; Catherine M. Desbarats, "Colonial Government Finances in New France, 1700–1750" (Ph.D. diss., McGill Univ., 1993), 177–81, shows outlays for fortifications; E. R. Adair, "The Evolution of Montreal under the French Regime," Canadian Historical Association, *Report of the Annual Meeting with Historical Papers* (Toronto, 1942), 35–36, indicates that the city walls had little military value.

8. John Hare, Marc Lafrance, David-Thierry Ruddel, *Histoire de la ville de Québec, 1608–1871* (Montreal, 1987), 30, 52–60; André Charbonneau, *Québec, the Fortified City: From the 17th to the 19th Century* (Ottawa, 1982), 47–57; Pierre-Georges Roy, *La ville de Québec sous le régime français*, 2 vols. (Quebec, 1930), 2:119–20; "Charles de Beauharnois de la Boische," *DCB*, 3:45.

9. "Antoine-Denis Raudot," *DCB*, 2:551; Miquelon, *Dugard of Rouen*, 11; Frégault, "Colonization of Canada," 98; Lunn, "Economic Development," 96, 386–401; "Bégon," *DCB*, 3:57, 60; Rumilly, *Histoire de Montréal*, 1:313–14; Richard Colebrook Harris, *The Seigneurial System in Early Canada: A Geographical Study* (Madison, Wis., 1966), 64–69; Adam Shortt, *Adam Shortt's History of Canadian Currency and Banking, 1600–1880* (compilation of articles pub. 1896–1906; Toronto, 1986), presents valuable material on money during this era.

10. Thomas Wien, "Castor, peaux, et pelleteries dans le commerce canadien des fourrures, 1720–1790," in *Le Castor Fait Tout: Selected Papers of the Fifth North American Fur Trade Conference, 1985,* ed. Bruce G. Trigger et al. (Montreal, 1987), 72–92.

11. In the mid-1730s exports of parchment beaver were worth about twice those of coat beaver. See Wien, "Castor, peaux, et pelleteries," 73.

12. Dale Miquelon, *New France, 1701–1744: "A Supplement to Europe"* (Toronto, 1987), 3–5, 167–89; Jean Lunn, "The Illegal Fur Trade Out of New France, 1713–1760," Canadian Historical Association, *Report of the Annual Meeting* (1939), 61–76; R. David Edmunds and Joseph L. Peyser, *The Fox Wars: The Mesquakie Challenge to New France* (Norman, Oklahoma, 1993), 119–57, 178–201.

13. Lunn, "Economic Development," 94–103.

14. Frégault, "Colonization of Canada," 98; Lunn, "Economic Development," 96; Miquelon, *Dugard of Rouen*, 95–96; James Pritchard, "Commerce in New France," in *Canadian Business History: Selected Studies, 1497–1971,* ed. David S. Macmillan (Toronto, 1972), 41; Corinne Beutler, "Le rôle du blé à Montréal sous le régime seigneurial," *RHAF* 36 (1982): 242–43; "François Bigot," *DCB*, 4: 61–62; Jean Kupp, "Could the Dutch Commercial Empire Have Influenced the Canadian Economy during the First Half of the Eighteenth Century?" *Canadian Historical Review* 52 (1971): 371–372, presents valuable figures for the trade of Louisbourg; Denys Delâge, "Les structures économiques de la Nouvelle-France et de la Nouvelle York," *l'Actualité économique*, 46 (1970): 93–96; Jean François Brière, "Le commerce triangulaire entre les ports terre-neuviers français, les pêcheries d'Amérique du Nord et Marseille au XVIIIe siècle: nouvelles perspectives," *RHAF* 40 (1986): 193–98; Jacques Mathieu, *Le commerce entre la Nouvelle-France et les Antilles au XVIIIe siècle* (Montreal, 1981), 238, makes a distinction between the original worth of the cod and the Caribbean valuation. Note also that the figures for Isle Royale include a few cargoes directed to Acadia.

15. Alan Gowans, *Looking at Architecture in Canada* (Toronto, 1958), 48–52; Frégault, "Colonization of Canada," 96–98; Harris, *Seigneurial System*, 114; *Historical Atlas of Canada*, 1: plates 55, 56. In the period 1727–1760 less than one-fifth of rural homes had stone walls.

16. Hare, *Histoire de la ville de Québec*, 31, 42; Lunn, "Economic Development," 90–91; Miquelon, *Dugard of Rouen*, 70–90. On the makeup of the Quebec merchant community, see "François Martel de Brouague," "Pierre Trottier Desauniers," *DCB*, 3:433–34, 631–32; Cameron Nish, *François-Etienne Cugnet: entrepreneurs et entreprise en Nouvelle-France* (Montreal, 1975).

17. Lunn, "Economic Development," 219–57; Hare, *Histoire de la ville de Québec*, 32.

18. Louise Dechêne, "La croissance de Montréal au XVIIIe siècle," *RHAF* 27 (1973): 173–74; Dechêne, *Habitants et marchands*, 182, uses the term "marchands-voyageurs" (merchant-voyageurs) to distinguish these traders who went west from the *engagés* (indentured servants) who also would be called voyageurs. I am indebted to Thomas Wien for pointing out this usage.

19. Dechêne, *Habitants et marchands*, 219–20; Rumilly, *Histoire de Montréal*, 1:325–26; Camille Bertrand, *Histoire de Montréal*, 2 vols. (Montreal, 1935–1942), 1:199; "Charles de Beauharnois de la Boische," *DCB*, 3:43–47; Innis, *Fur Trade in Canada*, 86–101; Peter N. Moogk, *Building a House in New France: An Account of the Perplexities of Client and Craftsmen in Early Canada* (Toronto, 1977), 49–61; Moogk, "The Craftsmen of New France" (Ph.D. diss., Univ. of Toronto, 1973), 12; Gowans, *Looking at Architecture*, 43–52; Delâge, "Les structures économiques," 93–96; Guy Frégault, *Le XVIIIe siècle canadien: études* (Montreal, 1968), 291; *Historical Atlas of Canada*, 1: plates 55, 56. Fires in 1721 and 1734 spurred the shift to stone construction in Montreal.

20. Lunn, "Economic Development," 213–330; "Hocquart," *DCB*, 4:357–64; Frégault, "Colonization of Canada," 98–100; Delâge, "Les structures économiques," 107–108; Louise Trottier, *Les Forges: historiographie des Forges du Saint-Maurice, 1729–1883, 150 ans d'occupation et d'exploitation* (Montreal, 1988), 44, 72–73.

21. Dechêne, *Habitants and Merchants*, 96–113, provides an excellent analysis of the importance of credit in seventeenth-century Canada.

22. Hocquart to Maurepas, Oct. 27, 1732, quoted in *Society and Conquest*, 133; Miquelon, *Dugard of Rouen*, 39–48, 86; Dechêne, *Habitants and Merchants*, 70–71.

23. Between 1736 and 1741 the Crown lent or gave 500,000 livres to such enterprises as the Saint-Maurice ironworks and the Quebec shipyards. See Dechêne, *Habitants et marchands*, 182–212; Michelon, *Dugard of Rouen*, 76–80; Maurepas to Hocquart, quoted in "Gilles Hocquart," *DCB*, 4:358–59; Lunn, "Economic Development," 293–318, 400–17; Frégault, *Le XVIIe siècle canadien*, 289–363; Lambert and Stewart, *Opening the Gates*, 28.

24. Lunn, "Economic Development," 364, 368, 477; Frégault, "Colonization of Canada," 97; Mathieu, *Le commerce entre la Nouvelle-France et les Antilles*, 177, 212; James S. Pritchard, "The Pattern of French Colonial Shipping to Canada before 1760," *Revue française d'histoire d'outre-mer* 63 (1976): 195–97, 201–8. The figures for imports and exports do not agree with the detailed breakdowns we have for trade in 1736 and 1739; cf. Delâge, "Les structures économiques," 93–96; Frégault, *Le XVIIIe siècle canadien*, 291; Moore, "Other Louisbourg," 86–90, 93.

25. James S. Pritchard, "Pattern of French Colonial Shipping," 201–10; J. F. Bosher, *Business and Religion in the Age of New France, 1600–1760: Twenty-two Studies* (Toronto, 1994), 464–86.

26. Lunn, "Economic Development," 243–79, 319–41, 415–26; Frégault, *Le XVIIIe siècle canadien*, 338–50; Frégault, "Colonization of Canada," 99; Emilion Petit is quoted in "Bigot," *DCB*, 4:67–68.

27. "Hocquart," *DCB*, 4:363; *Historical Atlas of Canada*, 1: plates 40, 41. Those interested in the volume of the fur trade should consult several graphs: (1) figure 8.5, showing the weight of beaver received by the companies; (2) figure 9.5 indicating fur shipments to La Rochelle; (3) graph of fur trade employees leaving Montreal, 1700–1764, in *Historical Atlas of Canada*, 1: plate 41; (4) Canadian beaver exports to France and Britain, 1645–1786, ibid., 1: plate 48; and (5) fur and hide imports to La Rochelle and London, 1718–78, ibid., 1: plate 48.

28. Lunn, "Economic Development," 118–24, 151–53, 175–76, 279.

29. Ibid., 112–115, 176; "Bigot," *DCB*, 4:64–66; Innis, *Fur Trade in Canada*, 111–112, 119–145; Marcel Trudel, *Introduction to New France* (Toronto, 1968), 125; William L. Marr and Donald G. Paterson, *Canada: An Economic History* (Toronto, 1980), 56–58; *Historical Atlas of Canada*, 1: plates 40, 41; Bosher, *Business and Religion*, 464–86.

30. Dechêne, *Partage des subsistances*, 142–46; "Gilles Hocquart," *DCB*, 4:362–63; Charles de Beauharnois de la Boische," *DCB*, 3:48–49.

31. Adolph B. Benson, ed., *Peter Kalm's Travels in North America: The English Version of 1770*, 2 vols. (1937; rpt. New York, 1966), 1:400 (July 23, 1749), 2:411 (Aug. 1, 1749), 2:416 (Aug. 2, 1749); Kalm's description of the farmhouses exaggerates the presence of stone construction. Most buildings were made of wood. See also *Historical Atlas of Canada*, 1: plate 52; Dechêne, *Partage des subsistances*, 141–59.

32. "Beauharnois de la Boische," *DCB*, 3:48–49; *Historical Atlas of Canada*, 1: plate 42; Dechêne, *Partage des subsistances*, 146–47; George F. G. Stanley, *New France: The Last Phase, 1744–1760* (Toronto, 1968), 192, quotes Bigot.

33. Lunn, "Economic Development," 103–4; Dechêne, *Partage des subsistances*, 147–53; Guy Frégault, *François Bigot: administrateur français*, 2 vols. (Montreal, 1994), 2:341–82; Dubé, *Les intendants*, 122–26, 152; Bertrand, *Histoire de Montréal*, 1:265–69; "Pierre de Rigaud de Vaudreuil de Cavagnial," *DCB*, 4:670–71; "Bigot," *DCB*, 4:64–66.

34. Dechêne, *Partage des subsistances*, 147, 152–55; Lunn, "Economic Development," 106–7.

35. Stanley, *New France*, 192–95; Dechêne, *Partage des subsistances*, 152–55, and see figures for flour imports on p. 203; Lunn, "Economic Development," 106–8.

36. Lunn, "Economic Development," 301–41, 376–77, 439; Jacques Mathieu, *La construction navale royale à Québec, 1739–1759* (Quebec, 1971), 17–26, 48–49; Réal Brisson, *La charpenterie navale à Québec sous le régime français* (Quebec, 1983); Pritchard, "Commerce in New France," 41–42; "Bigot," *DCB*, 4:59–71; George M. Wrong, *The Rise and Fall of New France*, 2 vols. (Toronto, 1928), 2:826–33, 881–82; José E. Igartua, "The Merchants of Montreal at the Conquest: Socio-Economic Profile," *Histoire Sociale/Social History*, 8 (1975): 275–93; Mario Mimeault, "Les enterprises de pêche à la morue de Joseph Cadet, 1751–1758," *RHAF* 37 (1984): 557–72; Bosher, *Business and Religion*, 464–509; Desbarats, "Colonial Government Finances," 177–81.

37. Stanley, *New France*, 191–96, quotes on pp. 192–95; Hare, *Histoire de la ville de Québec*, 37–38, 53; Dechêne, *Partage des subsistances*, 142–59; Desbarats, "Colonial Government Finances," 177–81, shows the sharp increase in government spending for "food and merchandise."

38. Lambert and Stewart, *Opening the Gates*, 38, 46–49; Bertrand, *Histoire de Montréal*, 1:262–65; Frégault, *François Bigot*, 2:62–70.

39. During this era, as earlier, there was industrial activity outside the towns. Iron making continued at the St. Maurice Forges. Like the Quebec shipyards, this foundry

became a state enterprise, the private investors having declared their bankruptcy. A lack of skilled labor slowed the expansion of the works, but during these years the forges added implements of war to the broad range of finished and unfinished products produced. The ironworks operated until the end of the French regime, although returns fell off after 1754. See Trottier, *Les Forges*, 67–82.

40. Lunn, "Economic Development," 91, 276, 376–381, 423–424; Pritchard, "Commerce in New France," 199; Igartua, "Merchants of Montreal," 275–293; "Bigot," *DCB*, 4:63–69; Pritchard, "Patterns of French Colonial Shipping," 198; "Hocquart," *DCB*, 4:363; Mathieu, *Le commerce*, 192–94, 232–66; Louis-Philippe May, *Histoire économique de la Martinique, 1635–1763* (Paris, 1930), 306.

CONCLUDING NOTE

1. Paul Kennedy, *The Rise and Fall of the Great Powers: Economic Change and Military Conflict from 1500 to 2000* (New York, 1987), 148–50, 198–202, discusses the changing balance of economic strength and provides several tables that illustrate the ascent of the United States during the nineteenth century.

2. Dean M. Hanink, *The International Economy: A Geographical* Perspective (New York, 1994), 60, 350–57; J. Foreman-Peck, *A History of the World Economy: International Economic Relations Since 1850* (Totawa, N.J., 1983); U.S. Bureau of the Census, *Historical Statistics of the United States, Colonial Times to 1970*, 2 vols.: (Washington, D.C., 1975), 1:200–2, 225; B. R. Mitchell and Phyllis Deane, *Abstract of British Historical Statistics* (Cambridge, Eng., 1962), 469–73. For a dissenting view, see Brinley Thomas, *Migration and Economic Growth: A Study of Great Britain and the Atlantic Economy*, 2d ed. (Cambridge, Eng., 1973). Thomas emphasizes the differences between patterns of growth in the United States and Britain in the nineteenth century.

3. Mohammed H. I. Dore, *The Macrodynamics of Business Cycles: A Comparative Evaluation* (Cambridge, Mass., 1993), 14, 27–28, 745–75, provides graphs and tables showing how between 1790 and 1982 business cycles in various countries became increasingly similar in timing and intensity; Victor Zarnowitz, *Business Cycles: Theory, History, Indicators, and Forecasting* (Chicago, 1992), 27–29, 77, 190–94; G. Moore and V. Zarnowitz, "The Development and Role of the National Bureau of Economic Research's Business Cycle Chronologies," in *The American Business Cycle*, ed. R. J. Gordon (Chicago, 1986); C. Michael Aho and Bruce Stokes, "Managing Economic Interdependence: The European Challenge," in *Europe and the United States: Competition and Cooperation in the 1990s*, ed. Glennon J. Harrison (London, 1994), 339–59; Dick K. Nanto, "The U.S.-EC-Japan Trade Triangle," in Harrison, *Europe and the United States*, 360–78; V. W. Malach, *International Cycles and Canada's Balance of Payments, 1921–33* (Toronto, 1954).

Index

Numbers in boldface refer to the graphs or tables on those pages. Also the regional distinctions discussed in the text are used here. *North* refers to the northern Thirteen Colonies, reaching from New Hampshire to Delaware. The *Upper South* includes Virginia and Maryland, while the *Lower South* consists of North Carolina, South Carolina, and Georgia.